SOMETHING
TO OFFER

SOMETHING TO OFFER

*Developing An Agenda
for All Canadians
for the 21st Century*

Editor
Dennis Mills

for The 21st Century Study Group

First Published 1989

Canadian Catalogue Information in Publication Data

Something To Offer

ISBN 0-929066-00-6

1. Canada - Social policy. 2. Canada - Economic policy. 3. Canada - Social Conditions. 4. Twenty-first century - Forecasts.
I. Mills, Dennis (Dennis J.)

HN107.S65 1989   361.6'1'0971   C89-093851-2

Printed and bound by The Alger Press, Oshawa

HEMLOCK PRESS
680 Queen's Quay West
Suite 702
Toronto, Ont M5V 2Y9
Printed and bound in Canada

89 90 91 92   6 5 4 3 2 1

Dedications

To the people of Broadview-Greenwood, Toronto, who voiced their concerns on behalf of fellow Canadians. The issues discussed here are their issues, the priorities are their priorities, the questions are their questions. This book is their book.

To Professor Sissela Bok who has been a special inspiration to me.

"In the 21st century, if, as I do believe, the issue of trust is so central, then government leaders are going to have to systematically think through what kinds of actions increase trust and what kind of action decreases it."

Sissela Bok
Christian Science Monitor
October 22, 1986

To Lou Gallucci, my campaign manager and good friend, my special thanks. For almost a year Lou fielded my ideas, quelled my doubts and answered my phone calls at all sorts of unreasonable hours.

ACKNOWLEDGEMENTS

Special thanks are due to the many people who helped to make the Conference on Developing an Agenda for the 21st Century come to life:

Our Sponsors
Ahead Realty; Ainsworth Electric Co. Ltd; Akropol Bakery; Albert Jewellers; Amherst Greenhouses Inc; Apple Canada Inc; Ashland Video Corp; Astoria Shish Kebob House; Bakery Delite; Billiards Academy; Budget-Rent-A-Car; Byzantium Restaurant & Tavern Ltd; Carling O'Keefe Breweries of Canada Ltd; Chan's Peking Resaurant; Christina's Restaurant; Cinespace Studios; Dac Hoa Restaurant; DECA Publications Co; Ed Hou Realty; Faros Restaurant; Grand Restaurant; Hong Ning Restaurant; John McAndrew; Knob Hill Farms; Laserplex; Loblaw Companies Ltd; Lucky Shop; Maddever Associates Inc; Magna International Inc; Master Linen; Mister Greek; Multi-Tech Services Inc; New House Restaurant; North Pole Bakery; Odyssey Restaurant & Dining Lounge; Omnicom; Omonia Shish Kebob Place; Palace Shish Kebob House; Pallas Bakery Ltd; Pape IGA; Pappas Grill; Patris Dining Lounge; Pearl Court Restaurant; Plaka Shish Kebob House; Pride of Erin; Rogers Cable TV - Toronto; Sea Castle Seafood Restaurant; Sun Valley Fruit & Grocery Ltd; Sunland Fruit Market; Swiss Patisserie European Desserts; Telav Audio Visual Services; The Upper Crust Bakery & Cafe; Tier One Communications Inc; The Country's Best Yogurt TCBY; Tu Do Restaurant; Unique Bakery; Victoria Canada Ltd; Whistler's Restaurant; Woods Bag and Canvas Ltd.

Our Organizers and Helpers
Mohammad Al Zaiback, Fulvio D'Amico, Bill Bartos, Kevin Callen, Vito Ciraco, Jim Conrad, Evie Christakos, Chris Fermanis, Tom Fragos, Mike Franey, Jim Frohlick, Christina Georgakopoulos, Judy Goodman, Anne Grealis, Donna Hobson, Ed Hyjeck, Jim Kaludis, Fred Langan, Mary Lansitie, Richard Lant, Mike LeCour, Bill Macheras, Michael Marzolini, Dick Mathieu, Rob Moore, Christine Murphy, Mohamed Nayed, Donna Peacock, Paul Pelligrini, Angello Persichili, Paul Raina, Dan Rider, Roberto Roberti, Dale Robertson, Diane Scharf, Jeff Shamie, Mary Shih, Bob Singleton, Paul Stergiou, Frank Stronach, Deborah Thadaney, Charles Thibault, Paul Thibault, Barbara Tinker, John Upper, King Wong, Norman Wood, George Zivontis.

Our Moderators
Denise Chong, Jim Coutts and Michael Homsi

Our Media Team
Randy French, Bruce Lewis, Michael Malone, Barbara Frances Sack

Our Newsletter Reporters
Jennifer Baker, Mike Braun,Stephen Clarkin, Mary Connolly, Jean Cox, Tracey Davids, Carol Dervaric, Doug Gordon, Carol Gruber, Al Hoffman, Julie Holliday, Sam Hunting, Gord Jones, Diane Laucys, Arlene Nicole, John Reid, Arvo Reitav, Dennis Roberts, Mary Rudolph, Lillian Salmon,Jon Schill, Sabita Singh, Valerie Street, Jodi Windover, Laura Zeitz, and the faculty members of Centennial College - Ross Maddever, Lindy Oughtred and Gary Schlee

Our Community Groups and Associations
Blair Court; Chester Village; Eastview Neighbourhood Community Centre; Estonian Association; Finnish Golden Age Club; Francis Beavis Manor; Greenwood Towers; Ina Grafton Gage Home; Nesbitt Lodge; Woodgreen Community Centre; Danforth By the Valley BIA; Danforth Village BIA; Gerrard India/Bazaar BIA; Pape Village BIA; Queen Broadview Village BIA; Cabbagetown Riverdale News; Leslieville Community News; Midtown Watch

Our Transcriber
Wayne Woodman of Alfred Devenport's.

Our Technical Consultants
Bonnie Burnet, Ron Gosbee and Michael Gaughan of Lazerline.

Our Audience
Everyone who came to the Conference and listened; all the speakers who, unfortunately we were unable to name in this book; all the viewers who have watched the telecasts on Rogers Cable TV, Toronto, Channel Ten.

We thank each and every one of you for your support and encouragement. If the book earns any praise it must be shared with all of you; any mistakes will remain our own.

The views expressed in this book belong to the individual writers and do not necessarily reflect the opinions of any of the above.

CONTENTS

Forward

In our complex and rapidly changing world, now is the time to set new goals for the 21st century. Although we need strong leadership, this goal setting process should not be undertaken by a few on behalf of the many. People in Broadview-Greenwood, in Canada and all over the world have clearly demonstrated that they want a dialogue with, not a monologue from, their political leaders.

They are demanding a say in what happens to their physical and social environments. They want to be heard on issues such as peace and disarmament and international relations. For them, democracy does not simply consist of voting at intervals for political representatives. They want it to be an open, ongoing process of consultation and participation.

Our initial response to this desire in Broadview-Greenwood was to hold a conference with the aim of sharing our concerns and exploring the possibilities for solutions. This was only the beginning and we were not able to cover all our concerns in this first session. Neither were the problems we discussed open to quick or easy resolution. We will need to keep the dialogue alive and continue exchanging our ideas and experiences in order to agree on and achieve our goals.

We are coming to realise that in a situation of constant change, ideas must evolve over time to reflect current realities and we must resist allowing ideas to harden into rigid ideologies that encourage division and conflict rather than provide solutions to problems. We are aware that the rights we have all fought so hard to achieve come complete with responsibilities and must be continually guarded against erosion.

You will read about some of our concerns in the following pages. You will also discover some of our visions for the future. If one thing is certain in this uncertain world it is that we cannot afford to enter the next century burdened by old conflicts and antagonisms; race against race, region against region, language against language.

If we can work together to shed these burdens, it is my belief that in the years to come Canada will be provided with an unique opportunity to show the rest of the world a way forward into a more peaceful and prosperous age. This opportunity will come from the very special nature of our current Canadian culture - its multicultural and regional diversity.

In order to do this we will have to protect our culture and the values we hold dear. It is for this reason that many people are conceerned about the Meech Lake Accord and the Free Trade Agreement with the US. The arguments about the Accord are ably presented later in this book but I would like to take this opportunity to draw your attention to a particularly worrying aspect of the Free Trade Deal.

Section 16 effectively removes Canadian control of investment in Canadian industry. We must regain this control. How else will we be able to realise such goals as employee equity sharing? We should be able to welcome foreign investment without allowing it to shape our culture in ways which are foreign to our value system.

For Liberals, opposition to the free Trade deal was not a negative reaction but a positive belief in our national identity; an identity based on the political values we believe important to Canadians: Integrity, Approachability, Caring, Concern and Action.

The Liberal Party's Agenda for the 21st Century will assuredly be based on those values and sensitive to the voice of the people. This conference in Broadview-Greewood, and the book that was inspired by it, is but one element in the shaping of this new policy for the future. Yet we believe that the sentiments expressed by the constituents of Broadview-Greenwood fairly reflect the hopes and fears of all Canadians. We also believe that the future will be one of a new generation of political conduct, whose clearly defined value system will increasingly govern Canada's destiny.

Dennis Mills
Broadview-Greenwood
April 1989

Photo: John Fred Sharp

Our children are already learning to work together - a hopeful sign for Canada's future

Introduction

Setting the Agenda

Dennis Mills

Dennis Mills was born in Toronto and studied at the University of St-Thomas, Houston, Texas. He worked as truck driver, tobacco primer, construction worker and successful businessman. After working for the Hon Jim Fleming he was a communications advisor to the Right Hon Pierre Trudeau. He was elected M P for Broadview-Greenwood in 1988.

First, I would like to give you some background to this Conference and its aims.

During last year's election campaign I spent several months knocking on doors in Broadview-Greenwood and time and time again people told me that they wanted to see more active participation in their community by their Member of Parliament. What they did *not* want was someone who, once elected, stayed in Ottawa and only came back to the constituency in times of crisis. The people here wanted a politician who would listen to their concerns and try to do something about them.

This conference is the initial step in responding to these concerns. The issues that are on the agenda are the very issues that the people of Broadview-Greenwood want addressed by their governments: the environment, drugs, crime, employment, illiteracy, urban planning, education, defence, Canadian culture, multiculturalism, regional disparities and the constitutional issues of the Meech Lake accord. These are issues that also affect all Canadians.

Canada and the world are undergoing profound transformation. The planet is threatened with global warming, deforestation, over-popu-

1

lation, and general environmental degradation. The country is faced with problems related to acid rain, environmental decay, inefficient technology and poor industrial management. Environmentalists give us ten years to undertake comprehensive changes before the damage to the Earth is irreversible. They suggest that without strong leadership and radical lifestyle changes there is no way out of this downward spiral.

It seems to me that the time has come for a new plan of action and, because the problem is so overwhelming and the challenge so great, the opportunities are unlimited. I think the coming decade will be far more exciting than any other Canadians have known.

Last week, while I was in Quebec City, I picked up a book on early Canadian history. It was the story of our first immigrants; they included the poorest of the poor - the rejected, prisoners, prostitutes. They also included farmers and merchants; people from all social classes. They had overcome tremendous hardship on the way to the New World but, once they settled in, there was more than peaceful co-existence; there was social consensus - a consensus born of need; born of the necessity to fight harsh winters and tame thick forests.

A sense of community soon became the driving force of the new land. Soon the *filles du Roy* became the wives and mothers of the new settlers. The troubled youths of the old country became the heroes of the new. Some, like Dollard des Ormeaux were the greatest of heroes. Dollard, who now has schools, a city, and a federal Riding named after him, is known throughout Quebec as the man who saved Ville Marie - now known as Montreal. It is said that he and a few of his friends fought off aggressive Iroquois who were on their way to attack Montreal; he died in the battle. While the myth is probably slanted by European writers, and while the history of French-Indian relations is open to interpretation, there is no question that these young nobles' sons had found their niche in the young community.

What is not well known is that the Colony probably owed the arrival of Dollard and his friends to the fact that their fathers couldn't handle their renegade, misfit sons in France, and shipped them off to the New World. With deep faith, pioneering spirit and lots of hard work, these early Canadians began to build a nation and they were soon joined in their efforts by peoples from the four corners of the Earth.

2

Always they turned to the basic values of care, concern and hard work to keep them going. Well, we have to draw on these same values once again. In the face of our social and environmental crises, we have to start to work together towards our common future. We are condemned, as the old proverb goes, to "live in the most interesting of times".

What are the environmental issues that must be dealt with? When I speak about the "environment" I include our family and community environment; our workplaces; our country. Environment is more than ecology; a healthy environment means healthy family life, a hopeful future for our youth. It means an ability to address the social issues affecting our communities and workplaces.

Working towards improving our environment means fostering good will through our schools and in our neighbourhoods, by attending to the learning needs of our young; by coming to the aid of our new Canadians struggling to learn English or French; by pitching in and working in our seniors and youth programs; and by making sure everyone is included when working towards the building of a common future. It also includes making sure our workplaces are healthier and more humane; by keeping our factories safe and our workers happy; by recognizing that a job is more than a job, it is a source of dignity and of self-worth; by recognizing that our neighbourhoods are more than just places to live, they are the breeding ground of hope.

Everyone wants to be a part of the building process, and I think we have reached the point where none of our problems can be addressed in any sort of cohesive fashion unless everyone makes themselves a part of the process.

As to the environment in its traditional sense: everyone belongs to this planet, and the planet belongs to everyone. That is why people are experiencing such extreme discomfort when faced with problems like global warming and deforestation and air and water pollution closer to home. There is, I believe, a growing consensus: more and more people are prepared to address these environmental concerns. All we need is a plan of action and a little momentum.

I had a friend, Stuart Lawson, one of the great entrepreneurs that Canada has known, whose life motto was, "Never better." No matter

3

what crisis Stuart faced, when asked how things were going he always said: "Never better." He'd roll up his sleeves and get to work. There was no place in his world for gloom and doom. The way he saw it, "A bad attitude leaves you with nothing, but a good attitude is like a shot of hope, and hope is contagious." It may sound a little hackneyed, but "where there's a will, there's a way." There's no question that we have the will; and there are a number of ways to choose from.

In British Columbia, they've developed new, clean-air technology. One of these products is, essentially, a clean-air engine; it runs on methanol and causes next to no pollution. Canada is rich in methanol. We have the resources; we have the technology; and we certainly could use the new jobs that will come from the mass-production of the solid polymer fuel cell. That's just one example; there are plenty of others being developed as alternatives to the smokestack industries. Once all these goods are marketed, there will be jobs created at all levels of manufacturing as well as in the service industries.

A clean environment is good business. It saves money and creates new opportunities. Once we develop this engine for new jobs, it will be an easy second step to begin setting an example for the entire world. We are not just talking high-tech, high-skilled jobs and projects, either. If Canada can harness its energy and use its creative talents to spot the project, there's no limit to what we can achieve.

When the American space program began under John F. Kennedy, a whole generation was mobilized by the idea of putting a man on the moon. Let's make Canada's space program a caring, environmentally conscious society. In order to do so, we can no longer afford to allow conflicts to persist between labour and management, between government and industry, or different tiers of government. We must act cohesively, as one community.

One of the most brilliant Parliamentarians Canada has ever known, Edward Blake, wrote, in the first years of Canada's nationhood, that "the future of Canada depends very largely upon the cultivation of a national spirit." We must find some common ground on which to unite, some common aspiration to be shared. Once it is found, our national spirit will be uncovered. The need for a national will, for cohesive national programs, is greater than ever before. At stake are our rivers and lakes, our communities, our future. We can no longer afford a multitude of splintered ideas. We must look to the past to remind us of what unity has to offer; look to the future to see what we can become; and then get down to work. We must keep in mind the old Haida saying: "We do not receive the Earth from our parents; we borrow it from our children". There's no shortage of things to be done; nor do we have to look any further than Broadview-Greenwood. My father used to swim in the Don River, and I see no reason why my children shouldn't be swimming there in the next five years.

A growing number of young people come before the justice system today as a result of drug and alcohol abuse. There are too many people collecting welfare and UIC because they cannot slot themselves into the workforce. We have a number of Seniors who are alone and lonely, and who would be willing to play an active part in our society. The Don Valley Cleanup will offer opportunities to all of these groups. In so doing, it will alleviate the discomfort Canadians feel when faced with problems such as drug abuse, unemployment, pollution, and inertia.

Everyone agrees that global environmental problems will not be resolved until we change our lifestyles - from country to country, from coast to coast. Changing your lifestyle means a lot more than putting out a blue box; it means getting involved, caring, working together. It involves *caring, concern, approachability, integrity* and *action.*

My plan of action involves the greatest job-creation project this country has ever known. The plan is to create a National Environmental Programme (NEP) that incites the development of "ecotechnology" and encourages the active participation of all members of society from students to senior citizens. It is inspired in part by the Institute for Environmentally Sound Technologies (IET), a watchdog organization currently being set up in Sweden. The Institue was recently profiled in the following way:

IET is being set up in the belief that environmental considerations must become an integral component of strategic decision data both in government planning and industry. And the hope is that it will develop into a technology assessment institution serving the world community by helping to define ecological imperatives, ethical considerations and social values. [Update: United Nations Centre for Science and Technology for Development No. 36/Winter 1988/9]

5

A National Environmental Programme would make everyone a part of the building project, and it would make a prosperous society in a clean environment its principal objective. This conference is the first step and one of its aims is to share with you all my excitement and hope for the future.

In this book we have added some discussion papers on issues of concern by people who were not able to be with us on the day of the conference. Even so, there remain areas which demand attention: employment and re-training, industrial relations, poverty, childcare, opportunities for young people, fiscal and financial policies. We have not forgotten these issues. A second conference will be held to explore them. If you have any other concerns *you* would like explored, please write to me at the House of Commons.

In 1910 people could skate on or swim in the Don River. Not so today.
Perhaps by the year 2000 we will once again be able safely to use the river
for recreation and enjoyment.

Photo: J M Carisse

One of my constituents, Charles Sauriol, has devoted a lifetime to the preservation of the Don Valley. He is seen here with his wife, Simonne, and myself after receiving the Order of Canada for his services to the environment.

Section One:
The Environment

Corporate Responsibility

Paddy Carson

Paddy Carson was born and educated in Belfast, Northern Ireland and came to Canada in 1974. He is convinced that Canada can take a leadership role in worldwide environmental issues. He is presently Vice-President, Environmental Affairs, for Loblaws Companies Ltd.

Photo: Jerry Hobbs

If a weather forecaster indicated to you that there was freezing rain imminent, you would drive carefully or, perhaps, you would stay off the road. If it was pointed out that an electric fixture or appliance within your home was hazardous, you would have it repaired or remove it. If health authorities warned you that the insulation in your home contained cancer-causing agents, you would take steps right away to have it removed, or you'd look for alternative accommodation.

However, environmentalists have been warning us for the past fifty years or so that our planet is dying because of poor environmental practices yet we have failed to react. Why? Because we feel that it is someone else's responsibility, and we don't perceive that it affects us as individuals.

For their own political survival, governments must be perceptive of their citizens' needs. The recent actions of governments around the world show that they are aware, at last, that a Green Revolution is under way.

For instance, Prime Minister Thatcher of the United Kingdom recently held a special meeting of her Inner Cabinet to look at what environmental initiatives Britain would take to gain a leadership role in the world. President Bush recently appointed an environ-

9

mentalist to his Cabinet. Italy's waste-management laws have been stepped up. Nordic countries have voted environmentalists into their Parliaments. Israel, with all its problems, two weeks ago, not only appointed a Minister of the Environment but made that Ministry a super-Ministry.

Canada realizes that it, too, must change and our provincial and federal Governments have started to take new initiatives. We have blue-box programs going on throughout the country, and we have coming into vogue within the next year or next month, perhaps, a program called the EFP Program, which means that products will receive a stamp which will designate them as "Environmentally Friendly Products".

The heads of large corporations, such as mine, are basically no different to politicians; politicians react to their citizens and presidents of large organizations react to their consumers. I can assure you that business in Canada is very much aware that its consumers are demanding greater corporate responsibility towards the environment.

At Loblaws Companies we believe that, as retailers, we can act as the catalyst between manufacturers and consumers. We can help educate the consumer and, by feeding back to the manufacturers the consumer's wants and needs, we believe that the manufacturers will change, and that safe environmental practices will mean good business to manufacturers.

My own particular company is responding to that Green Revolution. Earlier this year, I was appointed as Vice-President of Environmental Affairs. I think we are the first retail company in North America to make an appointment at that level. We're holding weekly strategy meetings on initiatives on the environment. We're changing the very coolants that are in our refrigeration to more environmentally friendly freons. We are now monitoring the emission levels of our trucks. We're even looking at changing the chemicals that we use in cleaning our floors, meat rooms, deli counters and bakeries. We're working with environmental groups such as Friends of the Earth, Pollution Probe and the Environmental Network people, to try to get better guidance and become better corporate citizens. Come Spring of this year, because we are in business and we must make a profit, and I make no apologies for that, we're introducing a line of products under the name of "Nature's Choice". These products, hopefully, will be more environmentally friendly because we're putting a lot of work into ensuring that.

It may be very frustrating to people like Julia Langer and Colin Isaacs and other educated environmentalists, that business is not moving as quickly as they would like to see but, when large companies make a move, they can affect the manufacturers and that, in turn, can affect their employees; it can affect them adversely. In an organization as large as ours, if we make a change in a product or in a manufacturing practice, we can affect the livelihoods of employees; we can affect the capital investment of a manufacturer - who is not necessarily large. So we've got to be very responsible and I'd like to say that, while business has a responsibility to the *environment*, it also has a corporate responsibility to *people*.

As I travel around the world, I find that Canada is looked upon as an environmental leader; unfortunately that perception is not always a reality. However, with conferences such as this, and the communications that we have initiated between us, we can go forward, acting in concert, to ensure that the perception becomes a reality.

I would appeal to government bodies, regulators, environmental groups and consumers to recognize that Canada has a tremendous opportunity to be known throughout the world as a leader, exporting environmental products that are safe and sound, exporting technology that is appropriate, and exporting people who care about this world.

I believe that today can be the beginning of Canadians showing greater environmental responsibility. I believe that the environmental summit that Dennis Mills is going to hold later on this year, in September, will be the first international conference and show-and-tell symposium in the world. We need you to assist us. We need you to be responsible so that when we, as Canadians, travel this global village we will be recognized as committed environmentalists.

Possibilities for Action

Tess Quilty

Tess Quilty's background is in education. She is presently a Development Officer with the Canadian Environmental Network. Her work there focusses on resource development for Network projects such as a nationwide toll-free environmental hot-line.

Photo: Jerry Hobbs

In 1988, more than ever before, the environment became an extremely emotional issue. Recent events, such as the PCB accident at St. Basile le Grand, the oil-spill off Pacific Rim National Park, and even the problem with waste management right here in Toronto, have forced more Canadians than ever to become aware of the urgency of the environmental crisis.

For anybody who is aware at all, the state of our environment and its prospects for the future are overwhelmingly frightening. The emotions that result from this quandary are frustration, a sense of helplessness, apathy; the desire to pull the covers over one's head and just wait for it all to go away.

Let us make no mistake. The state of our environment is serious enough that anybody in his or her right mind *ought* to be frightened. But let's *not* pull the covers over our heads. There are things that we can do. The very fact that we are here today indicates that we are frightened enough, or better still concerned enough, to actually do something as a step towards environmental responsibility.

In my work at the Canadian Environmental Network, I meet a lot of new environmentalists; people who describe themselves with words like "conservative". They are non-radical but very concerned. They're not sure that they should call themselves "environmentalists" but what they're really doing is breaking down the old stereotypes of the flower-child/environmentalist. And they're no longer saying that the environment is somebody else's problem. They're saying, "The environment is my responsibility".

This new face of environmentalism is not a passing fad. Our current rate of environmental destruction far surpasses our rate of response or the Earth's ability to recover. So, environmentalists are here to stay.

Environmentalists are also now in big demand, and I predict that into the 21st Century they're going to be in far greater demand. When I say "environmentalists" I'm talking about politicians, corporate executives, scientists, teachers, engineers, parents; we need *everybody* to become an environmentalist.

One might say that there are three steps towards environmental responsibility: Awareness, Education and Action. The fact that the state of our environment is now identified regularly as one of the top three issues of concern to Canadian citizens is an indication that we are at last becoming aware.

So, how will we get from this state of awareness to a position of action as quickly as possible? Well, as individuals there are a number of relatively simple things that we can do which, when multiplied, will really make a difference. Things such as recycling, re-using plastic bags (or, better still, not using plastic bags at all), using mugs instead of disposable cups, things like that.

What will be a little more difficult will be to re-educate ourselves as a society to start to re-think the way we make decisions about what we produce, what we consume, what we keep and what we throw away; re-defining euphemisms like "disposable" and "landfill sites", words that change the way we think about the actual relationship between what we do and our environment.

I don't believe we will discover a miracle technology to save this planet. Rather, if there is an answer, it will be found in traditional adversaries working together without political, economic or social boundaries. It will be found in people realizing again that we are a dependent part of our environment but not separate from it.

13

The educating process will also mean learning facts about the issues, about alternative products and technologies, about sources of pollution, and about initiatives of sustainable development. It will mean joining with other like-minded individuals and making our concerns heard.

At the Canadian Environmental Network, we've seen our membership rise from 1,500 to over 1,800 environmental groups in this past year alone. I think that most people are both surprised and encouraged to hear that there are so many Canadians out there right now working actively for our environment.

More and more people are coming to the Network as a starting point. One of the goals at CEN is to make it easier for individuals, corporations, groups and governments to be environmentally responsible. By facilitating communication and interaction, the Network acts as a neutral catalyst for environmental change.

I think that the role of the Network and other support systems for environmentalists will become increasingly important into the 21st Century. Government and private industry must take the initiative; must act as leaders to provide positive support for environmental initiatives. They must invest now in our common future.

One such initiative for which CEN is seeking support is a network of environmental hot-lines. In the Fall of 1989, we plan to launch a series of environmental hot-lines which will give practical information and referrals to Canadians calling from across the country. The hot-lines will catapult Canada's ability to act as a leader in the environmental realm, not only by encouraging greater numbers of people to become active but by enabling public and private sectors to share information and to work together towards common solutions.

The coordination of information and interaction and cooperation between sectors is not only an idea whose time has come, it is a necessity if we are to face the 21st Century with a fighting chance. I urge other leaders to join companies like Loblaws in supporting us on this project, so that we can work together for our future.

In summary, the messages that I'd like to leave with you are quite simple. Let's make sure that our great grandchildren are here and are able to meet like this a hundred years from now and, to borrow from an often-used expression, "As individuals, we should think globally and act locally".

As to government and industry leaders, the message is, "Support environmental work by providing a climate where people can and will work together towards common solutions".

Finally, to all of us, let's live on this Earth as if we plan to stay!

"Better to be Frightened Now Than Dead Hereafter"

Warner Troyer,

Warner Troyer is a veteran investigative journalist who is also an author and award-winning filmmaker. His current book A Canadian Green Consumers' Guide is to be published by McClelland & Stewart in September 1989.

Photo: Jerry Hobbs

I guess it was about ninety years ago that George Santayana, when he was teaching at Harvard, wrote a letter to a friend which opened with the words, "This will be a very long letter as I don't have time for a short one." That shouldn't concern anybody too much. As I used to tell people, when I only gave them five minutes for a television interview, "The Gettysburg Address only runs three minutes and twenty-four seconds, and the Sermon from the Mount runs five minutes and forty seconds"; but I don't expect to match either of those gentlemen with what I have to say today.

It was Sam Johnson, I guess, who noted very wisely that, "Nothing so wonderfully concentrates a man's mind as the knowledge he is about to be hanged" and that, I think, has a good deal to do with our lengthening attention-span with respect to the environment. We've seen some of the sentences and some of the warrants, and we're paying more attention.

It is neat, by the way, that this occasion today is being held in Riverdale. I was briefly a member of the Toronto Board of Health when some of the manufacturers in this area were telling us that "lead is good for you" and I know that Riverdale contains within its boundaries the most effectively activist people in Metro Toronto (maybe in Ontario, maybe in Canada) viz. the Commissioner Street Incinerator. Let's hope the Rouge Valley is next.

I think that there have been two or three really significant things that have happened in respect of the environment. The first one, in my mind, was Rachel Carson's book, *The Silent Spring*, in the '50s, which was a very alarming book; and it made us all relentlessly aware that we couldn't just carry on hoping for the best, that we were doing irreversible things which were just bloody awful. So it jacked up our awareness and it frightened us to a degree, and I think that was very healthy for people generally - as it is all the time for politicians. A little fright is terrifically therapeutic.

The next really significant thing that happened, I think, was the publication two years ago this April, of the World Commission on Environment and Development Report - now called the Bruntland Report. Because what the Bruntland Report did (in the face of that anxiety, that fear, that understanding of the problem) was make it clear that "we don't have to roll over and die" or "put our head under the covers" but that we can survive. We can even develop, if we do it in "sustainable" terms - a word that you're going to hear an awful lot of, I hope, over the next decade.

The main thing is to do things consciously; and the irony is, of course, that it's bloody good economics. Anybody in any industry will tell you that a retrofit of any kind, "to fix a problem" is not the best solution. Generally speaking, the rule of thumb in industry is that a retrofit costs 40 times more than it would have cost to fix the thing at the design stage and have it right the first time around. Whether it's a five-cent gasket in a car or something else, it's good economic sense to do environmentally sound things; and it's stupid economics not to - really stupid. If you don't believe that, speak to those battery makers who were in Bhopal!

I guess the important thing is to figure out how we, as individuals, can do something about it. I'm sure you know all of these things already, but sometimes it's useful to remind ourselves that we have enormous power as individuals, working together. If that were not so, Bull Connors would still be the Sheriff in Selma, Nixon would probably still be in the White House, the Americans would still be in Vietnam and Anthony Eden would probably still be in Suez.

Because of mass communications, we now have the opportunity to

17

recognize areas of common concern. Especially through television, we've been able to cut across all the boundaries - of culture, of education, of economics, language - and work together, to do things together effectively. So, that's the first rule.

It's okay to be sceptical; indeed, it is necessary to be sceptical. Corporations are by nature amoral. This is not a pejorative; it's a recognition of a fact of life - they have to be. It's their job to look at bottom lines. But individuals within them can be persuaded and moved.

So, when you go to the dry cleaners, ask them if they recycle their solvent. It would save them a hell of a lot of money every year, and it wouldn't be going down the drain. Do the same thing with your photography shop. Ask your service station what they do with the oil they take out of your car; it can be recycled. Recycled paper uses about 60 percent less energy per ton of production than new paper.

Recycling is nothing new. When I was a kid, recycling involved the old Eatons catalogue, which is the one we kept in the out-house for the obvious purpose. It served a double function; I got my sex education from the corset ads! So recycling is not a new thing and we can do it.

I guess the other thing I want to remind myself and all of us about is that everything we do has some impact on the environment, and anything we do to help might be life-saving in the future. For example, we cannot continue practices which cause the extinction of biological species which have yet even to be named, let alone studied. More than 50 per cent of prescription drugs are based on substances found in some wild species. So, by burning rain forest, for example, we may be destroying species with some substance that might prove to be a cure for cancer , or whatever. That's dumb and we can't afford to do it. We can't afford to go on playing Russian roulette with the environment, because that means with our future. The good news is it's not too late. We can resolve these problems.

Winston Churchill, about 35 years ago in a speech at Tallahassee University in the States said, "We should beware. The Dark Ages could return on the gleaming wings of science". I suppose, although talking about nuclear energy at that time, he could just as easily have been talking about PCBs, and many other substances of that kind.

We just have to pay attention; that's the main thing. We have to look at inter-relationships, not at simplistic solutions. I was in my local, friendly, neighbourhood, store-front boozeteria last night, and they gave me a plastic carrier bag with very proud letters across it saying "Photo-degradable". That's a scam! If that plastic bag goes into the garbage, it goes into a landfill site where there ain't no light so it won't ever degrade. I can hang it on the clothesline in the backyard for a couple of years and I'll end up with a whole lot of itsy-bitsy pieces of plastic which, in aggregate, will be just as much as I started with.

So it pays to ask questions; it pays to be sceptical; it pays not to take the easy answers from anybody but we can still do a lot and we've made a hell of a good start.

Individual, National and Global Issues

Julia Langer

Julia Langer is an Honours Graduate of the Environmental Studies Program at the University of Toronto. She has served as Policy Advisor to the Ontario Minister of the Environment. She is now Executive Director of Friends of the Earth

Photo: Jerry Hobbs

I work for an organization called Friends of the Earth. We're an advocacy organization. We also undertake public education and research. We have sister organizations around the world which gives us a very good perspective on some of the issues which are happening in countries and geographic regions other than Canada.

We do try to be quite pushy because we feel the environment is worth being pushy for. We do our homework first but, in the long run, we think that there are such pressing problems, and there are so many things that are possible to do to help protect this environment, that we'd like to be very active and very, very vocal.

Now I know that everybody is tired of hearing that the environment is going to hell in a handbasket but the fact of the matter is *it is.* The questions I have to ask are, "Are we really up to the task? Can we really do it? Can we really fiddle around a little bit, buying a few things that are better for the environment, casting our vote at the cash register and really help the environment?"

On one hand, Friends of the Earth is certainly going to give it a good shot because that's something that, as individuals, we can do. Sadly, we are in an incredible, incredible rut - as individuals, as a political system, and as an economic system. We believe that if we are going to develop, and develop sustainably, and be able to feed ourselves and be able to breathe and have some place for our children and our grandchildren to live, we're going to have to stop doing some of the things that we're doing that are keeping us in this rut.

We really must make a change and that's what I feel this Conference is, hopefully, going to achieve in a variety of areas. It is looking at that Agenda; looking at what we're going to have to do to get out of the rut.

There are some basic rules. One is really an old-fashioned concept - as Warner Troyer has pointed out - and it's really doing more with less. It's something that has been employed, certainly, in the commercial sector. How do you get the best gizmo? How do you get the best mechanism? How do you do something better; make a better mousetrap? Without relying overly on technology as an agenda for getting us out of the rut, there is really a great opportunity for employing new technologies; putting our brains into gear and actually moving in the direction of doing more with less.

In a country like Canada, we depend so much on primary industry -primary resource extraction - but resource extraction has meant, to a large extent, resource *exploitation* and not care for tomorrow. So we're going to have to start winding down those inefficiencies; doing more with less, especially in energy. Did you know that Canada is just a shade - just a shade - under the United States in per-capita energy consumption? We're about even with, let's say, China and India in terms of energy efficiency in our industry and in our domestic sectors. That means we're energy gluttons. No doubt about it.

There's a lot of fat to trim here and that doesn't mean having to give up lifestyle. In fact, we are probably going to lose "lifestyle" pretty quickly if we don't do more with less and if we don't trim some of that fat. That is when environmental problems will come knocking at our door. So, doing more with less does not mean losing lifestyle or losing quality of life. In fact, we make a very strong case that it is *adding* to our quality of life. This kind of economic motivation- doing more with less - has already shown itself to be a growth industry.

The same can be said for water use. We are one of the most profligate water-users, per capita, in the world. We think we've got a lot of water. Do we really have a lot of water? What's happening to the

21

Great Lakes? What's happening to the Don River? I think the answer really is, "No". So let's try and find solutions to that.

In trying to find solutions, one of the things which arises - and this is definitely another Agenda item, and one which Friends of the Earth has been pushing for very strongly - is that it's very hard for me or you as an individuals, to go knocking on polluting corporation X's door and say, "Excuse me. Can you please stop that? We don't like it any more." There has to be a transitional mechanism and we feel that that has to end up being national regulation. I say *national* very forcefully because that is our agenda. We don't want to see bits and pieces of regulations here and there, however well-intended. Every Canadian deserves the same treatment right across Canada and that means having strong national regulation but it's something that we're getting less of rather than more! We would like to see that changed around, hopefully before the 21st Century.

The other issue that were going to have to address is: how does Canada relate on the international scene? With a trillion dollars in debt worldwide, how responsible is Canada for what's happening in Brazil? The fact of the matter is we're incredibly responsible. There's not just a little bit of tinkering involved here. There is a *huge* amount of economic turnaround - probably a lot of debt forgiveness - if we're going to survive and not do it at the expense of other countries.

In short, the Agenda is getting ourselves out of a rut economically, as individuals; making sure that we can and do push for strong regulations that are going to achieve some of the goals and aspirations for a clean and healthy environment that we all have; and taking some responsibility for what is happening to the environment in developing countries.

We can do it as individuals; we should expect our governments to do it; and we will work, certainly, with the corporations who will probably end up being the people with the know-how and the investment potential to develop technologies. I think that working together - all of us together - we can press for our own Agenda, which is a clean and healthy environment for ever and ever, not just for our own sake but for our children's.

Photo: Henri Keleny

Agrobiology: A New Vision

Jean Boutet

Jean Boutet has studied education, mathematics and computer science and has worked in catering and food processing. He is involved in the Canadian and Québec environmental networks, is President of the Fédération nationale des associations de consommateurs du Québec and is Executive Director of the Mouvement pour l'agriculture biologique.

I am pleased to have this opportunity to tell you about Québec's strategy for the conservation and development of natural resources. In actual fact, a great deal of expertise has been accumulated by a number of creative individuals who are at the forefront of major social trends. For example, the development in Québec of a type of agriculture that is genuinely respectful of the environment was the work of pioneers who at the time was at odds with the dominant developmental trends of the agri-food sector, which were research into productivity at any cost without concern for the conservation of resources. Public participation is important because a conservation strategy can only be effective if all the social sectors, the governments, industries and consumers collaborate towards its success. It is a step forward in this dialogue to be able to outline for you the direction that the Organic Farming Movement is taking in Québec agriculture in helping the Québecois to respond effectively to the environmental challenge.

During the 1970s, it was acceptable within official circles of the agri-food sector to claim that organic farming could only result in famine for mankind. This spectre flourished when we left the gardening realm and entered the serious world of productivity and profitablility

23

in agriculture. Fortunately, such attitudes did little to discourage the early pioneers who worked relentlessly to establish viable farming methods covering every aspect of livestock and plant production. Today, it is possible to argue to the contrary that large scale development of agrobiology is indispensable if the human race is to escape famine, disease, destruction of the environment and depletion of natural resources. If I succeed in showing you that this new system of agriculture is within arm's reach in Québec, I will have achieved my goal.

The keystone of agrobiology is based on the optimization of living ecosystems. Special attention is focussed on micro-organisms of the soil that act as a link between the living world and inanimate nature. Fertilization consists of feeding this micro-fauna and micro-flora with organic matter and with minerals in their natural state. Through close association with vegetable roots, these organisms provide plants with their daily subsistence, at the same time playing an active role in stabilizing the soil structure. Through this method, the soil not only ceases to degenerate but improvements in soil fertility and structure result.

The concern in parasite control is to cease the practice of exterminating harmful insects and to understand their place in the scheme of things. This does not mean letting them loose but rather controlling them through management of the ecosystem. The diversification of cultures and milieus results in the presence of predators, and the practice of rotations and green manure reduces the risks of infestation. An infestation is a sign of imbalance. In optimizing the balance of the ecosystems, the infestations are greatly reduced. In an emergency, organic substances, biological and mechanical techniques are available to control the situation. In a paradoxical way, the parasite epidemic presents less of a problem in agrobiology than in conventional farming.

Agrobiology places emphasis on use of many varieties adapted to their specific ecological niches that are resistant to disease, rather than on the monoculture of just a few varieties grown on a continent-wide scale. Besides contributing to the growth of genetic resources, the diversification of cultures leads to greater stability in farm enterprises in protecting them in part from fluctuations in the marketplace, climatic hazards and production problems.

24

Investment in the practice of ecological methods has proven to be a profitable venture. At the present time, hundreds of Québec dairy producers have converted their farms to growing organic products for economic reasons and have found that they are better off and the system is more financially sound. Production is adequate and overhead has been greatly reduced. A Vermont researcher has shown that manure production is equivalent in market value to dairy produce. Manure as a resource had been neglected while costs of chemical fertilizers and veterinary care mounted. These costs have now been minimized and the health of herds has improved. At present the market for organic food products is virtually unlimited. The benefits of agrobiology are evident everywhere, namely in quality food products and in lower health costs. In the future, this new science will prove itself to be crucial in the face of overwhelming environmental problems that confront mankind. With their focus on ecology, agrobiologists fully understand the ever-changing interactions that occur amongst the living species, amongst themselves, and finally their interaction with the physical conditions.

Like any new science or technology, agrobiology faces many obstacles. The major factors obstructing the development of organic farming are the need for research and for professional and public education. The isolation and disunity amongst the interveners, the problems related to technology transfer and technical boards, agriculture policies that do not take into account the needs of organic farming, and the departmentalization of responsibilities in institutions are all drawbacks that must be overcome. Agriculture is in the hands of the agronomists, but biologists, entomologists, ecologists, sociologists, anthropologists and others can all make useful contributions to agriculture. We are seeking more technical know-how rather than basic research. This work must take into account the needs of farmers and in fact it should be carried out in close collaboration with the farmers themselves. Up to the present time, it has been they alone who have conducted any research worthy of the term, and very often they pursued it at their own expense. They alone know now what is needed and researchers must constantly refer to environmental realities.

The Organic Farming Movement of Québec has, since its inception, brought together all those interested in organic farming methods. It is only organization on a province-wide scale that brings together all interested interveners under their respective area of expertise. Rather

25

than just talk, they have acted. At the moment, organic farming has made a modest inroad in Québec agriculture but the time is ripe for a big push forward. What is needed to ensure the future development of organic farming are adequate funding and a clearly articulated political will. We need to ask some basic questions. Should governments support the status quo of the conventional agricultural system which, as the experts would say, has resulted in increased productivity at the cost of major disadvantages which are gradually surfacing? Should governments and main interveners of the sector invest progressively in a system of agriculture oriented towards the rational use of resources and sustainable development? Should we go ahead and change our methods in favour of an organic farming system that requires investments on a more modest scale, a system which, based on present practices, results in minimal impact on the soil?

Productivity is a relative concept. In actual fact, it depends on the frame of reference. In standard economies, it appears in a limited context and results in many externalities. For example, in conventional agriculture, if we apply to production costs the added costs of decontaminating the water, of restoring depleted soil in addition to medical expenses related to intoxications caused by the use of pesticides, etc, productivity will be compromised. When we refer to the productivity of conventional agriculture, we are in a sense dealing with a myth that does not hold true in an analysis of reality. In Beauce, one-third of greenhouse produce is organically grown. Often the producers of organically grown tomatoes obtain yields per flat which exceed the average yield of Québec's regular greenhouse tomato producers. For the same output per square metre, fertilizer costs in organic farming are only one-third of those in conventional farming, including labour. In dairy farming, comparisons show that organic farming can cut production costs by up to 50% over conventional methods.

During a recent conference of the Québec Association of Biologists, we showed how the introduction of soluble manure and synthetic pesticides in themselves constituted the very source of the process of soil degredation through the harmful action of micro-organisms and the breakup of the network of living ecosystems. The nitrogenous fertilizers make the plants more appetizing for the parasites, and pesticide use leads to the reproduction of the parasites in question! Withdrawal of the soluble fertilizers and herbicides from pastures results in an improvement of up to 80% in the health of livestock; so just imagine the effect on the health of human beings.

Agrobiology promotes a viable form of agriculture on a long term basis because it is based on the preservation of optimal soil fertility. In basing its fertilizing methods on the recycling of organic matter, it eliminates at source one of the causes of pollution in conventional agriculture, in addition to developing a renewable resource. We must remember that the production of fertilizers and pesticides requires the use of oil. They are in actual fact petrochemical products. Organic farming can lead to spectacular results in restoring the structure and fertility of impoverished soil when it is treated by organic farming methods for a period of several years. Although it cannot perform quick miracles on soil that has completely degenerated, a big improvement can occur in a few years to the damaged soil.

The government remains undecided as to whether it should support the status quo or whether it ought to invest progressively in a sustainable system of agriculture. In this regard the government is behind the times on environmental issues. In actual fact, 25% of consumers are seeking organic products, according to Agriculture Canada. At the Farm Producers' Union, some of the directors predict that in 15 to 20 years, 40 to 60% of total farm produce will be of organic origin. The giant food chains are introducing organic food. It is estimated that 70% of Québec's organic food produce is sold in these chains. The British are prepared to charter 'planes to import organic fruits and vegetables from Québec! The government's participation is essential. On one hand, some of the work already falls under normal government routine; the control of the term "organic" to ensure that the definition is registered according to the standards of the International Federation of Organic Agriculture Movements (IFOAM) who set up scientific meetings. Education and some aspects of research also fall under the government's domain. In addition, government participation eliminates certain inconsistencies in its policies: for example, how to reconcile the Ministry of Energy's plan to invest $200 million to set up a fertilizer plant in Québec versus the need for the conservation of resources?

The challenge lies ahead; will the growing interest in organic farming result in an alliance between politicians, entrepreneurs and agrobiologists? For this alone can truly unite agriculture, environment and economic development into a viable and sustainable force.

27

Questions and Comments from the Audience

Question:
You've all talked a lot about your role in re-educating consumers and re-educating ourselves. The topic is Developing an Agenda for the 21st Century. So, what are some of the words that are going to be new words that are going to become part of our vocabulary in the future, with regards to the environment? Maybe you can just throw out a few words that you think will come, hopefully, into more common usage.

Paddy Carson:
I would think that the words have begun, and they are: "environmentally friendly/environmentally unfriendly practices".

Tess Quilty:
I believe that we're going to have to look at "efficiency" as a very key word; efficiency in our use of resources. You can even apply that term to our population growth. You know we are, in biological terms, reaching and exceeding our carrying capacity. That's not a very efficient way of managing our growth and managing our consumption. That's definitely key.

Question:
Well, in terms of "efficiency", does that include words like "recyclable", "biodegradable" and so on? Because "efficiency" has taken on a very commercial sense.

Warner Troyer:
We don't need new language and, pray God, we won't get any more acronyms. We've got all we can handle now. The key word is one that we're all familiar with - "responsibility" and, under that rubric, obviously "efficiency", obviously "forethought", obviously, "planning" - and all of the kinds of things that we know and love, but don't practice. You know, it's like going to church on Easter Sunday and for the Christmas Eve Mass and then saying "That's it, Charlie.

We'll see you next year." We all *talk* a good fight, but we have to start *doing* these things as individuals and we have to beat on all the people who don't do them. And they *will* respond; pain is a marvellous motivator - it really is.

Question:
It's a comment and a question and they're separate. The comment has to do with national regulation. I think that's a terrific idea but, at the same time, let's not forget that cities like Toronto, with organizations like its citizen-manned Board of Health, can and do, effectively lead the way. The lead cleanup in this area that Warner Troyer mentioned was largely, but not entirely, due to this plant right across the laneway. That's Canada Metal. That was the source of the lead that we just cleaned up here. A thousand homes got cleaned up, or are in the process of being cleaned up. So there's no reason for cities - whether it's a city like Toronto or a city like Trail, B.C. or any other city of this country - not to not lead the way to a national regulation.

Julia Langer:
I did say that provincial and local regulations are needed but we feel very strongly that a lot of issues have to be and *should be* dealt with by the federal government. In fact, I have supported municipal regulation very strongly; partly because it's a jab in the side of the federal government which is not taking responsibility.

Question:
I just didn't want people here to think that the initiatives in Toronto weren't worthwhile .

Julia Langer:
No. They are certainly worthwhile.

Question:
My question is about priorities, and specific issues. It seems to me that the greenhouse effect is very alarming and I just wondered what Friends of the Earth is finding now that it has begun to work on this issue. I wonder what you're finding in terms of things that we can do in our daily lives as well as in our national lives?

Julia Langer:
Well, in fact, we are going to launch a greenhouse campaign in the

29

early Spring. What we're finding is that Canadians, per capita, are incredible energy gluttons and that there is a lot of opportunity - by reducing energy consumption in industry, in commercial institutions and in our households - to decrease the amount of carbon dioxide that is emitted into the air. At an individual level, that involves using energy-efficient appliances, applying old standards like having well-insulated homes, and not using coal but switching to natural gas for heating at the power plant. That could make an incredible difference - I would say gains of between twenty and thirty per cent just in the household sector, and that means up to twenty per cent less carbon dioxide going into the air. It makes a very significant difference.

Warner Troyer:
One of the things that I think I have learned as a journalist is that it's usually a mistake to over-state a case and frighten people because then, if they find out later that they are still alive after all, they don't believe you the next time. The greenhouse effect is very serious - no question. We can all do a hell a lot about it as individuals - no question - but we should bear in mind that this week the U.S. Climatology Service said that, after surveying weather records going back to the first year they had them (98 years ago I think), they can find no evidence of any impact on North America's climate, so far, by the greenhouse effect. There isn't a one-degree-Centigrade difference in a hundred years. That's not to say it's not happening - it is - but it *is* to say that we don't , again, have to roll over and say, "Oh God, we can't do anything about it." There *is* time; we *can* do something about it. One of the things that irritates me is that I know there are such things as energy-efficient refrigerators, vacuum cleaners, electric stoves but I don't know anybody who will tell me how to find out which are efficient and which aren't. We have to hit on the retailers, the manufacturers and, most of all, the politicians, so that some kind of labelling is required that *will* let us know.

Julia Langer:
There used to be just such a program but unfortunately the federal government cancelled it and that's something which certainly should be re-instated - if not at the government level, certainly within an industry association. It's inexcusable.

Question:
I was curious to see what was going to go on here and I am really very

heartened by what I've seen and heard so far. Back in the '60s, in my salad days, I used to go to things like this and there was talk of change and there were protests and there were demonstrations and they had songs. Since then I've watched in disbelief as all these things were absorbed into our culture and exploited by industry - clothing, music etc.. I guess I'm worried that this environmental thing is going to be used in the same way, because I already see it happening. It was mentioned about the biodegradable bags. I went around during the recent election campaign handing out biodegradable bags in the belief that I was presenting something worthwhile; now I find I was being used, I think. How do I prevent that or how do *we* prevent that? I've seen it happen before and I don't see any changes in the system that are really going to prevent it happening again.

Warner Troyer:
I talked about *photo*degradable bags and not *bio*degradable. Photodegradable plastic does have uses to which it can be put. The cellophane on the outside of a pack of cigarettes should be photodegradable because a hell of a lot of people throw it away and at least it will break down.

But look, it isn't just rhetoric any more; things *are* happening. For example, in Japan, between 1975 and 1985, the amount of energy used in the production of any unit of manufacture, whether it was a pocket calculator or an automobile, went down by 50 per cent, because it was good economics. It was also damn good for the environment.

I was talking to a lady at the FDA in Washington yesterday about cosmetics and she told me that five years ago when the FDA phoned cosmetic companies and said, "Hey, what's in that eyeliner?" they wouldn't tell them. Now the cosmetic companies are phoning her, trying to give her information. There *is* an understanding, an appreciation, an awareness that change has to happen; and change is happening. There's a lot of change, but still not enough. You know, if you're wearing a polyester shirt instead of cotton or wool, you're not doing the environment a hell of a lot of good and you're not as comfortable either.

Question:
How many people would consider themselves "environmentally

31

corporate conscious"? In other words, if you owned shares in a company
that was polluting the environment, would you do something about
it either by voting at a Shareholders' meeting or selling those shares?

Warner Troyer:
What you have to add to that is that the mutual funds in North
America with the best return over the last ten years are in that very
small group of mutual funds which only invest in "environmentally
good" corporations.

Question:
The largest polluter in this province right now is not Loblaws or
Allied Chemicals or anyone like that; it's a Crown Corporation that
we all have control over and it's Ontario Hydro. So I'd like to pose a
question to Paddy Carson. As a member of private industry, you've
got a competitive challenge. You have a problem in that you have to
raise and invest a lot of capital in order to take a leadership role in
environmentally good products. What about your competitors from
outside this country, like the United States, or throughout Canada
who may not have to face those costs? What do you suggest we do to
make sure that everybody is "put on a level playing field"? In other
words, so that there's not a level of corporate bashing directed only
at one certain industry, and that everybody has equal opportunity to
meet the legislation and meet the requirements for "environmentally good" products.

Paddy Carson:
I come from a country where confrontation hasn't solved a problem
in eight hundred years and that's why I came to this country. I sin-
cerely believe that what you can do is to differentiate between corporations by your expenditure and they will listen because we're all
motivated in business. My job and my family's lifestyle is dependent
upon the profitability of the corporation I work for.

I will give you an instance of good environmental practice making
good business. About eight years ago, we embarked upon a re-cycling program for our garbage. Our bill at Loblaws had been $1.2
million per year and, by recycling the cardboard, we reduced it by
$570,000. Now we're very conscious at Loblaws and we know that
the manufacturers that we're dealing with are also becoming more
and more conscious. They're calling me and they're saying, "What
about these environmentalists? How are you handling them?" and

I'm saying, "Well, please, don't look upon the environmentalists as the chains on your profitability but rather look upon environmentalists as acorns of new-growth business." What you can do, as citizens, is differentiate at the cash register, at the gas pump and let it be known. I can assure you that the presidents of large corporations and their shareholders will respond very quickly.

Question:
"Environmental" is a big, generalized word that means the "the world". My question is trying to bring it down to specifics. I was wondering if Mr. Carson could tell me if Loblaws considers irradiated food an "Environmentally Friendly Product"?

Paddy Carson:
Absolutely not.

Warner Troyer:
Start with your M.P. Ask him to ask some questions in Parliament. It is against the law in Canada to sell irradiated soft fruit but, in order to make some money for Atomic Energy of Canada Limited, the Government of Canada is loaning (not even loaning - giving!) a very large amount of foreign-aid money to Thailand so that it can buy an irradiation factory from AECL, in which they are going to irradiate soft fruit, a good deal of which may then be exported to Canada.

Question:
I'd like to ask Ms. Quilty if you are getting ahead at all in persuading the government to take the salt off the roads?

Tess Quilty:
I should point out, first of all, that the Network does not work on issues itself. What we do is support the groups and their activities. I think the point that you're raising is that there are a lot of issues that we don't know whether we should call environmental issues or not. Certainly, things like irradiated food and salt on the roads do affect the environment and they should be considered environmental issues - as should a lot of things that affect our physical health. I think that generally we have to take a very holistic attitude towards products that we consume, practices such as salting roads and so on, and ask environmental questions in a lot of areas that we don't traditionally think of as being the "environment".

A view of the famous Toronto skyline seen from Riverdale Park.

Using public transit in Broadview-Greenwood

Section Two:
Cities in the 21st Century

New Plans of Action

Alan Tonks

Alan Tonks was born and raised in the city of York. He has earned four degrees and, after a successful career in teaching, followed his father's footsteps and entered politics. He was recently elected Metro-Toronto's sixth Chairman.

I'm very pleased to see how many of you are concerned about all aspects of life as we plan for the next Century. Certainly, the kinds of issues that we are dealing with now can be a springboard for us to reach into the year 2000, not just reacting to past issues and past problems, but identifying them and managing them and dealing with them such that we can look back and say that we were in a watershed in 1988 and 1989 and we took the advantage to prepare for the year 2000. I hope that we can reflect in that way, and consciously say that we did accomplish things in such a fashion.

I'd like to begin these reflections with a story. A surgeon, an engineer and a politician were having a conversation one day about whose was the oldest profession. The surgeon claimed his was the oldest because when Eve was created she was formed from Adam's rib; hence, surgery was the first profession. The engineer disagreed with the surgeon. "A long time before Adam and Eve, the Universe and everything in it was created from chaos" he said. "I think that particular feat of engineering makes mine the oldest profession." The engineer and the surgeon seemed to agree on that point but then the politician piped up, "Ah, but you're forgetting something," he said. "First there was chaos!"

Now I can relate to that story with ease because my first profession,

35

of which I am still proud, was teaching. As a teacher, I was responsible for order, not chaos. More specifically, I had creatively and responsibly to develop the minds of my students. I also had to enforce some days too and, believe me, keeping a couple of dozen young people in order is a breeze compared to chairing my thirty-three colleagues on Metro Council.

My second career, in politics, has also involved enforcing order although, to be more specific, it has meant creating order out of the all too frequent chaos of modern life. It has meant learning and refining the delicate art of managing change; and then teaching those lessons to others.

We live in a society of rapid growth and unprecedented prosperity but many of our society's complexities have become so burdensome that we must now derive new plans of action. Not only have the old solutions become passé, but we have even had to find new ways of defining our problems; we've had to re-think the questions that we ask about our society and ourselves. This is why I'm so glad that Dennis Mills has convened this Conference, and why I'm especially pleased that he has recognized the importance that cities should have on the Agenda for the 21st Century.

By the year 2000, well over half of the world's population will reside in cities. This is mainly because cities have become our societies' centres of economic growth but does this mean that people choose to live in the world's cities or, rather, does it mean that economics makes this a necessity? In the case of Metropolitan Toronto, I think it means both.

Metro Toronto, in some respects, is a model city. Since this municipality was formed, our citizens have enjoyed a quality of life that is unparalleled but Metropolitan Toronto has only been around for three-and-a-half decades. The men and women who have guided this community's growth have had few Canadian urban examples from which to learn - certainly few examples that possess the size and scope of Metropolitan Toronto. In spite of that challenge (or, perhaps, because of it) Metropolitan Toronto has come up with some good ideas, and has taken action.

Metropolitan Toronto was a leader in the development and financing of rapid transit. In turn, Canada's first subway line did much to influence massive re-development in the core of Toronto and, over the years, northward. Even as, some years later, the east-west line directed a renewed focus on development and growth eastward and westward, it developed this growth within Metropolitan Toronto.

Expressways seemed to be the sensible thing back in the '50s and '60s, in responding to the growth that was transforming no-car families into two and three car families. So the expressways were built but now they're having trouble coping with three and four and five car families. The enormous expansion of apartment living, and the steady rise in traffic density quickly made the need for rapid transit evident enough; and rapid transit was built.

Maintaining law and order and public safety was challenge enough in a huge, sprawling, urban metropolis without trying to do it under a dozen different regimes. The police joined forces, and then that was followed by the ambulance services.

Meanwhile, Metro welcomed and accommodated the transition of hundreds of thousands of rural Canadians to urban life. Concurrently, Metro welcomed hundreds of thousands of immigrants who contributed hard work and devotion to their chosen land, and we all prospered from the economic growth that they brought us.

While all this was going on, new focus was given to the construction of housing for the poor and for the working poor. Metro's leaders of the day tried to make some order and sense of development by imposing stricter planning. As they built expressways through our valleys, they also established our greenbelts.

As low-density or decaying housing was torn down to make way for townhousing and high-rises, they worked to preserve the best examples of our architectural heritage. Metro is growing into a premier arts, cultural and entertainment centre with Roy Thompson Hall, the O'Keefe, the St. Lawrence Theatres and Hall, the Royal Alex, the Metro Convention Centre and the new Dome, the Museum expansions, the Ontario Science Centre, and a proliferation of other theatres, workshops and cultural centres.

We have brought the world to Metropolitan Toronto, with hundreds of international conferences and conventions at the Metro Convention Centre; especially with last year's international Economic

37

Summit which welcomed, again, the world's most influential leaders, thinkers and writers to our doorstep.

All of these successes have occurred not by accident but by design over the last 36 years. Apparently the 2.1 million people who live in this Municipality believe we have done the right things despite obstacles. The 77,000 business establishments in Metropolitan Toronto that provide employment and wealth to our economy, also believe that we have done some of the right things. In the past great cities have simply evolved, but these days that natural evolution is augmented by foresight and action.

As I look ahead eleven years towards the next century, I can see that Metro has become a great Canadian city; even a great North American city. As the world changes, with the rise of the Pacific Rim, the massive restructuring and opening of the Soviet Union, and the creation of a Unified Europe in 1992, Metro - like so many other burgeoning cities - must also change. Local action is still crucial, but it should be local action with an eye to the experiences and opportunities in the rest of the world. As I said earlier, the lessons we have learned in managing change (and that we have, in turn, taught by example) will have to be re-learned and re-taught as we marshall our community towards becoming a major world city.

First, there is a need to build on, and strengthen, our economic development for the year 2000. In this municipality, a multitude of people in the public and private sectors have crafted an economic engine that has driven the prosperity and growth that this region enjoys, and that other jurisdictions envy, but changes are still needed, not only here in Metropolitan Toronto but also in the rest of Canada. This municipality, like other cities, should use its influence to increase the level of prosperity shared by our residents through higher and more value-added jobs and through higher-paying jobs. Before that occurs in Metro, however, we must recognize that our best chance to achieve increased economic prosperity is with increased research and development; with the creation of several indigenous world-scale companies and with a smooth but thorough process of industrial re-structuring.

So, having declared myself in favour of economic development, I will swing my other leg over the fence and into Metro's 21st Century by declaring that the secret to our success - our key to the viable City of

Tomorrow - will be, I believe, the creation of the transit-oriented city.

The first half of the 20th Century saw governments and taxes chase the public's demand for roads, then highways and expressways, to accommodate our society's love affair with the automobile. By the second half of the century it has become evident that the cars which prosperity had made affordable were by no means clear winners over the convenience and economy of good public transit. Having bought in to bigger highways and urban expressways, politicians and planners were buying in to subways and rapid transit, too. By the 1970s, "expressway" was even becoming a dirty word for some. Then Premier Bill Davis started to talk about a "balanced" transportation system; the Spadina Expressway Extension was torpedoed; and the lean toward public-transit solutions to urban traffic problems began.

So, the concept of the transit-oriented city is not new. It is no accident, nor bad planning, that the Metro Convention Centre has limited parking space; it's not an accident that the Sky Dome planning is based on patrons overwhelmingly relying on public transit and not private cars. We are already, if you'll forgive the pun, on the road to the transit-oriented city. The major problem is that most people have yet to realize it.

Certainly, we will need to complete a few missing links in our road system, and undertake a few road widenings and extensions, because these are needed to ensure the continued mobility of our commercial traffic and our surface transit system, but there is no question that many of the trips now being taken by private automobile can and must, in future, be taken by public transit.

There will be many benefits in that transit-oriented city of the 21st Century. It will encourage housing and economic development to be planned rationally and coherently, in conjunction with rapid transit's development and expansion. The costs of the new transit systems will be bearable to a tax-oppressed society because the proceeds of the housing and commercial development that will parallel rapid transit's expansion and growth will help significantly to pay for it.

Along with sensible growth linked to extended public and especially rapid transit, a key issue for the City of the 21st Century which relates to the transit issue is, obviously, the environment. These days we tend to think primarily of "environment" in terms of garbage or acid rain. The word can, and does, encompass much more than that.

For Metropolitan Toronto, garbage clearly tops the list of environmental problems at the moment. In fact, much is happening right now to deal with the immediate garbage crisis we currently face. I'm optimistic that the problem will soon be under control. Even more important, however, is the establishment of long-term solutions. There is growing evidence that the cost of garbage is going to soar. That reality alone may drive us to some obvious solutions. Perhaps prosperity has made many of us environmentally lazy. There's nothing like the almighty taxman to make us sober up and share in problem solving.

By the year 2000 - and probably long before - the four "R"s: *Reduction, Re-use, Re-cycling* and *Recovery* of waste materials will have to become universal and compulsory. Individual households will have to take time each day; people will have to be better educated in what to do, and how to do it. Very little of what we now consider waste will be accepted as waste in a few year's time. We will be forced to care, because the price of not caring will have become too great. In turn, as the public and their governments learn to participate in the solution, we (collectively) should be asking industry to tag along and creatively pursue environmentally sustainable development, as the 1987 Report of the Bruntland Commission has suggested.

Cities have also got to consider new ways of thinking and doing. Metro Toronto has led the way, experimenting with new ways of managing the community. Currently, our new initiatives range from the successful introduction of community-based policing to this year's directly elected Council of thirty-four Councillors, who will be identifying and getting on with the business of strategic planning for the kind of city we want.

New styles of management continue to be required. We especially need to build and strengthen relations between Metro's police and our minority communities. We also need to think regionally, as well as locally, recognizing that our regional partners in Durham, York, Halton and Peel are affected by the same problems of solid-waste disposal, airport congestion, stable economic development and rapid transit as Metro.

40

We need to look seriously at the comparative wealth of properties and re-examine our municipal taxation system and its ability to pay for local, general and school-board expenditures on an equitable basis. We also need to remember that our taxpayers will not foot the bill for Metro's continuing development on their own. On matters like community services and transit improvements we need new capital and operating cost-sharing arrangements with our federal and provincial partners.

Finally, I believe the success of the 21st Century city, including this metropolis, will depend on a broad re-birth of individual and family values. The costs of things to be done, the challenges we face, will be of a size and nature that municipal governments will, in their tax expenditures, be limited to covering the basics and caring for the poorest.

Community interest and participation will be essential for the maintenance of law and order in the 21st Century city. Quality of life will depend upon an increasing focus on group and community sharing of responsibilities. In today's complex society, all the money in the world won't buy real public safety. Only the kind of community involvement and sense of responsibility that gives life to a community will be able to provide the foundations and confidence within which safety, caring and community can prosper in an urban environment.

To sum up, the main items on the Agenda for the City of the 21st Century are:

* *well-planned economic growth;*

* *rapid-transit expansion and development linked to that growth;*

* *a more caring and participatory response to the environment;*

* *new styles of management to address new problems and opportunities;*

* *a return to emphasis on familial and societal task-sharing to ensure quality of life, community caring and community safety.*

I am being very forthright on these issues because, as Metro and

41

other cities look to their future in the next century, they must also be honest about their problems and imaginative in their solutions. Metropolitan Toronto has good resources to meet these challenges in the experiences of its people, the present strength of its economy, and the excellence of its infra-structural facilities. A creative and responsible approach to building and maintaining our cities is possible; and I believe that order can prevail over chaos.

Towards Solutions to the Housing Problem

Chaviva Hosek

Chaviva Hosek was educated at McGill and Harvard. She has been Associate Professor of English at the University of Toronto, a Research Partner with Gordon Capital Corp, a member of the Economic Council of Canada and President of the National Action Committee on the Status of Women. She is currently Ontario Minister of Housing.

The housing problem is not one that will give way to either smoke and mirrors or quick fixes. Instead, I am confident, it will give way to long-term solutions - so long as we stand united as a community.

In my view, Canada has achieved its enviable quality of life, relatively high living standards, and economic and social stability through an unique combination of compassion and pragmatism. We maintain a free enterprise system so that risk-takers and entrepreneurs can create wealth. But we also provide a solid social safety net so that all Canadians can share in it. One of the things that makes our communities work is our concern for each others' needs.

Canadian business people do not object to paying their fair share, in taxes and decent wages. It's a reasonable price to pay for a social environment blessed with low crime rates, relative labour harmony, and a highly educated workforce. In Canada, business knows the advantages of prosperity and optimism over poverty and despair.

This Canadian attitude has been tested in depression and recession. Now, ironically, it is being tested in prosperity.

Here in Toronto, and in other large southern Ontario cities, we are living in the midst of a paradox. The province is enjoying its sixth consecutive year of economic growth. More than 100,000 jobs are being created every year, while consumer price increases are running at less than 5%. But at the same time, we face a housing crisis that threatens the very basis of our economic buoyancy.

Over the past couple of decades, Ontario's economy has been transformed. Where once we depended on resource-based industries to provide jobs, today we live in a service economy centralized in our large cities. Our booming service sector has become a magnet for people from all over the country. In 1987 alone, net migration to Ontario exceeded 110,000 people - more than the population of Thunder Bay.

This huge influx, along with other demographic shifts such as the increase in one-parent households and the coming to adulthood of baby boomers, is affecting our province in many ways. Certainly it is having an enormous impact on the availability of housing.

The numbers tell the story. The average resale price of a home in Metropolitan Toronto in January 1989 is $254,575. More than a quarter of a million households in this province spend more than 30% of their income on housing. Up to 20,000 people a year use the province's emergency shelters.

The extent of our housing problems is apparent to anyone who has tried to buy a home or find an apartment - or even picked up the newspaper. Moreover, this housing crisis could turn the current era of economic growth on its head. The shortage of broadly affordable housing is hurting not only people who are trying to find a home, it is also affecting people who are trying to maintain a business.

In Markham, for example, there are local firms that send buses to Toronto every morning to pick up employees because there simply aren't enough places to live in Markham that most people could afford.

This shortage of workers has grown beyond being an irritant - it is starting to threaten the very economic boom that fuelled the housing crisis in the first place. As the cost of housing rises, so must wages and benefits. In the Toronto area, wages are already higher than the national average. But even that hasn't solved the problem of attracting workers.

Historically, people have moved to where the jobs are. But that's starting to change. People are asking: What's the point of having a decent place to work if I don't have a decent place to sleep? The executive you try to recruit may simply decide that a higher salary is no great inducement to move to a city where you have to pay more than twice the price for less than half the space.

Hardly a day goes by that I don't hear from someone who is unable to fill an important job because people won't move their family to a city where they can't find a house they can afford. Just the other day, the head of one of the University of Toronto's faculties told me he had been turned down by several potential job recruits in a row - all because of the cost of housing in Toronto.

Make no mistake about it, this housing crunch is a major problem for anyone who owns or runs a business - indeed, for anyone who lives in or near any large Ontario city. If there is no place to live, how will you find middle managers? Where will you find people to work in your factories, fix your car, wait on your table?

The problem that faces Ontario now is also beginning to appear in other parts of Canada from Vancouver to Halifax.

If you want to consider the dimensions of the economic problem we may be facing, just cast a glance south of the border. In the United States, human resource managers report that housing prices are responsible for the loss of from 20 to 30 per cent of potential employees to areas of the country where costs are lower. The problem is having serious impact on the bottom line. A study conducted two years ago by Merill Lynch found that some 1,300 US companies lay out about $17.5 billion each year to relocate new and transferred management-level employees.

Housing shortages have already distorted corporate decision-making, resulting in significant loss of jobs in many high-cost areas. The Grunman Corporation, one of Long Island's leading employers, recently had to shift nearly 1,500 jobs to the Sun Belt because engineers refused to work where they could not afford to live. High housing costs have forced the same kinds of decisions on many other

US companies - including Mobil Oil, J C Penney, and International Paper.

Moving plant and equipment can cost a company tens of millions of dollars but even that enormous expense may offer only temporary relief. Housing problems have a way of pursuing companies all over a country.

That is the US experience - and it is one that we must attempt to avoid. The housing shortage could place businesses in Ontario and other parts of Canada between the rock of expensive plant and equipment relocations, and the hard place of rising wages and a declining pool of workers.

Moreover, if people are no longer able to afford to live in places like Toronto, they will no longer be spending money there. Every man or woman unable to find a place to live represents a potential decline in the local consumer market. If people are unable to find a place to live, to whom are you going to sell insurance and furniture? You can't buy a washer/dryer if you have no place to put it.

If Ontario and other regions are to enjoy continued growth, we have to be able to accommodate it. That means we have to be able to ensure there is enough accommodation for the people who live here. Quite simply, broadly affordable housing is good for business.

It is in everyone's interest to solve this problem. But no one should believe that will be quick or easy. I'm not going to try to tell you we have all the answers, and that the solution is just around the corner.

The creation of broadly affordable housing is a top priority for the Ontario government. In the past three years, the Ontario Ministry of Housing has been playing a more aggressive role in initiating policies and programs.

In order to better meet the needs across the province, the Ministry took over primary responsibility for social housing and assumed a greater cost-sharing role. The Ministry of Housing has emerged as a proactive partner in the promotion and production of new housing stock.

At the same time, we realize that you can't just throw money at a problem until it goes away. We have to target our resources. Our strategy consists of four elements: Building, Land, Partnerhips and Rules.

First - building. The Ontario budget last April provided $2 billion for the construction of non-profit housing units - up to 70 per cent of which will be geared to income. In October 1988, we announced the largest non-profit housing program in the province's history. The program, called Homes Now will create 30,000 homes over the next three to five years. Indeed, in 1988 we doubled the number of non-profit housing units we are committed to producing.

Second - land. We're putting unused government land into the housing market. Under the Housing First policy, we identify surplus government land that is suitable for broadly affordable housing, and make it available at an appropriate cost. At least 35 per cent of the housing that will be built on these lands is relatively low-cost, to create more accommodation for low and moderate income earners. Through this policy, we have already committed to eight sites, including six in the greater Metro Toronto area, that will be used for thousands of homes.

We're delighted to see that Metro Toronto has also committed itself to a Housing First policy for its land holdings. And we're encouraged by the fact that the federal government is making land available for housing at the Downsview Airport site. However, we are still waiting to learn whether the housing that is built there will be priced to meet the need.

I was deeply disappointed in the federal government's decision in October 1988 to sell a large block of post-office land in Mississauga, without receiving a commitment to a single affordable unit. When we are in the midst of a housing shortage, the last thing the government of Canada should be doing is simply selling the land to the highest bidder. I understand the federal government is reviewing their overall land sales policy. I urge them to make a commitment to Housing First.

Third - partnerships. Solving this housing problem requires the involvement of a great many people. Under our unique Partnerships program with municipalities, we have signed agreements with the City of Ottawa and the City of Peterborough. We will work together for affordable housing through special projects, allocations and land

An aerial **view** brings statistics to life. Almost half the residents of Metro Toronto live in high rise buildings. In my constituency of Broadview-Greenwood almost half our community are tenants.

use approvals. We are working towards similar agreements with several other municipalities.

In July 1988, we worked out an agreement with the City of Toronto to create a $1 billion housing development - St Lawrence Square - which will provide homes for 12,000 people in downtown Toronto. Approximately 60 per cent of these units will be developed under non-profit housing programs, and for ownership and rental by low-to-moderate income households. Again, we hope the federal government will also choose to make a full commitment to a partnership to create broadly affordable housing.

The final element in our strategy is rules, and making sure they encourage rather frustrate the creation of broadly affordable housing. We are working with the Ministry of Municipal Affairs to change the land regulatory process to make it easier to get housing developments off the drawing boards more quickly and smoothly.

The new approach includes a major emphasis on allowing residential intensification, which is simply a way of making better use of the developed land and the housing stock we already have. There is tremendous potential out there - commercial strips and shopping malls that could add a couple of levels over top for housing, basement apartments and attic apartments, single family homes that could be turned into duplexes.

Consider the fact that half of the homeowners in Ontario have fully paid off their mortgage. There are tens of thousands of senior citizens in the province who are asset-rich but cash-poor. By allowing them to rent out part of their home we could make it possible for them to increase their disposable income - and help to solve the housing crisis by making better use of established neighbourhoods. The roads are already there, the sewers are there, the schools are there. There is no reason why there cannot be more people there. It makes simple common sense.

Make no mistake about it, when it comes to planning policies across this province, it can no longer be business as usual. From now on, municipalities planning new communities will have to ensure a full mix of housing, at least 25 per cent of which must be broadly affordable.

These last two policies - the 25 per cent affordable housing allocation and the residential intensification - have aroused more heated opposition than any other aspect of our housing program. We are seeing many examples of an attitude known as NIMBY - Not In My Backyard. We all want people to have a place to live, but some say "Not in my backyard". We all want broadly affordable housing available, but some say "Not in my backyard".

The issue is one that is clouded by disinformation. There is considerable confusion about what intensification means, and the impact broadly affordable housing has on a neighbourhood. It reminds me of something the philospher Montaigne once said: "Nothing is so firmly believed as that which is least known".

The people who blindly oppose programs to create broadly affordable housing in their neighbourhoods are no doubt acting on honest emotion but emotion won't solve the problem. We have to respond with cool reason. We have to act on the basis of facts, not myths.

I would like to take this opportunity to clear up several myths on which the NIMBY attitude is based, myths which have arisen about intensification and the overall issue of broadly affordable housing.

Myth: Intensification will force senior citizens and others to take in boarders.

Fact: Intensification will not force anyone to do anything. All we are asking is that homeowners be *allowed* to rent out part of their home, and that landlords be *allowed* to add housing units to plazas and shopping strips. No one will be asked to do anything they don't choose to do. As a matter of fact if there is any interference in people's preferred lifestyle, it comes from those municipal governments that try to regulate against homeowners who wish to rent out part of their homes.

Myth: Intensification will disrupt neighbourhoods and create traffic and parking problems.

Fact: The neighbourhoods we are talking about are already well set up to handle the traffic and parking that would result from two or three more people living on the street. If a household with a family that includes two teenagers with cars does not disrupt traffic or

51

make parking difficult, why should a home with an empty nester and a new tenant?

Myth: Intensification and affordable housing developments destabilize communities.

Fact: Several thousand homes have already been converted for rental use, and more than 17,000 affordable units have beed built in the past three years and no community has been made any less stable as a result. Indeed, many neighbourhoods are strengthened by intensification and affordable housing. They create a more balanced mix of communities and a more balanced mix of housing.

Moreover, the stability of all neighbourhoods depends on the stability of our cities. Healthy, stable communities depend on a healthy, stable supply of housing. The creation of broadly affordable housing and improved use of existing housing stock only furthers that goal. Neighbourhoods are not going to be overrun by change - so long as *all* neighbourhoods get the chance to participate.

Myth: Broadly affordable housing developments are being foisted on people.

Fact: That notion has as much accuracy as the idea that people are being forced to take in boarders. All housing plans are subject to planning rules and regulations. Residents and their municipal representatives have the opportunity to express their views and make decisions at the local level. No community is expected to accept more units than is fair, reasonable and realistic. The entire housing policy is based on balance.

Myth: Huge public housing projects destroy the character of a neighbourhood.

Fact: Public housing mega-projects are as *old* as this myth. Ontario hasn't built one for *12 years*. What we are building is so well-developed, so balanced, so aesthetically pleasing that sometimes you don't even know that it has a public housing component - even if you live down the street.

Myth: Broadly affordable housing programs encourage dependency.

Fact: The homes we are creating are affordable but they certainly aren't free. The cost of rent is still significant - it just isn't out of reach.

The facts speak loud and clear. The creation of broadly affordable housing is good for all of us. And the huge majority of Ontarians realize that. By far most Ontarians want to ensure that everyone has a decent place to live. Throughout our history we have welcomed newcomers - to our neighbourhood, our province, our country. I would hate to see the day when Ontario's well-earned reputation for openness and generosity is tarnished because of the loud complaints of a few.

You know that Ontarians care about their fellow citizens, and whether they have a place to live. You can see that when a story about a homeless family appears in the media. All kinds of offers of help come forward - many from people who ask that their name be kept private.

It is time that the many people who care start speaking out in public. When 300 angry protesters come out to their local high school gymnasium to oppose a new housing development in their community, I know there are 3,000 others at home watching television shaking their heads and asking : "How are my kids going to be able to afford a home?"

Well your kids are going to be able to afford a home only if you stand up for that goal now. It's time for people to more than *care* about Ontario's housing needs - it's time to do something to make sure they are met. Silent support won't create more places to live. You can be heard only if you speak up. To those who say, "Not in my backyard" we must ask: Would you rather see people living in the streets? To those who say, "Not in my neighbourhood" we must ask: If not in our neighbourhoods, then where?

Many people who care about the future are already beginning to speak up. Fewer people are saying NIMBY, and more are saying LEAD - Let's Encourage Affordable Development. We need more people like that to take the lead.

We need people who recognize that the housing shortage is bad for business. It drives up costs, drains the workforce, and forces busi-

53

nesses to pour valuable capital into swelling recruitment and relocation projects. We need people who realize that housing problems threaten the opportunity for a bright future for all of us. Ask yourself: Where will your employees live? Where will your customers live? Where will your children live?

When people ask themselves these questions, they will come to the same answer they always have. It depends on us, it depends on what we do now, it depends on our commitment to a stable and liveable city, province and nation.

The Role of the Police in Drug Education Programs

William Bishop

William Bishop is a Staff Inspector with the Metro Toronto Police Force. A thirty-nine year veteran with the force and a holder of the Medal of Honour, he is responsible for No. 5 District, including the District Drug Squad, one of the most productive Drug Enforcement units in the Country.

I think that we're all agreed that the most precious commodity and resource of any country is its young people, its youth, and I can't think of a more tragic waste of a country's resources and commodities than the involvement of young people with drugs - the trafficking in drugs and the abuse of drugs.

The role of the police in enforcement is clear, but the role of the police in prevention and education differs from Province to Province, and between each police jurisdiction within the province. I'd like to give you a brief overview of what has been happening in Ontario in the last eight years, and our plans in the Metropolitan Toronto Police Force for the near future in the drug-prevention field.

In 1980, the Ontario Association of Chiefs of Police decided that they would attempt to reduce the demand for illicit drugs by becoming more involved in prevention programs. Studies were conducted and the results indicated that the effective alcohol and other drug-abuse programs should start in Grade 4. That's a very tender age but it does need to begin at that time - Grade 4.

In 1981, the OACP, in association with the Ontario Ministry of the Solicitor General, produced a program entitled *A Beginning* for use with Grade 4 and 5 students. It was just that; the beginning of Safety

Education Officers - they are the traffic officers that you've all seen with Elmer the Safety Elephant - giving alcohol and other drug-abuse presentations in the elementary schools.

In 1982, a second program for Grade 4 and 5 levels was developed by the OACP Drug-Abuse Committee in cooperation with the Ontario Ministry of Education and the Ministry of the Solicitor General. The program was entitled *Consider the Source* and is still in use throughout Ontario by police officers.

Moving into 1984, the OACP Drug-Abuse Committee, with the assistance of the Ontario Ministry of Education, developed and produced another program. It was entitled *With Friends Like That* and was developed to be presented at the Grade 7 and 8 levels by police officers. This program is still in use by police officers throughout Ontario.

In 1987, the OACP Drug-Abuse Committee, with the assistance of the Addiction Research Foundation, developed and produced another video *The Choice is Yours* for use in Grades 9 and 10.

Metro police officers not only use the programs developed by the Ontario Association of Chiefs of Police but our Community Programs Unit has purchased a number of other drug-abuse films and videos that are also used as teaching aids.

In Metropolitan Toronto, the drug-awareness program began in the public and separate school systems in 1981. The Metropolitan Toronto Police Force utilized their Safety Education Officers to make these presentations because they were already established as teachers of safety in the schools, and were accepted as friends by the students.

All Safety Education Officers have received a one-week course at the Teacher's College or a one-week teaching course at the Ontario Police College at Aylmer, Ontario. These Officers were also provided with a special course concerning drugs and how best to present an awareness program to the Grade 4 to 8 levels.

These Officers are still performing this function in the public school and separate school systems, as well as many private schools. They are continually presented with new visual aids, buttons and educational hand-out materials; and are given additional training sessions in order to upgrade their teaching skills and knowledge of drug-abuse concerns.

Since 1981, Safety Education Officers have made presentations in over 20,000 classrooms and to over 450,000 students about the dangers of becoming involved with drugs and how to avoid peer pressure in saying "No" to drugs.

High school students are also provided with drug-awareness programs. These are presented by non-uniformed Community Relations Officers who receive the same training as the Safety Education Officers. Both modes of making these presentations have, unfortunately, been limited due to other duties that must be performed by these Officers.

For the past two years, the need to expand the contact time with students has become recognized, and a program has been developed which will result in an additional five police officers conducting ongoing presentations to students in Grades 6 to 9. This new approach has started and will target students in Senior Public, Middle and Junior High Schools. These Officers have also received extensive training. These presentations are in addition to the alcohol and other drug-abuse presentations give by local Boards of Education.

What type of program is given by a police Officer in the schools in Metropolitan Toronto? The first thing I wish to make clear is that we do not give lectures, or preach, against drug abuse. Lectures and preaching turn young people off. We give a structured presentation from lesson plans that are developed with the assistance of experts from the Ministry of Education, Boards of Education, Addiction Research Foundation and other agencies.

This presentation leads to discussions with the classes. Some of the areas discussed are: Self Esteem, Peer Pressure, Coping and Refusal Skills, Problem Solving and Decision Making. Education and prevention programs must not only increase knowledge but must change attitudes and encourage positive behaviours.

Drug-education programs which focus on resistance-skills training and social-skills training have proved effective. Such programs provide appropriate knowledge, but also focus on the skills of communication, decision making and values clarification. They deal

57

with consequences that are important to the target group.

Whatever the program, it must be relevant, interesting, timely and significant. Our aim is to make students aware of factors that influence the use and abuse of drugs, and to offer other alternatives. Our objective is, through education and knowledge, to have the young person decide, from the facts, that he or she does not need to use drugs and that these substances are not the way you solve problems. We try to approach the students in a non-judgmental, supportive way.

The role of the police should also be as a resource for teachers, other staff, and parents. In Metro Toronto, our Boards of Education are all very concerned about alcohol and other drug abuse. All Boards have their teachers presenting programs to the classes. We, the police, should be reinforcing what should be taught in the home and the school.

So, what is the role of the police in substance-abuse prevention? We are the enforcers of the law; we are counsellors, advisers, educators, resource persons - but most important, we hope we are are friends to our young people

Drug Awareness, the Local Community and the RCMP

Ben Jenkins

Ben Jenkins was born in Summerside, PEI. He joined the RCMP in 1967. He has worked in undercover drug operations and is currently in charge of the RCMP Drug Awareness Program for the Province of Ontario.

I'd like to congratulate the organizers of this Conference because it is exactly what the RCMP sees as a necessary part of the war against drugs - community involvement.

As far as the background to police involvement in the drug-awareness part of drug prevention, is concerned, I must tell you that up until 1980 the police side of it was not very organized in relation to the drug-awareness theme.

It was a haphazard process where we went into a school and did a presentation, not all the time coming across with a consistent message from one end of the country to the other. Today, we are educating our Officers for those presentations and beginning to achieve the consistency that was alluded to in the previous paper.

In 1980, the Ontario Chiefs of Police Association started a consistent program for the schools and part of that was the formation of an organization known as the Drug Education Coordinating Council which is made up of provincial bodies. That particular organization aims at consistency; to try to get everybody on the same track. They hold a conference each year to encourage that.

As far as the RCMP is concerned, 1986 was the year when we offi-

59

cially implemented a Drug Awareness Program created within the RCMP. The program is aimed at youth and focussed mainly on Grades 6, 7 and 8. That's followed up, of course, through the other Grades but it's felt that if we talk to the youth at this age they are still receptive to authority figures, and also that education for prevention will probably be much more effective than enforcement alone.

In that program we use athletes to act as role models and they come into the classrooms and discuss such things as decision making and similar subjects. This gives the young people a chance to meet the athletes and also, hopefully, to look up to and emulate their behaviour.

Part of our program is directed at parents because it was found, from the questions that they were asking when we went out conducting the sessions, that there was a lack of knowledge (or at least a misconception) as to what the drug situation was.

In a nutshell, the drug situation can be described as a *business* - nothing more and nothing less than that. The whole objective for anybody being involved in it is to make money.

We also go out and talk to industry and, in that regard, we're hoping to come achieve a couple of objectives. One, as far as industry is concerned, is to prevent the loss of productivity and the loss of materials. The second is on a more personal level because we also talk to the employees as parents. Hopefully they'll take what they learn home; hopefully they'll spread the word from these sessions.

Another initiative that we took was getting together with the Addiction Research Foundation in 1986 and creating Drug-Awareness Week Committees all over the province. There are thirty-five of them active at the present time. The purpose of these Committees, of course, is to try to bring the communities together to achieve drug-prevention.

As far as the future is concerned, we are attempting, through these drug-awareness committees, to go out to each community and try to get them active in taking care of their own problems. This is based on the belief that the police, the government, and the education system can't fight this problem alone; it takes the parents and it takes the community itself to deal with its particular problems. Sitting in Toronto and trying to deal with a drug situation up in Dryden, or Kenora, or anywhere else, is very, very difficult because you have to take the local circumstances into account.

So I think it's very good that this conference has been organized in your community, and that you're out here taking part in it, because you're the only people who can identify the problem, say exactly what it is and the best way to fight it. That, of course, brings in all the ramifications of culture, etc that somebody from outside such as myself might not fully realize

This Conference is exactly along the lines of what the whole enforcement community is attempting to do - to organize local communities to help themselves.

Drug Prevention Programs for Youth

Catherine Strong

Catherine Strong has degrees in science and education and is an experienced counsellor and group worker with clients of all ages in the workplace and the community. She is currently a Community Consultant with the Addiction Research Foundation

I work with school boards, the police, administrators, superintendents and teachers, as well as parents, students, and many other organizations and people in the community.

I work in the area of alcohol and drug education, and promoting healthy lifestyles. Our aim is to reduce alcohol and drug problems and to enhance healthy lifestyles for families in Ontario.

This work is within ARF's Community Services Division, and the role of the Community Service Division is to establish a range of alcohol and drug-prevention and treatment programs in Ontario.

This is done by 30 offices through a community-development process which involves mobilizing local resources, assessing community needs, promoting ARF's research knowledge, and implementing its prevention and treatment models.

Through these activities, and by providing information and materials to health and social service personnel, agencies, the occupational community and the public, the CSD influences the adoption of prevention and intervention programs.

The CSD's work for the '89-90 fiscal year will be concentrated in a number of areas. In the area of treatment and rehab services, we'll be conducting community-based needs assessments, establishing new treatment services, as well as improving existing treatment services and facilitating earlier intervention with alcohol and drug problems.

In the area of the work force, we'll be establishing and improving work-force health programs.

In prevention programs and services, we'll be implementing the Addiction Research Foundation's Ontario school programs and providing the ARF's 40th Anniversary Conference in October 1989.

In the area of public awareness and knowledge, we'll be implementing alcohol and drug-awareness programs such as the EASAP Program in the East End of Toronto.

We'll also be implementing alcohol-safety programs, along with the police - some of which have already been mentioned. We'll be implementing a key-influencer's program, community action programs, and responding to community requests.

As is clear from the recent Ontario Task Force on Illicit Drug Use (the Ken Black Task Force), drug issues continue to be the focus of increasing public and political concern and attention. Mr. Black suggested that law enforcement by itself is not a solution to our problems. He suggested that if we're going to deal seriously with this problem, we have to reduce the demand and he goes on to say, "If we're going to reduce that demand, we're going to have to involve many more participants in the game than we've had to the present time." He says, "We're all part of the problem and we must all be part of the solution."

Because Ken Black's Task Force is focussed on illicit drugs and their use by our young people, it does not include two of the most common drugs among our youth: alcohol and tobacco. Many parents are more frightened about cannabis or cocaine than the more familiar drugs such as alcohol and tobacco. Let's not forget that alcohol is the most popular drug of all; it's easily obtainable, socially acceptable, vigorously promoted and most commonly implicated in drug-related deaths. For example, the greatest killer of Canadian youth is traffic accidents, and up to fifty per cent of these are alcohol-related. The 1987

Ontario Student Survey by ARF indicated alcohol was used by 89 per cent of students in Grade 13; 85 per cent of students in Grade 11; 65 per cent of those in Grade 9; and 44 per cent of those in Grade 7. These are telling statistics that indicate the need for a lot more work to be done with our youth.

As an organization, ARF is unified by the clarity of its stated mission: to help reduce the pain, suffering and lost human potential caused by excessive and inappropriate use of alcohol and other drugs in Ontario. To ensure that its work is focussed on social priorities, and that the investment of the provincial government yields maximum return, ARF's work is directed to four distinct but inter-related goals.

Virtually all sectors of the province have a role to play in helping to reduce the number of people afflicted with alcohol and drug-related problems. In recognition of this role, the Foundation commits significant human and financial resources to the development of prevention programs designed for use by Ontario's community service system, the education system, judicial services and the work place.

The efforts of the Foundation and its partners in prevention are the key to making a difference, now and in the future. We're committed to helping foster positive social change through the ongoing, creative and innovative work and influence of ARF in Ontario.

Photo: Jerry Hobbs

Drunk Driving: Our National Crisis

Dee Nicholson

Dee Nicholson has worked in the advertising industry for fifteen years and founded Project Live Audience in which famous musicians took part in a series of rock star vignettes, urging their fans not to drink and drive. She is now Executive Director (Canada) for Sandy Golden's Campaign Against Drunk Driving.

Despite the millions of dollars to counter the problem, despite government intervention in unprecedented amount, three thousand Canadians die and over half a million are injured every year; half a million maimed, scarred, wounded - all needlessly, all preventably - because of drunks on our roads.

Obviously, our counter-measures system is not working. Officials may tell us, "Look at what we're doing; look how much we're spending" but people are still dying - not decreasingly but *increasingly*. We are now back up to 1984 levels of alcohol-related death and injury. The odds are fifty/fifty that, in your lifetime, you will suffer or die because of a drunk driver; the odds are virtually 100 per cent that someone you know and someone you love will be hit by a drunk driver.

We lose billions of dollars from our economy every year, and tragedy strikes thousands and thousands of Canadian families and our system does not work. In fact, our system is not a system at all but, rather, a hodge-podge of groups whose effectiveness, by virtue of their isolated existence, is vastly exceeded by their dedication.

The problems are the same in the United States, multiplied by ten

65

and it was these problems that spurred Sandy Golden - investigative reporter, acclaimed author, first volunteer Executive Director of Mothers Against Drunk Driving and now perhaps the world's leading authority in the fight against drunk driving - to form his own campaign. Over the past four years, Golden has been lobbying hard to have drunk driving declared a national crisis by the United States Surgeon General, Dr C. Everett Coop; to focus the nation's attention and galvanize the governments, the groups, the organizations and individuals involved in the issue into action - action organized in a total-systems approach to fight a systemic problem.

This goal is a hair's breadth away from being achieved. Through the national-crisis declaration, Golden will be able to assist, nationwide, in forming a blueprint for action, unifying forces with weapons that work. Under Golden's format, the process of bringing drunk driving under control starts with an audit of all programs and efforts in the country; to cross-reference all the things that work and take into account all the regional differences. By a careful audit, weak links become instantly obvious and strong points come to the fore. Further cross-referencing leads to universal methodology for funding and management, with the overall outcome being a complete blueprint for success where only `haphazard, "gee-let's-try-this-one-next" approaches existed before.

With the federal government committed to doing everything in its power through the national-crisis declaration, all the support systems are then in place, all the gears well oiled, in an efficient, proven program. For example, there was, in one year, a reduction in alcohol-related crashes in the State of Maryland to an 18-year low; in Montgomery County Maryland, a 71 per cent reduction in one year in alcohol-related death and injury. We have seen the written endorsements of every major medical organization in the USA, of state and local governments, of police and paramedics, the entire U.S. Senate and House of Representatives, and of the newly inaugurated President, George Bush - all calling for a national-crisis declaration and for the unified action necessary to eliminate drunk driving as the leading cause of death of young Americans.

This is President Bush's position on alcohol:

Alcohol must be recognized for what it is, a drug; and drunk driving must be recognized for what it is, a crime; and both should be dealt with as such. We must tell our children: "Alcohol is a dangerous drug, a drug which does not enhance life but destroys it.." When coupled with an automobile, alcohol becomes a terrible weapon, a weapon called drunk driving - a crime that is as real as murder or rape."

Bush states that he has nothing but admiration for dedicated groups such as the Campaign Against Drunk Driving and he says further that, "I agree completely that drunk driving is a national crisis and will do all I can, as President, to provide effective leadership to bring drunk driving under control." For a statesman of Bush's stature to take a leadership position this strong is an historic move but what better way to "a kinder, gentler nation" than to eliminate the leading cause of death of American youth?

We need our Prime Minister to exhibit the same kind of leadership in this country, where drunk driving kills more young Canadians than any other cause; where all of us are at risk every time we so much as step into the street. Some say that we have made great strides in raising public awareness. It is true that we have but with the wrong segment of the public. We now have a lot of people out there not driving after drinking but who weren't doing it anyway. The statistics speak for themselves. We have huge numbers of people with alcohol-abuse problems, people who deny they have a problem and don't want our help. They're the ones we have to fear most because they cannot hear the message and they comprise the majority of drunk-driving offenders. Indeed, there are those who, despite protestations to the contrary, would not want the message about drinking and driving to be too forceful.

Statistics Canada reports that, in 1987, per-capita consumption of alcoholic beverages included 322.07 bottles of beer, 12.24 750-millilitre bottles of wine, and 8.5 750-millilitre bottles of spirits. Somebody out there's drinking a huge dose of my share and somebody out there is probably drinking a huge dose of your share, too. This means there are a lot of Canadians who are consuming abusive amounts of alcohol. In the commercial process, they have to buy it before they can consume the estimated 6,207,002,400 bottles of beer per year, 313,960,000 bottles of wine, 218,266,668 bottles of spirit. Amazing! What would happen if everyone in North America drank in moderation? According to the numbers, the alcohol industry would lose billions upon billions of dollars. Is it, therefore, in their best corporate interest to be responsible in the sales and advertising of their potentially deadly products? Of course not. I believe that the alcohol industry is the most irresponsible corporate citizen of North America, indeed, in the world.

One of the main reasons keeping governments from intervening effectively is the huge revenue they receive - the so-called "sin taxes" - on alcohol. Governments have thrust upon them a huge conflict of interest; they have to juggle numbers - numbers that balance the well-being of the people with the well-being of the national debt - and ultimately, we all lose. Interestingly enough, drunk driving (the most immediately lethal form of alcohol abuse) is an equation. The number of deaths and injuries is directly proportionate to the level of government activity in intervention.

I hear it said that there are lots of government programs but these are smoke with no heat. We need to ask a lot of questions. Questions like:

Why is the drinking age virtually unenforced across this nation?

Why do levels of police enforcement vary so widely, despite uniformity of the law?

Why do police officers need to take up to three hours of valuable enforcement time processing paperwork on a D.W.I. suspect, when they can simply drop off a prostitute at the station and get on with their work?

We need to get our governments acting at all levels in unison, and rivet the nation's attention on this life-threatening situation through the declaration that drunk driving is a national crisis. It's more than that; it's a national disgrace. The loss of life, the pain of victims and families, the loss of dreams and human potential in stupid, preventable wrecks, is a disgrace.

Sandy Golden's Campaign Against Drunk Driving is now mustering support to send a message to Prime Minister Mulroney, a message that says, "Canada cares, and we won't tolerate drunk driving any more." As part of this effort - and with the kind support of Dennis Mills - we are sending a busload of student leaders from SADD Ontario to Ottawa to meet with Prime Minister Mulroney and ask that

Parliament declare drunk driving a national crisis and commit all available resources to eliminating drunk driving as the leading cause of death of Canadian youth and the leading criminal cause of death of all Canadians. But we must do more, much more. We must all join forces to sway the government. Please join us by sending a letter to the Prime Minister telling him you are concerned, asking him to have Parliament declare drunk driving a national crisis and do everything in his power to bring this killer under control. You don't even need to put a stamp on the letter.

There is no time to waste. Every day of delay kills more of us; every day of delay puts more of us in hospitals, in wheelchairs, or in the ground. We have no time for apathy. If ten 747s each carrying 300 people crashed each year killing all aboard, would there not be a huge furor? Would *you* be very anxious to get on a plane? Given the numbers of dead and injured, why would you be eager to get in your own vehicle and hit the road?

Here is more food for thought. At any given time, every fourteenth driver on our roads is impaired; count the cars. Between 11:00 p.m. and 3:00 a.m., especially on weekends, the proportion of impaired drivers increases to about one in four. One hundred thousand convictions are registered each year against impaired drivers but each one represents well over a thousand more who are never stopped. This means there are over a million drunks on our roads every year. The odds are you could be the next one hit - you, or your child, or your spouse, or your friend. If you don't believe it now, the next time some of your friends are hit, you're going to believe it. Our roads are not safe. We have to stop this insanity.

The agenda of Sandy Golden's Campaign Against Drunk Driving is to ensure that more Canadians have the chance to enjoy the privilege of living in this great nation in years to come. Help us in achieving our goal of a safer, healthier Canada in the 21st Century. We need all the help we can get.

If you want to send a letter to the Prime Minister, just address it to him in Ottawa; get all your friends and neighbours to send a letter, too. If you're the head of an association (or if not have the president) send the letter on behalf of your association. You can say something very simple, like:

"Dear Prime Minister Mulroney,
We are concerned about the drunk-driving issue in Canada. We believe it is a national crisis. We ask that you have Parliament declare drunk driving a national crisis and we ask that you do everything in your power to eliminate drunk driving as the leading cause of death of young Canadians and the leading criminal cause of death in Canada."

Street Kids

Mike Faye

Mike Faye has worked for the past twenty years with children, youth and families in Toronto as a child care worker, social worker, supervisor and program manager. He has been Director of Programs at Covenant House, Toronto, for six years.

Photo: Jerry Hobbs

About 80 kids stay at Covenant House each day. There are 30 beds so that leaves 50 sleeping on the floor. Who are these kids? Why do these young people run to the streets? Why do they end up at Covenant House?

It's very important, before we talk about that, to know that every one of these kids *uses* drugs or alcohol. We estimate 80 per cent of them *abuse* drugs and alcohol (meaning that it gets in the way of their carrying out their lives, doing what they're supposed to do every day) and about 10 per cent of them are *addicted* (meaning that they need drugs every day to survive their day).

These kids come mainly from the Toronto area and suburbs (about 65 per cent of them), 20 per cent come from the rest of Ontario and about 15 per cent of these kids come from across Canada - and a couple from the 'States.

Who are they? They're high-school dropouts. These kids have no skills to gain employment; they come from dysfunctional families; about 50 per cent come from middle-class families and 40 per cent of these kids come from families in which both parents are there. These kids have experienced physical and sexual abuse in their homes before leaving, and certainly on the streets after running away.

71

In 1987, in a study of about 200 of the kids at Covenant House, they reported significant figures in terms of this abuse. Physical abuse was reported by 74 per cent of the boys and 90 per cent of the females - and this is in their own home, before leaving. Sexual abuse was also considerably high: 50 per cent of the males reported they were abused and 86 per cent of the females reported sexual abuse in their homes before leaving and running away to the streets.

So, we may get a very different profile, or understanding, of these young people between the ages of 16 and 21, particularly at Covenant House - why they're on the streets and what they're trying to accomplish. They're simply running away from dysfunctional families and they're running away from dysfunctional situations.

The problem is that a myth exists. The general public thinks that these are bad kids running away to the streets. How does that relate to drugs and crime? Well, the reality is that once these kids hit the streets, there are very few ways to survive. They have no skills and it's very difficult to get jobs; very difficult to maintain employment at a rate that can support them.

Ultimately, they have to steal and sell what they steal to survive. Unfortunately, a lot of the time, they're selling their bodies which, of course, gets them involved in prostitution. So we're looking at a very damaged kid who uses drugs and who gets involved in crime in order to survive his or her day-to-day existence.

This week, you may have read in the paper of a young 20-year-old woman who had experienced drug-induced mental health problems. She is a former client of Covenant House and was a young lady who was very typical of the kid who comes to us - who comes and goes, and experiences a revolving door in and out of the system that is trying to help them. The drugs really do take over and gain control of their lives, and it's very difficult for them to lead a life, because they are addicted to drugs and they are addicted to the subculture of downtown Toronto.

I think that the main message from Covenant House, to anybody who is concerned about the youth of today and where they are going, would be that, if they're supposed to be our future, there must be a political will to see these kids as young people in trouble who need our help, not looked down on as trouble makers who refuse to accept parental control and parental authority.

That's not to say that they aren't trouble sometimes at Covenant House. They aren't perfect kids but they aren't the bad, violent kids that people seem to think they might be.

I had an opportunity to speak about six months ago to a group of home owners in the Scarborough area, when we were trying to support the development of a Shelter in Scarborough. I can understand their fear because it was related to ignorance of not knowing what these young people are all about, assuming that these kids were living in, or coming from, a halfway house or a correctional system, and might possibly injure one of their family members, rape one of their family members.

I understood their fear but I was shocked, watching people literally being screamed and yelled off the podium when they tried speaking in support of these kids. So I think that it really is essential, in addition to the political will that I talked about, that the general public sees these kids as young people who need our support.

We need to develop and provide programs (which ultimately is an issue of money once the political will is there) to provide prevention; to provide treatment and to provide a continuum of services that these kids need.

We are providing an alternative to prostitution by offering them free room and board and support while they get a job. That seems like the answer to the problem but, if you're addicted to drugs and you're addicted to the street style, it's not going to happen over two or three weeks or months at Covenant House. These young people have been running from problems in their background and have a major mistrust of adults and this is a significant factor which we have to understand as we try to help them.

In summary, what we require is political will and a will on the part of the general public to see these kids as *damaged* kids who need our help and not to see them as acting-out kids who need to be shoved somewhere out of sight.

Questions and Comments from the Audience

Question:
You spoke about giving talks in front of home owners in Scarborough, and maybe we're victimizing those home owners as being average Canadians who might not know what's going on in the streets. What's the difference between the awareness level of people who aren't exposed to drugs, compared to the awareness level of people right in Covenant House? Is there a huge gap?

Mike Faye:
I'm not sure I understand part of that question

Question:
What are some of the questions that the youth in the street throw out at you people who are exposed to drugs and alcohol abuse and so on? Can you tell us so that we, who might not be exposed to that and might not be aware, understand what's going on in their minds.

Mike Faye:
One of the issues is that we try to respond to as quickly as possible when one of the young people "discloses" that they have a drug problem. If a kid is likely to stay anywhere from two days to five weeks, you have to act quickly. If they have to be put on a waiting list for treatment somewhere, you can forget it. The kid'll be quickly gone. So when you talk about responding when kids ask questions, it's mainly a question of how do we help them once they've decided they need it.

Unfortunately, the majority of our kids don't realize they need help, or haven't admitted that to themselves yet. I think we would all agree that, in trying to treat drug and alcohol problems, the first step is that the individual needing help has to *accept* that they need it. So for us the limitation is simply being able to find something to support these kids very quickly, as soon as they request it.

Question:
This is a statement and a question, mainly directed to the two police representatives. The prevention programs and the education programs for the children in our schools, I think, are fantastic. And I agree with what you're doing there but my question is: What is the level of awareness with respect to drug abuse and drug programs of normal police officers in the street? What sort of education is involved? Because I have encountered numerous times repugnance and ignorance among the people at your representatives in the streets. As a structured sort of educational system that you're directing to our youth and to our public, how does it work internally?

William Bishop:
We have ongoing training of our officers at our Police College in Aylmer. In each police station we also have a Sergeant who is dedicated as a Training Sergeant, to bring Officers up to date on the various trends, changes in the law, and procedures in relation to all types of crime and enforcement and, in particular, drugs.

We have six Drug Squads in Metropolitan Toronto, one for each Police District plus the Morality Drug Squad. The members of the Drug Squads attend police stations and give ongoing lectures to Officers. They pass on to them the knowledge, up-to-date, current knowledge, of what is transpiring on the streets.

Ben Jenkins:
I'd just add that in the RCMP we have a similar training program, where you start off with the basic training out in Regina, and then it's followed up by in-service training. But the point that you bring out is probably fairly accurate; that if you have a policeman who's engaged in, let's say, commercial crime enforcement rather than drug enforcement, he might not be as knowledgeable as the drug enforcement officer. He is covered on the generalities but he might be a little bit rusty on specifics.

Question:
Are there drug-awareness programs within the RCMP or within the Metro Toronto police for your own officers? I think the question was: It's directed at the public, but do you also reflect back internally?

Ben Jenkins:
Yes, we do. If you look at industry as a whole, you'll find that approxi-

mately 7 per cent of industry, on average, will be involved and have a drug problem. That is true of any industry, whether you're looking at the police or any other area of society. And we do have an internal education program, as well as the one that we spoke of.

William Bishop:
Also, the Metropolitan Toronto Police have an employee-assistance program, which the officers and members of the Force are encouraged to attend should they feel the need of personal instruction or personal guidance in relation to any problem. I'm sorry to say that, as in any organization, from time to time the drug problem does arise.

Question:
I live in the Riverdale area and I'm a parent of three boys in the school system. I'm impressed with the prevention materials. My six-year-old comes home from school and says he's "not going to do drugs". That's not language I taught him so someone taught him that. I'm also very concerned, as a resident in this area and as a parent, about a gap between the enforcement and the prevention activities.

I'm a nurse, and I've studied epidemiology in the health field, and I really feel that some of this needs to be applied to the police field, though I'm sure to a certain level it is. I'm concerned about the youths who are experimenting, or who are just entering into drugs, who are taking soft drugs or crack for the first couple of times, and are getting involved in minor crime. I just wonder what relationship to minor crimes, even to break and entry, there is attached to drugs, which is attached not just to apprehension but treatment and counselling of the kids involved.

On our street, over the Christmas period, I was aware of five attempted and successful break and entries (one at nine o'clock on a Friday night when a lot of people were home) and the woman came home and the person was in her house. There was a size 11 Adidas shoe in the snow outside. I think we've got to look at the early treatment in relation to crime, and understand and act on the connection of drugs and crime very early and I just wonder what the police force is doing about that?

William Bishop:
There is a definite connection between drugs and crime; I think

that's a foregone conclusion. I can say that our Chief of Police has handed down a mandate to all members of the Force, particularly those of us who are engaged in the drug-enforcement areas, to step up our enforcement against street dealers.

Question:
I'm not talking about the dealers; I'm talking about minor crime as an entry-way into early intervention.

William Bishop:
Are you talking about minor crimes with the youth?

Question:
That's right. Things like shoplifting, and break and entry for stereos and radios.

William Bishop:
Well, again, there is a connection in many cases, to drugs. We feel that by removing, as effectively and consistently as possible, the dealers from the streets, that we can cut back and solve an awful lot of this type of crime that is going on in the community.

Question:
Are you saying that your main, or sole, approach is through the dealers, and not through the kids that are doing these crimes?

William Bishop:
We have to deal with the situation at its grassroots and we feel that just to attack the major dealers and importers is not enough; that we must deal with the people that are right out on the street.

Mike Faye:
If I might just add some comments to that. Certainly, having some background in my previous job working with young offenders, I would think at this point, after a couple of years of the Young Offender's Act, which, for example, does not allow charging kids under 12 with crimes, that we've lost an ability to respond to the kid who's doing petty crimes. So, if a 10-year-old kid is doing a B and E as a front runner for a 15-year-old kid, the 10-year-old kid cannot be charged. I think that there really is activity now, between police support and people in community and social services looking at that because it certainly has tied the hands of police in their ability to respond to

dealing with these young kids. Although I asked people to consider these kids as kids with problems and not to kick them out but rather support them, I certainly don't have any problem with young people being apprehended for crimes and then dealt with in a social-service support way as well as a correctional way. There's nothing wrong with a consequence being attached to some kid ripping off people so he can buy drugs.

Ben Jenkins:
I'd just like to build on what the previous two speakers have said. In relation to the property crimes, I have a study in my office, and admittedly it's from the United States, which shows that over 70 per cent of property crimes can be attributed to those people who are involved in drugs. The second issue that I'd like to address is that the communities themselves have to take on a lot of responsibility as far as the prevention of these types of crimes. And that's where your committees can be made up from your community, including parents, treatment personnel, educationalists, business people, politicians, and media and take care of the problem in your community.

Question:
It was said here that alcohol was the major drug that was the subject of abuse. During the past two or three years, there has been a significant change in the attitude of our society towards drinking and driving; it has become much more socially unacceptable to be drinking and driving. Are any of you finding a greater reception from the people you're talking to about that kind of thing: that it's not socially acceptable to be involved with any type of drug?

Catherine Strong:
Let me respond to the first part of your statement, that there has been a change or, seemingly, a trend towards a change, in the drinking and driving habits of the public. That is so. However, it has stabilized somewhat or even dropped a little bit in the past year. That seems to be because the rest of the supports aren't there; the community supports, the law supports. The same thing happened with tobacco. Twenty-five years ago, the Surgeon General came out with warning labels for tobacco. It's been a long, uphill climb to reduce the number of smokers and it's got to be the same thing for alcohol. You can't just have RIDE programs and drinking-and-driving advertising. You have to change laws and you have to change the whole thinking of society about how acceptable alcohol in general

and also its excessive use is.

Question:
I'm just wondering (you're all involved with any type of drug, basically) are you finding a greater reception, from the people that you're talking to, to the idea that it is socially unacceptable within their peer group to be involved with those substances - with illicit drugs?

Ben Jenkins:
I would say yes to that, and what we're trying to do is promote the healthy lifestyle. We find that the young people who are refusing drugs are doing it for health reasons rather than from a fear of being prosecuted and they're coming across much more actively in their conversation to their friends; if someone's using drugs then they're trying to convince them not to. So, we are finding this attitudinal change; at least, that the feeling I get from the presentations I make.

William Bishop:
I would like to comment on that as well. I think that you'll find, amongst your own family and your own friends and so forth, that perhaps it's now becoming a lot less expensive to host a social function because people do tend not to want to drink the way they did some years back. That's an encouraging sign, and it's also there with drugs as well.

Question:
What are you finding with respect to the use of alternative-measures programs in order to help kids who are just breaking into crime and being involved with drugs?

Ben Jenkins:
What are we finding that works as an alternate program?

Question:
Yes.

Ben Jenkins:
You have to give the young people something. You can't just take away the drugs and leave a vacuum there; you have to create an atmosphere that's healthy for them. You have to fill that vacuum with some activity, like sports or reading or hikes or outdoors. In

other words, we can't sit back and just say, "Don't use drugs." We
have to get out, as a community, and get actively involved, and show
them that there's much more to life than sitting around smoking pot
or dropping acid or this type of thing. Yes, you're a hundred per cent
right; there has to be an alternative for them and, as a community,
you can develop that.

Question:

I'll address this question to Mike Faye, because you've had the most
recent experience with the problems out in Scarborough - bringing
a halfway house, if you want to call it that, to that area. A lot of the
kids that you see downtown come from the suburbs. What are some
of the alternatives that we can offer these young people if they're
forced to leave their homes in Markham, Scarborough, Etobicoke,
Mississauga, wherever? What are the alternatives so that they are
not forced to go downtown where they are quickly assimilated into
the subculture, as you have indicated?

Mike Faye:

The alternatives firstly, should be talked about in terms of prevention. What we try to do is ensure through our high-school program
that kids are aware of what the streets are like before they run to
them. We're not saying to kids, "Don't run." We acknowledge to kids
in the classroom that they have, in fact, been abused or may have
been abused; they may have friends who have been abused. We acknowledge the need to run. We simply say, "Know where you're
running to before that happens." We describe the downtown culture.
So, that's the first step.

The second, an alternative really, is to use the system in which they
live. There are social service supports in almost all the suburbs.
There are places that kids can go in terms of counselling. The limitation is that they generally have nowhere to go in terms of an actual
residence as temporary shelter. Currently, other than the downtown
area, there is only one other shelter, called Youth Without Shelter,
in Etobicoke. Originally that started to develop in North York, only
they couldn't put it through there so it ended up in Etobicoke. There
is an ongoing inability to develop temporary shelter.

There really are, currently, no alternatives other than teaching kids
that they can stay with friends; that they can get help through adults
who can be trusted; and also to ensure that, if they don't get any help

from the first adult, that they should keep moving to a second one because not everybody out there has the answer or the support. But literally, in terms of temporary shelter, if a kid has to leave home, other than immediate family and friends, there is nothing; there are not enough beds in the suburbs.

Question:
I think it's important that we make distinctions between three different things as we're approaching this topic. One is the kids themselves. There are very few kids under twenty here today to speak about the Agenda or this particular topic. I think if one has to deal with this question realistically, we have to find out what it is that the kids think, and how they address this and the peer pressure that they have to deal with.

The second is the parents. I was rather aghast at the statistic that was pointed out on the abuse that goes on within the homes, I assume by parents or by other adults, against kids. This is something that I've never heard before. I think it would be great if the adults in this room, or in this Conference, start to think how we in the society can do something to stop the abuse of children. Perhaps that is a totally separate thing from dealing with the problem. In my view we need to get the kids themselves involved in the question and secondly find out how we as a community can deal with the abuse that's being practiced by the adults on the kids. The third aspect is the role of the police (whether it's RCMP or the local police) in all this. It's unfortunate that the police are always being asked what they are doing about this situation. I feel that the police are, fortunately or unfortunately, being placed in a position of "It's your problem." It's not their problem; it's *our* problem. One of the good things is that we're here but, I think in order to analyze this problem properly, we have to separate this into the three areas that I'm suggesting. I would like to know, so I can deal with the police problem, is there anything that you could recommend that we can do in society to stop the expansion of crack houses in Toronto?

William Bishop:
Well, anyone who has any information in relation to drugs or illicit dealing in drugs, the first thing that I would suggest is that you contact the police; either the drug squads or your local police station. Speak to any of the officers there, particularly the Community Service Officers, and this information will be passed on. There's also the

Crime Stoppers program, and if you wish to remain anonymous use that. I can say that we have had a great deal of success in my particular Drug Squad with the Crime Stoppers program because we can't be everywhere and, as you say, it's very true; people in the community can assist the police in a great many areas.

Another approach is to contact your local police Division station and speak with the Community Service Officers who will be only too pleased to attend any of your groups or organizations. It doesn't have to be a large group; any size group at all, even individually, they will come and speak with you and give you some insight into how you can deal with a certain situation in relation to crime and drugs in your particular area.

Question:
Have you met any of the parents of some of those runaway kids that you put up?

Mike Faye:
Well, unfortunately, very few of the kids that come to Covenant House have an opportunity to return to parents. They generally, at that point, have decided they don't want to be there or their behaviour and their way of acting back against parents has been so bad that the parents don't want them back either. So when we talk about runaway and homeless youths, "runaway" means the kid has taken the choice to take a hike and "homeless" means that the parents have put the young person out. So we don't have a lot of experience with the parents. In fact, less than 2 per cent of our kids go home (which is a pretty sad statement when you think about it, but 3,000 different kids are admitted each year). These kids, at the age of 16, are trying to become independent citizens, which is very difficult.

On the issue of sexual abuse and what we can do about it, I think that the issue really is just accepting that it does happen. I mean, when I talk about percentages as high as 85 and 90 per cent of physical and sexual abuse, middle-class people don't want to believe that it's happening. I don't mean to point fingers (I don't even know anybody in the room) but I can guarantee you somebody in the room here is abusing their kid and that's a reality. As people begin to accept that, perhaps when the young person who happens to be the son or the daughter of their next-door neighbour tries to stay in their community by saying, "Dad is doing the following" (and certainly with sexual abuse, almost 100 per cent is done by men) the neighbour will believe that that kid is telling the truth. People don't generally lie about being sexually abused. It's so devastating to have to disclose that this kind of thing happens to you that I'm amazed neighbours don't believe - perhaps because the guy is an upstanding citizen, or he's the Cub leader, or he's whoever. It really is happening and I think that, over the last five years, the general public is beginning to accept that fact

I think a lot of it's due to the media attention, that has made it more acceptable for kids to disclose, and I think we have kids disclosing more frequently now. We have kids disclosing drug addiction as well. It's becoming more acceptable to tell somebody that you need help but the average guy on the street needs to be more accepting of that and believe that it occurs.

Question:
I agree that I don't think the problem we have with drugs and youth and crime has to do with what the police forces are doing. And I don't think that the Agenda for the 21st Century should be passing more regulations about the police force. Also I don't think we have a problem with youth and drugs and crime because of our schools. I don't think youths get into drugs because they don't know better. I don't think that's the issue. I guess my question to you is what is our Agenda, so that we don't come back here in the 21st Century and have this same conversation over again? What's your advice to us on what we should be focussing on to change the current Agenda?

William Bishop:
I think that you should try, with whatever means you have in your own particular home or your own particular community, to get the message across to the youth that drugs are not an acceptable way of solving their problems. As people here have pointed out, smoking is looked upon as socially unacceptable, and drinking to excess is becoming the same way (and probably it always has been in many areas) and now this is something that has to be done in the drug field as well.

We're seeing that particulary in the use of drugs amongst the athletes. We are having athletes come forward and say that they find it offensive; they find it demeaning that members of their organizations are using drugs and this is the message that has to get across;

83

that it is offensive and demeaning. I think when that becomes the norm, then this drug problem, although I suppose it may always be with us, will subside to a level where we won't have to be back here talking about it again.

Ben Jenkins:
I feel that we have to change the attitudes and, getting back to the question earlier, I think we as parents, or at least the older generation within the community, can go a long way toward this by organizing ourselves much along the lines of Neighbourhood Watch or whatever, creating a community committee, if you will, and go in and discuss the problem. The police can act as a resource in this venture. The young people can be invited to get their views on it. Just by talking openly about it and assessing the problem within the community, and then taking action within the community - preventative action - I think we can go a long way towards solving it.

Catherine Strong:
I think we have to start right in our homes, as well as all those other things that have been mentioned. We have to keep communication open with our children. We have to start very, very, very, very young - three and four - to start, not talking about drugs, but talking to our kids and part of that is *listening* to our children. So we need those kinds of skills as parents (of course, parenting is one of the hardest jobs in the world) and we need to do that well and keep communication open. That way we can transmit our values, be appropriate role models, and have our children cooperate in helping to reduce drug problems.

Mike Faye:
I can't improve on the former recommendations in terms of how one would actually respond but the one comment I would make is that, for years, I've been listening to a variety of ways that we can help improve the situation for our kids and for our families and they all make sense. Nobody can argue with the mom-and-apple-pie position of making sure that at age four your kid knows about drugs and that family relationships are healthy, and all those wonderful things that we like to do. But I've yet to see a significant amount of dollars in terms of the political will that goes along with that. You can look at any report on this subject! I hope I'm still employed after all this! I have the Catholic Church behind me at Covenant House, so I guess I'm okay.

84

I just think we should support providing that money every year and I would suggest that people support, through whatever means are possible, those governments who do provide the funds for these kinds of programs rather than simply talk about what we need to do.

Photo: J M Carisse

The Peace Tower, Parliament Hill, Ottawa

Section Three:
Peace and Defence

Photo: Photo Feature Ltd

Nurturing a Fragile Détente

John Lamb

John Lamb was educated in political science at the University of Toronto and in international relations at Columbia University. He has taught international relations at the University of Toronto and worked at the Department of National Defence. He is the founder of the Canadian Centre for Arms Control and Disarmament.

I guess you have probably all heard that peace is breaking out all over the world. People point to the Soviet withdrawal from Afghanistan; the Vietnamese withdrawal from Cambodia; cease-fires in Angola; the end of the Iran-Iraq War and every day in the news there seems to be some new evidence that Peace is breaking out. The President of Cyprus recently said, "Peace is breaking out all over. There's an epidemic. And we don't want to be left out." It's just extraordinary and the most important aspect of all is that the Cold War itself between the U.S. and the Soviet Union seems to be coming to an end.

Yet I think that there are questions that we all need to ask - and probably have asked at one time or another. Is this all something we can trust? Is this going to last? What does it all mean? The first thing to say is that the world doesn't stand still. Moscow and Washington are still going to be rivals well into the 21st Century, and there are going to be plenty of regional conflicts all over the world over a multitude of issues which are going to keep wars going and conflicts bubbling away below the surface. So, in general, peace will not have broken out everywhere in the 21st Century.

At the same time, I would argue that we are witnessing a major shift

87

in world affairs that will endure, which holds out great promise for the future and which will lead us away from the precipice that we have lived on over the last 40 years or so. One of the most important aspects of this is that there is a growing recognition around the world (including important political circles) that security can only be mutual; that one side can only be secure if its adversary is also secure.

In historical terms, that's a brand-new thought. In the past, one country's security has depended on its capacity to defend itself. If it did a good job, it didn't get invaded; if it did a poor job, maybe it did get invaded. Well, the situation has now changed. Nuclear weapons have wrought a change which means that only if your adversary is secure will you be secure as well.

I guess another major change which is contributing to the sea-change in thinking on this, is that people are beginning to recognize that you cannot assess security in military strength alone. Increasingly, people are coming to understand that the mountain of debt that's looming over us is also a security issue, and that the destruction of the environment that we see going on around is another security issue - conceivably an even more immediate and pressing security concern than armed conflict.

One of the consequences of all of this, of the broadening of the security agenda, has been that some people are turning away from arms control and concern about military security, and saying that now that Gorbachev's arrived and repealed the old, aggressive policies of the Soviet Union, can't we all go off and save the whales and trees? I think we need to remember one thing, and that is that every year now, worldwide military spending has reached a trillion dollars and I would argue that there is simply no way that we can reverse the destruction of the environment, repair our economies, deal with urban blight, and so on, if we're going to allow that kind of haemorrhaging of our financial and human resources into as unproductive an activity as the arms race.

This is, by the way, one reason why I think that this is not an ephemeral development; this is something that's going to continue. It's not simply a matter of how durable Mikhail Gorbachev's tenure is in the Kremlin because I think what is motivating him, and what is going to motive the United States, is a recognition that they cannot sustain the kind of spending on the military that they have in the past.

Gorbachev knows that if he keeps that up, he will lead the Soviet Union into the 21st Century as a third-world country. I don't think he will allow that to happen; and the same thing goes for the United States.

Now, nobody's about to disarm unilaterally; it simply isn't going to happen and that's why negotiated arms control is going to become an even more important aspect of security as we go into the 21st Century. If we're going to lift the burden of arms spending, negotiated arms control will be absolutely essential and Canada has a role to play in this. I think a lot of us look back with a degree of nostalgia at the '50s when Canada was known as "the internationalist country", as "a helpful fixer", as a country that really contributed to international peace and security. Well, it seems to me that, as the Cold War comes to an end and the superpowers settle down for a period of national consolidation and renewal, we're going to be entering a period when middle powers, like Canada, can come to the fore again.

I think, looking ahead to the 21st Century, that it won't only be the challenge of the superpowers' arms race that will be of concern. Another important issue will be the spread of nuclear weapons. Can you imagine what the world would be like if Libya, Iraq, South Korea, maybe Brazil and Argentina, all had nuclear weapons? How much harder it would be to keep the lid on in the Middle East, being held hostage by the likes of a Khaddafy. Our children and our grandchildren could well inherit that kind of world unless we begin taking very seriously the spread of nuclear weapons now.

Nuclear weapons may not be the only hazard. What about chemical weapons? Remember, Canadians were the very first in the whole world to be exposed to poison gas in World War I. They're now calling it "the poor man's atom bomb" because anybody can get it.

Those are all items, perhaps, that will continue to be on the Agenda but let me just say that there is a more immediate problem. I believe that the real challenge facing us in Canada is to to make sure that the new détente between the East and the West is not reversed and defeated. Remember, we've been through this before; there was a détente in the 1970s, too. It was unravelled by hard-liners on both sides, in the East and the West, who didn't want to see a détente happen.

So the main challenge for Canadian foreign policy for the foreseeable future - well into the 21st Century - will be to help sustain and to nurture the fragile detente that is now in the process of being built out of the ashes of the Cold War. Yet, I would suggest that Canada is strangely unprepared for this role.

The government's Defence White Paper, presented as a blue-print for the '90s, actually looks more like something out of the 1950s. It reflects cold-war thinking; it shows red arrows across Europe; red arrows across the Arctic; red arrows coming at us across the Pacific. The nuclear-powered submarine decision is also completely out of sync with global realities and Canada's Defence needs going into the 21st Century. Canada does need armed forces - no doubt about that - but it needs them suited for the requirements of the 21st Century, not for the Cold War. They need to be oriented toward peace-keeping, sovereignty protection, and securing Canada a seat at the table on the important arms-control negotiations that we will be faced with in the future.

Most of all, I think we need to re-create a sense, as Canadians, that this country has a genuine role to play in making the world a more secure and peaceful place. This is going to mean developing a more independent approach, a more independent view, toward these issues and a role less closely attuned to the United States.

Now, however you may feel about Free Trade, I think you should know that the present government's continentalist policies are not restricted to trade. At a time when our security policies should be becoming more global in their focus, they are instead becoming more narrowly focussed on the defence of North America. I think that's wrong, and is going to preclude our developing an independent approach.

Only if Canadians with a concern about our global future inform themselves of the issues, and get involved, will Canada take up its proper and independent role in the peace process. I think that peace has been breaking out all over, but it will need to be nurtured and built into the institutional structures required for the 21st Century. That's what our challenge is: To build a peaceful and secure world for our children.

Vigilance for Peace

Graeme Nicholson

Graeme Nicholson is the author of Seeing
and Reading, *a book on the theory of knowledge. He has been active with nuclear disarmament groups in Canada, the US and
Germany. He teaches modern European
philosophy at Trinity College in the University of Toronto.*

Photo: Jerry Hobbs

In years gone by, war was a way of pursuing international policy. If
diplomacy failed, the generals led armed troops out onto an open
plain; their fighting continued a few hours, a few days, or even a few
years. The country that won on the battlefield got to achieve its
policy goals. One great writer said war was "the continuation of
policy by other means." Another way of putting it is that war was "a
dispute-settlement mechanism". But nuclear war would not take
place on a plain; nor would it last a few weeks or a few years; nor
would there be soldiers fighting. Instead of that, a few scientists
underground would push some buttons, and destruction would rain
down upon the Earth in a matter of minutes. Nuclear encounters
should not even be called by the name of war; nor should these
nuclear devices be called by the name of weapons. The language
deceives us into thinking there is some continuity with the past.

Since 1945, human history has changed completely. The great powers
now possess the power to destroy every human life and every form
of life on this planet in a matter of hours. That's not just making wars
and pollution even worse than before. The great powers can now
bring history and global life to an end.

All human traditions up until 1945 recognized the power of God to
create the world and to end the world; but now human beings have

taken over the power of God. Therefore, from now on, every form of decision making in all perpetuity is going to be different from what it was in all the past. About every single human undertaking, every human being will have to ask the question "Does this tend to promote universal destruction; or does this tend to reduce its likelihood?"

Moreover, these devices are becoming easier and easier to build, and to build in secret. Their blueprints are easy to get, and will become increasingly easy to get, store, and distribute. That means that vigilance for peace, for the preservation of nature and history, will be a worldwide imperative of every human civilization in all foreseeable future. It will be a part of every issue addressed at every level; every local issue, even every educational issue.

Every national and international issue will, for the foreseeable future, indeed for all future, have to be guided by that most important single question. Thus, in a nuclear age, war cannot be understood as "the continuation of policy by other means". A nuclear encounter cannot be the continuation of any policy.

Nor should we believe, in my opinion, in the development of what are called "tactical" nuclear weapons of which we hear more and more in the '80s. Generals and scientists, many of them, say that now they are developing highly sophisticated systems with nuclear devices that fix one target quite exactly, and won't spray nuclear fallout all over the planet; they are supposed to be "clean" nuclear weapons, these tactical devices.

What they're saying is that they can build a nuclear weapon that will act like a conventional weapon. So, why do they need it? The answer lies in the link between the military establishment and the research and development industries of the world powers. I could invent, for example, a new kind of fingernail clipper that would have a new kind of power (a fingernail clipper equipped with electrical battery power that has all the advantages of a conventional fingernail clipper) and I could say, "I can invent a high-powered fingernail clipper that will be just exactly like your conventional fingernail clipper, and I'll sell you one." The question is, why would we want one? And the truth is a battery-powered electrical fingernail clipper could, in fact, be murder.

I want to address the question not of the superpowers and their relationship in the nuclear age, but rather to talk about the question of a national policy for Canada. I'm proud to borrow the term "national policy" from Canada's first Prime Minister. I want to address the question of how Canada can secure room for manoeuvre, for a National Policy on peace and defence. We are, at this date, held tight in an alliance, a western alliance, and as John.Lamb said "closer than in the past" to our neighbour to the south.

How can Canada now gain room to manoeuvre? We are, of course, a western country; we should be proud of that - proud of our history and culture as part of the West - and I see no likelihood that we would wish to detach ourselves from military alliances with our western neighbours. However, I think we must do so under conditions set by ourselves. We must articulate a National Policy for our participation in military alliances.

In the first place, we should not yield to the pressure from our Allies to take on greater and greater defence expenditures. I don't think, by the way, that we should cut them but I think the pressure to raise the proportion of our budget allocated to the military up to the NATO level is dubious, especially now in the present situation of Soviet retrenchment. We should stand firm and not raise our military budget and, in that way, seek to point the way to other powers - even other Western powers.

Secondly, in my opinion, Canada should never, under any circumstances, assume any form of nuclear weapons; nor should we allow the testing of missiles to continue on our soil. We have now an Agreement until 1993 for the cruise-missile testing; this Agreement should never be renewed.

Canada's contribution to peace can be, among other things, to remain a nuclear-free zone and I think that should certainly be included. I do not wish to call for conventional disarmament; I do not think that Canadians would want, or hope, to abolish the armed forces, nor to save money in that fashion by reducing the proportion of our budget allocated to defence. I am simply saying that we must have a National Policy on defence; to eliminate our defence budget is to give up having a National Policy.

Surely it is possible for Canada to draw this distinction once and for all between weapons of war and defence on the one hand, and nuclear

93

devices on the other. I think there's nothing wrong with giving arms and uniforms to a designated body of citizens; some acting as a police force in the municipalities and others acting as a military force for the nation.

It is not wrong for a country to have armed forces and conventional weapons but in the 21st Century, the role of the Canadian Armed Forces and conventional weapons cannot be to wage war. It must be to patrol our coastline. Indeed, when a French fishing fleet comes to approach Newfoundland, they should encounter the Canadian Coast Guard much earlier in that process than they do.

We should have non-nuclear forces and submarines to explore our Arctic. We have to have forces that stand guard at our borders. We need a standing army to meet national disasters; to meet the possibility of riots and to continue our role in peace-keeping.

The Canadian record on international aid and development is something of which we can all be proud. All Canadians have a record that is second to none in the world in these matters. The tradition of French Canada sending missionaries through the Western Hemisphere in the 19th and 20th Centuries is another accomplishment which reflects on all Canadians. The role of English and French Canadians, side by side, giving international aid and development is surely the central task in our international relations in the 21st Century.

Defence and Security

John Hasek

John Hasek has an MA in psychology from the University of New Brunswick. A 20 year serving officer in the Canadian army with tours of duty in Ghana, Cyprus and Vietnam, he was the first officer commanding the CAF parachute team, the Skyhawks. John is now an author and documentary filmmaker.

Photo: Antel Productions Ltd

This conference in Broadview-Greenwood is what participatory democracy should be; citizens in their own riding, discussing the future of the nation. There is no field in which participation is more important than defence and security but to take part properly the citizen should have some basic information on the subject.

Canada no longer has the means of teaching even the rudimentary military skills to its citizens. Everyone to-day accepts the hoary cliché that war is too important to be left to the generals, but it is equally dangerous to leave the study of peace to those who have no idea of even the basic principles of war and conflict. Canada has a smaller percentage of citizens with current military training than any other developed country in the world; 0.4 per cent of the population.

Knowledge dispels fear, yet the great majority of academics and activists who talk and write about defence have no practical military experience. This can be seen in the debate, largely based on fear, which is then reflected in so many of the attitudes prevalent in our society. We are being told that the nuclear clock is at five minutes to holocaust time at the same time as we are told that nuclear weapons have made war obsolete. These statements are contradictory nonsense, designed to spread fear and defeatism.

Yes, there is a danger and a possibility of the human race being annihilated by a superpower nuclear exchange, but that danger has receded considerably in the past thirty years. On the other hand, under the nuclear umbrella, war and conflict have proliferated, especially in the so-called Third World. It is the escalation of these regional conflicts which is much more likely to destroy society as we know it, providing that it is not destroyed first by any of the looming environmental disasters.

We have had more regional, revolutionary and terrorist conflicts in the eighties than any other time in the twentieth century but our obsessive fear of being wiped out by the Soviets has prevented us from exposing the roots and attempting to deal with the causes of these conflicts.

No one, save the pacifists, argues that we should do away with our armed forces. The question that we should ask is: what form should these forces take? How much integration should there be with our allies? Should the military have a role in the education of the citizens in questions of peace and disarmament?

The sharing of defence with allies can decrease the danger as well as the cost, but to what level should we integrate? And what sort of soldiers should Canada have.

There are many models we could follow, ranging from the almost purely professional, which we have had in Canada for the past thirty years, to the citizen-soldier model of the Swiss. It has now become obvious that an all-professional model is very expensive and has a number of potentially fatal shortcomings. Therefore one of the main defence aims listed in the '87 White Paper on Defence is the revitalization of the reserves. There is nothing revolutionary or even innovative in this proposal, we are merely following the lead of the Americans and the British, who have both been relying more and more on reserve forces.

The proposed increase is modest: to bring the reserves from the current strength of some 20 thousand to 60 or 70 thousand in the next decade. We need those reservists. Not only because they are cheaper than career soldiers, but because it is the reserves which best ground the military in the nation's society and because service in the military is the best way to learn something about war and conflict without actually taking part in war.

Over the past thirty years, our military has become so isolated and the small reserves so out of touch that, unless we make some fundamental changes in the terms of service and in the societal rewards for reservists, we will not be able to meet even these modest goals. The irony is that, apart from the military necessity, there is a need and a desire for service among the young.

This need is evident to anyone who deals with young people. The kids are as good as ever, but there are so many who have dropped out. The book learning that they miss out on is only a small part of the problem. More importantly they fail to learn the self discipline which would give them a chance to catch up.

The formal, authoritative military setting is not necessary for the majority. There will always be a fortunate few who find the inner motivation which drives them to excellence, as well as a great many who find other ways to learn the basic social skills which will fit them into the work force. But to-day there are fewer and fewer places and institutions which are strong enough to deal with the youngster who has trouble fitting in. Even families, let alone employers, are unprepared to enforce rules, while society is making it more and more difficult to impose discipline of any kind. It is simpler to let the undesirable youth drop out than to take the effort to train him.

Most of the young men and women in black leather jackets, weird hairdos and Doc Martin boots are not just nature's own fascists. They are kids who are desperately looking for some form of identification, for some respect, for some direction in their lives. If they do not get it from home, they are increasingly unlikely to get it at school, so they will form their own society, with all the perils that such enterprises entail.

In the year that I was researching my book, there were some hundred and thirty thousand inquiries at recruiting centres across the country. The regular force was able to take only about 10 thousand. Many were directed to reserve units, but did not join or dropped out soon after joining. The reserves have trouble keeping their strength at the very modest 20 thousand which is their current establishment.

The regular forces offer a career which is well paid but they can

97

afford to be choosy, so the rebellious youth with a poor education has no chance whatever of joining. Even if an applicant can meet the qualifications, it can take up to a year of waiting to join. It is easier to get into the reserves, but this is only a part-time job which is not very appealing to most young Canadians. Moreover, the training is difficult to fit into school and work schedules. The standards are usually not high enough or tough enough to appeal to the youth who needs a challenge. There has been very little attempt to attract those who could benefit the most: the immigrants eager for a Canadian identity; the academic drop outs; the economically disadvantaged.

The system needs changing. Although it is clear that the changes would save money, and would be beneficial to the great majority of Canadians, they seem impossible to make. Even at the most logical and basic level, that of various departments of the Federal Government, coordination is lacking. As an example, the latest glossy pamphlet, paid for by the federal government, which tells young Canadians about careers and career planning, fails even to mention the armed forces as a possible career. Coordination with the education industry is also non existent; every high school in Canada once had a cadet corps, every university a contingent of the Canadian Officer Training Corps (COTC) but they have all gone. The Defence Department has started a pilot scheme to re-introduce COTC in selected universities but it has been done in a half-hearted manner which is begging failure.

The first defence White Paper in a quarter of a century was finally tabled in June of 1987. It unequivocally declared Canada's continuing commitment to NATO and NORAD. It also listed as part of its program most of the measures which strategists had been urging for years as vital for the refurbishing of Canadian defences. But instead of making hard financial commitments for the pressing defence needs, such as the revitalization of the reserves, the number one priority, with a funding estimate to match, was a brand new one: Canada was to build nuclear powered submarines for the navy!

It became clear that the effects of the misinformed peace campaign, combined with muddled strategic thinking, had seriously affected the new defence policies. The rationale for submarines fails to distinguish between a possible legal sovereignty challenge to our arctic waters by our allies and a military threat from our adversaries. This lack of clarity casts doubt on the entire process of refurbishing badly neglected defences. For, while there may be excellent strategic reasons for the purchase of nuclear submarines, some of the other defence needs are certainly more pressing. Nuclear submarines would only make sense if they were to be part of a joint US-Canada force based on the example of NORAD, or even as part of a wider NATO venture.

The majority of Canadians have now become aware of the degradation of the forces. Both Conservative and Liberal parties have promised stronger defences. Even the New Democrats have given lip service to the refurbishing of the run down defences. and, although their official platform is still to pull out of NATO, their leadership is patently uncomfortable with this position.

Starting with the last Trudeau administration, politicians have been conscious of a much greater support for viable defences than the media indicated. However, any single issue such as official participation in the Strategic Defence Initiative, or Air Launched Cruise Missile testing in Canada, can be manipulated by propaganda to turn the public against it. This makes the introduction of new programs a hazardous proposition, especially when such a program has suddenly appeared without being part of a long range strategic plan.

With the climate favourable to defence, the anti-defence campaign is unable, directly, to cause more cuts as it did in the sixties, but it can cloud the issue sufficiently to influence the effectiveness of any defence effort. Thus, the current Conservative government's promised revitalization of Canadian defence is facing problems. The Defence White Paper shows how impossible such a task is without proper professional military strategic planning and a broadly based community support system for Canada's military.

The Paper talks of rebuilding the reserves and integrating them with the regulars into a Total Force. Although this would help to minimize the most dangerous weakness in the current Canadian defence posture (the lack of trained military personnel) it is not given priority in the White Paper. The coordination with other tax-funded parts of society, such as the education establishment, or other federal departments, without which the re-rooting of the forces in society at large is impossible, is not tackled.

The government falls back on a major new equipment program as the only possible way to beef up security. Only the injection of large amounts of funds into a relatively few pockets, as well as industrial development in key political regions, can generate the needed public relations. For, in the face of an anti-defence disinformation attack and a public innocent of even the most rudimentary principles of defence, no initiative can survive without such a campaign.

Even then, the government felt that the only way that the nuclear submarine program could be sold to the Canadian public was on the basis of anti-Americanism. A recent article [Thomas Dewey: *Backgrounder*, July 1, 1988, The Heritage Foundation, Washington] spells out the concerns of conservative opinion in the USA:

...many White Paper recommendations are dictated as much by political considerations as by military logic. Noted Armed Forces Journal International: *"Politically [the White Paper] is a masterpiece of sophistication and cunning... it wraps a revitalized Canadian defence structure around the pole of Canadian sovereignty. By doing so, it builds on the massive (and emotional) investment Canada made in establishing a distinct Canadian identity."*

The study goes on:

The basically political motivation for many White Paper proposals has raised serious doubts about its strategic rationale. For example, the development of nuclear-powered submarines, the most costly element in the White Paper, may create more problems than it solves. By the time Canadian submarines are in service, they may not be able to counter effectively the Soviet Arctic threat.

While the Americans are uneasy about the effectiveness of the proposed submarines, domestic opposition is now being whipped up for exactly the opposite reasons. On July 12, 1988 a half page advertisement appeared in the Globe and Mail attacking the Canadian government's decision to acquire nuclear submarines. Using innuendo to suggest that the submarines were armed with nuclear missiles the advertisement said that the vessels could start World War III.

The assault on the submarines continued into August with a headline in the Toronto Star; "Sub purchase a problem for nuclear treaty paper reveals". In fact the paper, prepared by an unidentified summer student, merely offered the opinion that "while Canada has a legal right" to acquire them, the submarine purchase "might undermine confidence in the 1968 Non-Proliferation Treaty". This was good enough to keep up the media pressure on the Defence Department, for two weeks later it was followed up by an editorial headed: "Why nuclear subs set a bad example."

The vocal peace movement in turn influences the media, which is ultra critical of defence initiatives. Despite the public and political will, a great deal of insecurity is generated, as a result of this activity in the media, about Canada's ability to take the proper measures to shore up our defences. Four months after the election the submarine contract was still not awarded. A change of Defence Minister in the January cabinet shuffle merely led to a further media outburst against the nuclear powered submarines.

There are no easy solutions. The problems of Canadian defence have been building for thirty years and it will take a lot of time, effort and money to undo the damage. What is needed above all is courage and thought. The first thing that must be tackled is the confusion. The smoke and mirrors of disinformation seem formidable but they are easy to neutralize. All that is needed is exposure. The politician who can sort out the true desires of the public from the disinformation campaign will be on a sure ticket for re-election.

Questions and Comments from the Audience

Question:
I wonder if wearing boots and entering the Army can change the
attitudes of young Canadians? That is my first query. I think Mr.
Hasek has misunderstood Professor Nicholson's assertion that the
military thought in the world has changed since '45.

Since '45 and the dropping of the atomic bombs, there have been
three currents, I think, that have run through all civilization: one,
the redefinition of society in light of ultimate destruction; two, an
increasing precedence of science and technology that has basically
taken over and preoccupied our society, culture, thought, all that is
almost obscured in the face of science and technology; and three, the
increasing economic definition of everything we do. The world is
divided. I think both the first two speakers pointed out that, with our
alliance with the States, it continues the division of the world into
imperialist blocs; Canada and the United States in the West versus
Soviet Union, their satellite countries and East Asia.

So, in the face of this division; in the face of the re-definition of
ourselves; and in the face of our attitudes with our youth, where do
you see Canada coming through? How can Canada be at all influential in a world that is divided into three major sections? Canada, as
a middle power, as it was in the '50s under Pearson, just can't exist
any longer.

Graeme Nicholson:
I think that the assertion I made was not that human beings or
human nature, had changed but that the human *situation* had
changed. I think that we now, for all perpetuity, have in our hands
the possibility of universal destruction; there could be no greater
change than that.

I think that the questioner also alluded to other changes which may,
or may not, accompany those directly. The economization of all our

102

thought, the division of the world into power blocs, and the insistent presence of technology as the central human project are all changes that do seem to me to accompany the drastic turning point in 1945. I would just like to add that I don't object to the notion of having a military force, nor to the culture of the military force, nor to the educational role of military activity for youth; I have not made that case, and I think neither has John Lamb.

John Hasek:
I get disturbed by this business of imperialist blocs. I think that one of the great problems that we face in Canada today, is this *mea culpa* idea that, somehow, we or the other democracies are responsible for the mess that's in the world today; certainly, we've contributed to it. However, if there is one chance that this world has, it lies in what is loosely known as "the first bloc" (that is, pluralist democracies in the developed world) bringing the rest of the world up to the same standards.

Unfortunately, in this we've been under constant, indirect attack - but attack nevertheless - by what is, again, loosely called "the second world" of the communist powers. We're now in an era of glasnost and peristroyka, but nowhere has Mr. Gorbachev ever said that he no longer believes that Communism is wrong, that Marxism and Leninism are wrong. They still believe in that particular system, and that particular system has been responsible for an enormous amount of misery and for a tremendous amount of death, and wherever it has taken hold it has caused an absolute disaster.

When you look at environment, the greatest environmental mess is, again, behind the iron curtain. So, you know, where do we stand? We stand very firmly on the side of democracy and I don't believe that the democratic nations are an imperialist bloc at all. Imperialism is one of these emotionally laden words. If there has been an imperial empire, it has been the Soviet one. Now, the Soviet empire is busily telling us how dreadful it's been but we here in the West are still not keeping up to date with what they're saying.

In the latest English version of Pravda, which is on sale everywhere, they're now talking about the seven million people that were killed during the forced famines in the Ukraine. Yet, at the University of Toronto, my son, who takes a course in Soviet history, is still being taught from a textbook which says basically that Stalin may have

103

broken a few eggs but how else do you make an omelette and, in the end, his goals weren't that bad. So I think that is a great problem as well - the disinformation that's extant at the moment.

John Lamb:
I would like to address one thing that John said right at the end. Gorbachev has, in fact, said on numerous occasions - and I think there is a fair bit of evidence to back it up - that the Soviet Union is no longer going to regard class war as the principle engine of Soviet foreign policy. I think that they are returning to much more nationally oriented motivations for their foreign policy behaviour. I think, to some extent, we're witnessing a retreat of ideology in international relations. It's amazing it took them so long, because usually following ideological paths hasn't been particularly constructive.

But to come back to the question, I think that the key to Canadian development of an independent stance on these issues is to recognize that there are no monoliths. You know, this three-bloc thing really doesn't work to my mind and I would like to give you three very quick examples.

In Europe, probably the most contentious issue that's coming up will be whether NATO modernizes its short-range nuclear weapons. These are, to my mind, the most dangerous weapons; they're the "use-em-or-lose-em", right-up-on-the-front-lines nuclear weapons, and NATO says that it needs to modernize them. Well, in fact, it doesn't. You've got the Germans and the Italians sayings, "Let's hold off; let's not be rash; maybe we can prevent that or avoid it." The Brits and the Americans are saying: "Let's go and modernize these nuclear weapons." In other words, NATO is divided. Canada should be in there, to my mind, arguing along with the Germans and the Italians, saying, "We don't need these things."

In the Pacific, the U.S. and the Soviets are rivals. Naval competition there is very dangerous; much more dangerous than Europe. Australia, New Zealand, Japan and Canada have all got a terrific incentive to see that rivalry reduced. We should be working with those countries to introduce confidence-building measures; pushing both the superpowers to come to agreements and stop playing chicken with their naval vessels, and so on. Finally, in the Arctic, superpower rivalry again. Canada has non-superpower, circum-polar neighbours. We should be cooperating with them to try to produce an Arctic Security Treaty, which we would then go with to the super-powers and say, "Listen, we don't want to put up with this rivalry." That's the way to fashion Canadian independence in foreign policy, to my mind.

Question:
My question, I'm afraid, may seem a very silly one, but it's one that troubles me. It seems to me that we have this tremendous set of personnel in our military that spend a large portion of their time playing war games; I guess that's what they do. Why are we not using these people in ways that are more immediately valuable to us - be it to help us with environmental cleanup or be it to help us with building bridges and sewers that are so needed in our municipalities? Is there not some way we can use this very valuable resource not only in the defence of Canada but in our more immediate economic and infra-structure needs?

John Lamb:
First of all, I think we should recognize that the Canadian Armed Forces do play a lot of roles in aid of the civil power, which includes search-and-rescue, help during natural disasters, and that sort of thing. I think there is room to expand that. I mean the oil spill out on Vancouver Island, is a good example. I think there's some resistance in the military to expanding that too far. I think the military would be a lot more popular with the public if they showed more willingness to be involved in things like that. I was at a meeting recently where about five military people stood up at one point in the conference, one after another, and said that they didn't want to be picking up dead birds on beaches. They found that offensive; maybe they need to be brought around to it.

I would also say that there are going to be military-related roles. We shouldn't just assume that we can put them on good works, but I think a re-orientation is needed. There's not going to be a land war in Europe so to keep training the military in traditional roles of that kind is not very sensible, even the militia. Get them trained-up for peace-keeping, for sovereignty protection, and that sort of thing. I think we should remember that there are some militarily related roles that remain valid.

John Hasek:
I'd like to correct a couple of grave misconceptions here. The first is

that there's a great Canadian military establishment. We have a smaller per-capita population in uniform than does any other industrial, developed nation and these people are not just wasting their time; they are, in fact, highly trained people and the skills that they need are tough to develop. The reason that the people you met may have baulked at picking up dead sea birds was not, perhaps, because the mission is repugnant to them, but because maybe their people have had no leave because of other training commitments.

You know, a soldier doesn't spring into being just by putting a uniform on a civilian; it takes a tremendous amount of training and the smaller the military you have, the less you are able to do in this sort of essentially public-relations effort. Because someone's a soldier he has been trained at some expense so it's cheaper, in the end, to hire a civilian to do these sorts of things. So, if you have a large army like the Chinese, then of course you can have them out helping with the harvest. If you have a small, professional army, then there's very little like this that you can do. And that's the situation that we are in.

Another thing - and I would like to re-emphasize this - is that you cannot be effective in peace-keeping, or any other mission, unless you have trained in the basic military skills and, again, that is the problem; there are far too few Canadians now who really understand what a military is all about.

Question:
Mankind has been around for 20 centuries; we've been fighting for 20 centuries. I don't believe we're going to stop. I would like to know if you would equip your police force with antiquated machinery, as opposed to keeping up to date with the budget?

Graeme Nicholson:
I'd like to say that it's a very common argument that the introduction of the bow and arrow was thought to be a revolution; the introduction of the bullet was thought to be a revolution; the introduction of the tank was thought to be a revolution. So every generation has quailed with fear at the new technology. The conclusion that people draw sometimes is that we're just like all the others; we, too, are frightened by the powers that are new to us. But I think it really is different in this case; the fact that we could have the universal destruction of life on the planet. That makes a difference the like of

which has never been seen before.

John Lamb:
Just one very quick point. I don't know what examples you were thinking of, but one example that's been used very recently is that the Defence Department has been portraying the issue of nuclear-powered submarines in the context of the choices between nuclear-powered submarines and old clunkers. In other words, unless we get these subs, we'd be denying the Armed Forces the kind of equipment that you were referring to. I would just like to say that that's completely false. The choice is between nuclear-powered submarines and modern, diesel-electric, non-nuclear submarines. And I'll just leave it there.

John Hasek:
I'd just like to say that I couldn't agree with the questioner more. There's nothing more demoralizing than to have a bunch of soldiers going around saying: "Clank, clack; I'm a tank" or "Bang, bang; you're dead" because you have no money for blank ammunition.

Question:
And, what about our fleet? I mean, we are supposed to be, not a superpower, but we are a world power. Half of our fleet in Halifax, as far as I know, is not up to NATO standards. I mean, we have a presence to keep, to present to the world. Why not at least show them that we mean business?

Question:
No sane person would want to see us go to war, yet if we do go to total war, that'll be because the politicians have failed to do their job. I've attended a number of these conferences, and I've heard speakers on TV talk about the field of national defence and policy. Yet nowhere and at no time have I heard anybody address the question and the issue of civil defence.

I wasn't around at the time, but a lot of you will remember the Cuban Missile Crisis; nobody expected it but it happened and I believe that the United States, or Canada, was prepared to attempt to protect citizens. Now, granted nobody knows what the outcome of a war will be but, I think if civil defence was addressed and looked at, and maybe even implemented even more than it is now, maybe it would make a big difference in how Canadians feel about the whole issue.

Do you believe we should have a stronger civil defence policy? And, if so, why? Or why not?

John Hasek:

Yes, of course. That is clearly part of the participatory defence that I'm talking about, and that is one of the roles that, in fact, your Reserve Forces could undertake because it doesn't just work for war and we're unprepared for all sorts of other emergencies. I was involved in that planning, and we have got pretty large holes in that whole business.

John Lamb:

I would make the opposite comment and say no, of course not - as regards war, that is. Civil Defence against natural disasters is fine. Canada is not going to be involved in a war in which Civil Defence would make a damned bit of difference.

If there is a nuclear war, it will not be limited or prolonged. If you get into global nuclear war Canada is targeted; no doubt about that. Even if it weren't, we would be thoroughly irradiated from the United States. There is no defence against that which is economically practical or, in my view, achievable. I think we need to recognize the fact that a nuclear war cannot be won and must never be fought.

Question:

I am an engineer and I am an Indian. Let me start with the second part first. India is only a thousand miles from Russia and about 5,000 miles from Britain, but I speak fluent English. That, by the way, is a form of fruit you get from the "language imperialism" if you like. I am very thankful for that because today I can even speak to Canadians and Americans quite fluently.

As an engineer, I would have to say that I agree that we are in a different age - 1945 has brought to us a discontinuity. But a greater discontinuity has crept in in the high-tech world in the '70s, or perhaps in the '80s, where the nuclear age has passed into the "automatic" stage of war.

We suffer now from the dangers of accidental nuclear war. I believe that in that situation, these old habits should die much faster than otherwise. Maybe you can comment on the "automatic" stage of the nuclear age.

Graeme Nicholson:
I think that it is true, that the automatic character of the war danger is, in fact, probably a further intensification of it. And that seems to be a very important point, yes.

Photo: John Rowlands

Danforth Technical School has been contributing craftsmen and women to our community for well over half a century.

Section Four:
Education for the 21st Century

The Challenge for Education

Pat Latham &
Michael Raggett

Pat Latham has taught all ages from Kindergartento University. She has worked in print and electronic publishing, the hotel and manufacturing industries and university research. She is currently writing a book on waste.

Michael Raggett, formerly Head of an Educational Research Department, founded an international publishing company specialising in educational policy and curriculum studies. He has also undertaken research in communications and set up a company which used this technology. Currently he is engaged in publishing, writing, and advising industry.

Photo: Ernie Kestler

The challenge of the 21st century has already arrived for the education system. Students in Grades 1 and 2 will be graduating after the next century begins, so educators have begun making decisions that will shape these future graduates. This is the time to take a good hard look at how the Canadian education system will respond to the challenges of the coming century.

The task now facing education is to anticipate what society will be like at the beginning of the 21st century. Some trends are already apparent and it is likely that we will see some dynamic contradictions The manufacturing industries will become more automated, demanding fewer but highly trained, creative and probably specialized, personnel. At the same time, service industries will expand and employ large numbers of creative, enterpreneurial generalists who may need a very different set of educational supports. Already 70% of the jobs in the USA are in the service industries and in most European countries it is over 60%.

Society will still be information driven in the 21st century and knowledge will be constantly in need of up-dating. This trend is in addition to the different "fashions" in knowledge which also influence education. In order to function, people will have to be able to cope with vast amounts of continually changing information.

The widening gap between the rich and poor countries, as new technologies and global trading blocs take hold, will exert pressure on developed countries to take more immigrants from politically or economically troubled areas of the world. There will therefore be a continued trend in developed countries away from monocultural societies (or even bicultural) to multicultural. This will necessitate continual re-examination of the "mainstream" or "dominant" cultural values that societies expect their educational institutions to foster.

A further dilemma for schools will arise from the fact that, while society is becoming increasingly urbanized, it is at last awakening to environmental concerns. How do we educate urban children (or adults!) in what have been traditionally rural preoccupations?

All these challenges to education will arise from the needs of the major "stakeholders" in the system: an information-driven, technologically-innovative but largely service economy; a culturally and politically diverse society; and individuals demanding a relevant education.

The economy can be defined, for the purpose of this discussion, as the entire commercial/industrial base of the country which contributes to Canada's GNP. The economy's major demand has been, and continues to be, that the system produce graduates at all levels with the skills and knowledge to operate the economy successfully. Industry and commerce will need technologically trained workers at all levels, from high school to doctoral graduates. This is a difficult task for education as the number and level of skills needed are rising faster than schools and teachers can adapt. However, solving this problem is critical to Canada's ability to develop technology-based enterprises and to decrease our dependence on resource-based industries. Canada has one of the worst trade balances in technology of any western country. With a highly educated, technologically sophisticated population, our trading position could be improved. For example, it could improve our ability to upgrade the resources we have rather than selling them as raw materials which have value added elsewhere.

To achieve this aim of producing sufficient technologically literate graduates will require not only continuing emphasis on a high standard of literacy and numeracy but also rewriting the science curriculum at all levels. It will also demand that half the population - women - are not discouraged from taking science. Canada cannot afford this waste.

A second issue for schools is how to educate for an information driven world. Some of the fastest developing industries are the information industries and everyone needs to be able to deal with their basic requirements. This ranges from an ability to handle a computer to understanding the principles of such basic software as a spreadsheet or a database. Disastrous mistakes, such as the IKON program in Ontario are not going to help. Clear leadership and the support of industry itself will be required to ensure that what is taught in the classroom, and the equipment used there, relates to the needs of the economy.

Turning to the needs of the second stakeholder, it has been said that "school cannot compensate for society" but not only does society expect just that - it also expects schools to instill values that are not always so apparent or adhered to outside of school. This is unrealistic, so education tends to reflect society and society often finds its mirror image unpalatable!

Before the 1960s, education reflected the so-called "old values" of obedience to authority, knowing one's place, keeping one's nose to the grindstone etc. But, sickened by two world wars and supported by the beginning of the information age, this changed in the 60s to a greater emphasis on the self-fulfillment of the individual. This was going to be a time of peace and love and self-realisation. Child-centred education and open classrooms became the norm.

During the 70s reality began to set in, this process being highlighted by recessions and seemingly continual conflicts in various parts of the world. Child-centred education (or at least the mis-use of it) had bred self-centred adults - the "me" generation. Some people unable to cope with the harsh realities turned to drugs or cynicism. Education floundered trying to make sense of the social shifts that were occuring.

By the time the 80s arrived the drive for self-realisation was now fuelled by the need for survival and success. Competition was back in vogue and the pace had become frenetic. Education began to reflect an increasingly splintered society, a society divided between the successful "beautiful" people and the resentful have-not-enoughs. Ignorance and insensitivity abounded and information that had begun so promisingly as a resource had become a commodity.

In Canada, our society has a wide range of expectations of its educational system but there is one area in particular which will present the greatest challenge in the 21st century - our immigrants. As we move away from the northern European majority to more mixed ethnic and geographical origins, we will find that assumptions previously be taken for granted can no longer be assumed.

Much of any culture is based on commonly understood conventions and accepted ranges of behaviour. When a cultural mix enters the school system, a range of behaviour and attitude, as well as knowledge, can no longer be taken for granted and many aspects of education and preparation for adult life in our society have to be made explicit. This may range from such simple things as the games and associated concepts of what is considered "fair", to complex ideas such as those which define the relationship of the individual to the group. In many cultures the concept of group loyalty may be much higher than in our current Canadian society. On top of all this is the fact that the early years of a student's life may have been in a family where no English or French is spoken. When schools teach these new languages, they may isolate the student not only from his family but also from his cultural roots.

Addressing these basic dilemmas was at the root of the concept of multiculturalism, but at the time it was originally conceived, the range of cultures and the size if their representation were different from those likely to be present in the next century. Now a new debate is beginning about which of the traditional Western European/North

American values and attitudes are critical to becoming a Canadian and which may be less important. How do we accomodate new cultural values?

Few would wish to see an aggresive indoctrination of WASP language and culture, yet schools with a numberless range of curricula which accomodate all cultures and all languages are not feasible. So where on the spectrum of total melting pot to fully multiethnic education do we want our schools located? This is a critical *political* decision that cannot be left to schools.. It is a subject for debate and one in which there is some evidence to suggest that current minority groups may actually wish a greater emphasis on "Canadianization" than on their own culture. The reason for this may be that multiculturalism, while designed to protect the roots and cultural background of new Canadians may sometimes, in operation, have the effect of culturally "ghettoizing" minority groups, thus denying them the full advantages of Canadian citizenship and the Canadian economy. There is at the same time evidence that people from the mainstream Canadian culture have recognised that there is much to be gained from other cultures and are willing to embrace the advantages of diversity. This suggests that it will be possible to strike a subtle balance but society needs to make this political decision, and *soon,* if schools are to achieve a coherent policy for the future.

Society also needs a population that can cope with the rapid pace of change. It can be argued strongly that the content of education (which can quickly become obsolescent) is of less importance than providing an individual with the skill of learning. Students need not information but meta-information - that is, information about information. In science and technololgy, students need the conceptual tools to evaluate decisions and their consequences. With rapid development comes the need to understand the methods of scientific thinking; and be aware of the societal implications of new technologies, rather than amass a detailed content knowledge of what were often 19th century discoveries. Participation in an original project for a science fair may be more useful than bookfuls of knowledge.

Students will graduate into a society in which the old truism - that the ticket you get on leaving school is your ticket for life - is no longer valid but merely a temporary pass that will have to be renewed. Education will therefore have to structure certification and higher education to allow for late entry and "date stamped" qualifications.

For the third group of stakeholders, individuals, the need to accomodate the change from "live to work" to "work to live" will be crucial as the boundaries between work and leisure become less clearcut. Is the ski enthusiast who becomes a ski instructor working? In our current society many individuals identify themselves with their job: "I am a doctor." "I am a plumber." In a world where work may not continue to be the salient experience, where people may change occupations many times, where serial marriage and geographic mobility may be the norm, and where the effects of aging can be kept at bay by intellectual activity, continuing education for adults will become an important part of the scene. Other countries have responded to this challenge with easy access institutions, universities for adults only, distanced learning facilities - all of which retain high academic standards and rigour. Canada is under-supplied in this area. In France, for example, not only are facilities provided by the state but employers must also give employees leave and payment for continuing education.

Individuals will also need to deal with large amounts of changing information for their own benefit. Canadians should not rely solely on the media to tell them what the politicians and the industrialists are up to, what issues are important and which are not. They cannot afford to remain ignorant of basic scientific concepts which would allow them to make informed decisions on such subjects as the effects of new technologies on the world in which they live. It is important that everyone becomes technologically literate to such a degree that they can follow debates about issues that will affect their lives. Schools should be encouraging this independence of thought.

Canadian education is not in a desperate state but is in a slow crisis that needs a deliberate response. This will require involving all the stakeholders in a careful consideration of all the issues. Much can be gained from this approach. For example, the real worries of leaders of industry that education is becoming more than ever decoupled from the needs of the economy can be addressed. At the same time industry can be exposed to the need of individual workers to participate creatively in the workplace.

McLuhan has said that the medium is the message and, in the case of teaching, one can say that the *method* is the message. So educationalists, supported by their stakeholders, will need to re-examine their teaching methods for the 21st century. Too often in the past we have been given mixed messages by a clash between what is being taught and the methods used to teach it. As the need is now for creative, independent thinkers, able to access and manipulate information rather than memorize and regurgitate it, the current methods may well be out of step. Some teachers still see learning as the ability of their students to ingest a given set of facts and recall them faultlessly during a test. This type of teaching/learning is often made even more useless by the fact that the content is outdated and irrelevant to a student's life after graduation.

Classrooms need to become sophisticated learning centres where the emphasis is on the creation of structured experiences of a type which model the use of that subject later in life. Too often classrooms are deadening experiences for the creative individual. Few teachers seem to have been trained to value the original mind - whether at university or in the kindergarten.

The main challenge facing Canadian education in the 21st century will be to produce people prepared for change, with a high level of basic skills in literacy, numeracy, science and technology but also with the highest level of creativity that they can attain. Canada will need every one of them.

117

Art and Design Education in the New Millennium

Maurice Barnwell

Maurice Barnwell was born in England and emigrated to Canada in 1967. He has taught in England, Hong Kong and Canada. Currently Acting Head of the Department of Liberal Arts Studies at the Ontario College of Art, he also lectures at York University.

Let me begin with three requisite tenets. Firstly cultural historians can point to social groups that have managed not only to exist but to prosper and develop without any formal math, science or written language. However, no known cultural group has existed on the face of this planet without practising some form of artistic creativity. Secondly, as Jacob Bronowski pointed out more than thirty-five years ago, the creative drive powers human evolution. Thirdly, the arts are a fundamental expression of human imagination.

Despite their variable qualities, the mutual relationship, the interdependence of the arts and society will remain one of the predominate characteristics of human culture in the 21st century. This should not be seen as a mandate for elitism or for cultural exclusivity. In the pluralistic world of the next millennium - just over 130 months away and coming fast - the relationship between art and society will be complex and ever-changing. And, as the cultural context changes, so must the objectives of art and design education.

The reality of the new millennium will accelerate social change and emphasize the unpredictability of the future characteristics of the arts and the structure and form of tertiary art and design education programs. The changing contextual influences will demand an educational curriculum policy relevant to the society of the twenty-first century.

Art and design education is concerned with stimulating imagination and with transmitting information - it recognises the visual, verbal and technological methods of transmission. The Liberal Arts provide visual, verbal and technolgical skills, and establish lifelong learning patterns. Students are encouraged to integrate information and ideas from different disciplines. Artists and designers are provided with an edge in determining future responses.

The next decade or so will be a period of exploration, a feeling out of the freedoms created by technological innovation. At the same time, encouraged by changing social requirements and by patterns of financial support, the hard edges between existing disciplines will erode.

As the cultural context changes so must the objectives of art education. The curriculum format will be revised to keep pace with changing social conditions and cultural values. It will form the basis of the contemplative, critical and evaluative knowledge needed by artists to respond in a creative, descriptive manner. The revised format will reflect the forces that are shaping society - changes in the demograhic profile, increasing levels of education, increasing participation of women, and the aging of the population - all of which will modify art-related activities in the twenty-first century. The curriculum will also admit of the essential character of economics in the post-modern economy.

Twentieth century myopic fascination with specialization, often reflective of narrow self-interest, will be replaced by an integrated process of learning. The post-Bauhaus vertical divisions of colour, two-dimensional design, figure drawing etc., often found in foundation programs, for example, will be replaced by a horizontal, integrated approach. Expressed in the most crude and unworkable terms this may mean "Monday - creative process; Tuesday - concept development; Wednesday - visualization skills; Thursday - literacy and communications..."and so on.

The associated curriculum theory should be projective rather than reactive; one that encourages the skills of enquiry and analytical thought, one that fosters literacy skills, one that develops a degree of fluency in communication and one that avoids some of the problems of cultural and gender bias.

Technology has increased the tempo of change. It is essential for creative survival to be able to foresee some of the qualitative results of changing values. Handling change in a vital and creative way will be one of the prime characteristics of art and design related activity in the years ahead. Technological innovation is providing us with access to staggering amounts of information. Curriculum planning will take exploitive advantage of these new technologies. This will require administration, faculty and students to leave the security of what is known for the challenge of what might be.

It is stating the obvious to talk about an information explosion. Data is available through computers, dishes and satellites and we must stumble out of our cloistered carols and devise means of access and evaluation for all members of the education community, giving weight to methods of integrating the information into a vital, analagous visual vocabulary. This is already a reality with the truly inspirational and provocative opportunities provided to students through access to the NETNORTH and BITNET database and communication facilities.

The foreseeable economic and political climate will likely reinforce geographic isolation and insular enrollment and staffing policies. This will be countered, in part, by increasing co-operative ventures and exchange activities. Lines of communication will be established between various educational institutions, professional organizations, business interests and government bodies. Local business interests, prominent studios and cultural organizations will be encouraged to accept students for short term, on-the-job training. Colleges will engage in international co-operative ventures that may require short term exchange of students and faculty. Such activities will strengthen the bonds of understanding essential to universal harmony in the 21st century.

Artificial divisions between full-time, part-time, evening and summer programs will disappear. The academic year may not be the same for all students and all faculty. Staggered "graduation" may be more responsive to social needs. Faculty members may welcome the chance of an extended winter break. Timetables will be more adventurous. Bands of study are at present the same "width" (three hours) and the same length (either 13 or 26 units) and flow in uniform sequence. Once again, this is convenience without logic! The amount of content can remain the same but the timing can become more flexible.

As for funding art and design education, traditional sources must be enhanced by endowments and changes in corporate taxation guidelines . Other financial structures must be explored as a means of acquiring additional funding. It is unlikely that the debate about tertiary education as a right or a privilege will be resolved before the end of this century.

What I am suggesting is not change for the sake of change but a clear and urgent response to a changing contextual situation. The future is out there and we have a choice: we can ignore it, hoping that it won't interfere with the way we do things now, or we can try to *prepare* our students for changing times.

This restructuring will encourage curious, enthusiastic, perceptive and co-operative students and produce people fully capable of functioning in leadership roles in the culture of the 21st century. Quite simply, the choice would seem to be between short-sighted, local isolationism which will maintain the *status quo* or adventurous explorations which could establish our colleges as vital nuclei in the international art and design education scene.

The most difficult problem to overcome is outmoded thinking and established practice. There is nothing magical or sacred about starting the study week on Monday or finishing a programme of study in April or May. It is, however, convenient! For the first time we have the technology to make creative curriculum planning, timetabling and administration possible, What is needed is the will to make it happen. Similarly, study programs can be exciting, meaningful and unique to each individual student, establishing creative attitudes by providing information access to all that the world has to offer. At the same time they can be more responsive to the society in which we all coexist.

The Challenge for the 21st Century: A Literate Canada

John O'Leary

John O'Leary was born in Toronto and educated at Michael Power High School and Carleton University. He has worked as a child care worker and teacher and is currently Program Director and Director of Development at Frontier College.

Photo: Jerry Hobbs

About two years ago, some corporate executives from Southam Incorporated who, I think, are the nation's largest newspaper publisher, came to me and said, "Mr. O'Leary, how many Canadians can't read or write?"

I think they came to me because they knew Frontier College had been teaching adults to read for many years and I said to them at that time, "I don't know. Lots." That was my answer.

At that time, 1987, we did not know. There had been no significant study of the number of people in this country who do not read or write well. So Southam went off and did the Southam literacy survey called *Broken Words* which was published a year ago.

This study confirmed what many of us had known from our experience, that illiteracy in Canada is a very serious problem. They tagged the number at five million adult Canadians in this country who are not able to read and write well enough to achieve their goals.

Now, a problem we have with this issue is defining it. Last June, I joined over 20,000 reading teachers at the International Reading Association Conference here in Toronto and, with a name like O'Leary, it caused something of a stir among my friends and family to be going to the IRA Conference!

What we did at the IRA Conference, for almost three weeks, was argue about the definition of literacy. If I had the occasion, I'd ask some of you to tell me what it means to be literate. What is the definition of literacy?

At Frontier College, and most of the other literacy groups that we work with, we turn the question around by asking the student what it is that she or he wishes to achieve. It's not up to us to set an arbitrary definition and say that everyone achieving this level is literate and everyone below it is illiterate. The student will have a goal they wish to achieve. In 15 years of teaching, I have never heard an adult say, "I am illiterate." Never. I've heard people say, "I want to read to my child"; "I want to get a job"; "I want to learn more about politics"; "I want to read the Bible". That, for them, becomes the level of literacy and we can help them achieve that. So, right off the bat I want to point out that the level of literacy is really something the student determines.

Another point is that being illiterate does not mean you are dumb or stupid; in fact, it's the opposite. A colleague of mine once said, "If you don't have an education, you really have to use your brains" and that's really true. To survive in our world with very basic reading and writing skills is really a sign of quite a high level of intelligence.

Three more points I want to make. Why is it that in a country like ours we have a serious literacy problem? Most of the time when I talk about this issue, the public says, "Well, it's the schools. Of course it's the schools. The schools are falling apart; teachers don't teach phonics any more. The Hall-Dennis Report here in Ontario, that destroyed our education system, didn't it."

Well, my response to that, especially in Ontario, is that last November over 50 per cent of our Trustees were acclaimed in this province; people couldn't even bother running for School Trustees. And, for the remainder, about 30 per cent of us bothered to go out and vote. Very few of us would know who our School Trustees are; many of us don't really care.

So, when people criticize the schools, my response is that I'm not particularly interested what you think about our schools because, in fact, you don't really know much about it at all and the evidence is there to show that.

Have you ever been to a parent-teacher night in most of the schools in this province? You could do cruise-missile testing in the hallway because no one would be there. I am very serious. I criticize our schools a lot and I don't mind, as an educator, hearing schools criticized. I just insist that it be informed.

I don't believe literacy is an educational issue at all; it is a cultural issue. It's eleven o'clock on a Saturday morning and what are children in Canada doing right now? They're only doing one of two things. They're either watching television, overwhelmingly American television, or they're playing sports - both of which are wonderful things. I love sports and I love television but it's gone completely out of whack in our culture.

Now, the good thing about illiteracy is that we know how to solve the problem. Frontier College and other groups across the country are solving it as we speak; we are teaching people to read. We're not teaching enough of them and we don't have enough money to do it but that's a separate issue.

I'd like to challenge everyone not just to sit and listen or talk about literacy but to get involved. At Frontier College, we can train each one of you to become a Tutor and we can do that right away, and put you to work in your neighbourhood, in your community, as a Literacy Volunteer.

We can put you in touch with a local literacy program, if there is one. I mean that seriously and I hope some of you will take up that challenge. Go back to your church or to your political constituency, or to your home and say maybe this is something we could do, some action we could take, to prepare for the 21st Century.

The second thing that needs doing, as well as teaching our adult students to read, is that we have to show our children that books and reading and stories and language have a place outside of the classroom.

I get very angry when people criticize the grade-school teachers because the fact is that the only people in our culture who, with any

124

consistency, are showing our children the importance and the value and the magic of books and stories are our teachers. We don't do it.

I'd like to offer you an opportunity. Frontier College is organizing reading-promotion programs in a hundred and forty public housing-buildings in this city. We've got one started on Monday nights from five to six and every Monday night about 70 kids up to age ten come teaming into that room. Children love books, reading and stories but we don't have anywhere near the number of volunteers required to get that program going. So there's the opportunity.

I look around this room and I see people who care about their community. I see organizers, political organizers and I see people who are seniors and you would all be wonderful story-tellers in this program to show our children that language and books and stories and literacy are a very important part of their complete life development.

You know children learn to read the way they learn to speak. Can you imagine if we taught our children to speak the way we taught them to read? Correcting them every time they made an error, or insisting that they do some kind of formalized exercise? No! Our children learn to read by reading and hearing stories.

Finally, I'd like to make an observation about the connection between literacy and poverty. I'd like to put it another way. I've taught a lot of adults with Frontier College and in doing that I usually make one thing clear. Many of those adults have been people living in poverty and I've never, ever said to someone, "If I teach you to read, I guarantee that you will escape the net of poverty." What I do say to people is, "If you do not learn to read, chances are you will not escape the net of poverty."

The Fight for Literacy

Joyce Fairbairn

Joyce Fairbairn was born in Lethbridge, Alberta and holds degrees from the University of Alberta and Carleton University. A former political journalist in the Parliamentary Press Gallery in Ottawa with United Press International and FP Publications, she was Legislative Assistant to former Prime Minister Pierre Trudeau for 14 years. She has been Senator for the province of Alberta since 1984.

In the previous session we heard over and over again about drug-awareness programs and about drug-prevention programs. I want to tell you that there is no national awareness program on illiteracy and there is no national prevention program aimed at illiteracy in this country. Dedicated people like John O'Leary of Frontier College and a network of others across Canada, many of them volunteers, are fighting their hardest, working their damnedest, to get the subject of illiteracy on the national Agenda - just to get it on the Agenda - for the 21st Century.

I would like to urge you, with all of the conviction I can muster, to join the battle against illiteracy; to join the campaign to help some one-quarter of our adult Canadians have the opportunity to take part in the life of this country. No country, however rich or powerful, especially with our small population in Canada, can afford to have an estimated five million people sit on the sidelines of our economic, our social, our cultural and our spiritual growth as a nation.

When we talk about these numbers, we're not just talking about statistics; we're talking about human beings. We're not talking about people who have come to Canada; this is not an imported problem to our country. Indeed, some 78 per cent of the functionally illiterate in Canada were born right here; some 70 per cent of them live in our cities and a whole lot of them live in Toronto.

As John O'Leary said, we are talking about poverty; almost an assurance that if you cannot break through this barrier of illiteracy, you are going to be on the lower end of our society. We're talking about mothers who run dreadful risks in their homes, because they cannot read or understand instructions on dangerous goods or things like the correct dosages of medication to give to themselves or their children. We're talking about senior citizens in frightening isolation because their difficulty in communicating just compounds the other serious problems, the natural problems, of the aging process.

We're also talking about students and I'll throw a shocker at you. The Southam Survey, for the first time, included high-school graduates and they found that 30 per cent of the functionally illiterate adults in Canada are high-school graduates and we have another one-third of Canadian teenagers who drop out of school before they even get to be that other statistic.

We're talking about farmers, we're talking about prisoners, we're talking about native people for whom this issue is hard to calculate in terms of the enormous effect it has on their lives. We are also talking about workers and I would like to say a special word about that today.

Sixty per cent of Canada's functionally illiterate people are unemployed. They don't have jobs; they're not looking for jobs; they cannot hold jobs. Today, in The Toronto Star there's an amazing quote from the Minister of State for National Finance, Tom Hockin, who tells the brewery workers just to read the Want Ads if they want to find a more exciting and perhaps a higher-paying job.

Well, I'm talking about the folks who can't read the Want Ads; they can't read the Classifieds; they can't read the Yellow Pages. To them, going to a Manpower Office is a numbing experience because they can't read the instructions and, therefore, they miss the opportunities. Also, these are people who, if they go to a literacy program to learn how to read, run the risk of getting cut off unemployment insurance because they're not out actively looking for a job. They get caught coming and going.

127

Now, one in six of our labour force in Canada is estimated to be functionally illiterate. I'd like to put that in the context of the debate we've been having in this country for the last two years on the Trade issue. One of the central elements of concern on the Trade issue, and in the recent election campaign, was what will happen to the workers who are laid off, whose companies close down, whose companies want to streamline? They will have to up-grade to get into the technological mysteries of our age. We are told that maybe there is no need for adjustment programs for these people because the ones we have are good enough to re-train and up-grade. Well, I'm talking today about the people who cannot re-train, who cannot up-grade, because they cannot read. They can't read the manuals that help them to learn how to run the computers.

These are the people that are threatening to become, unless we can help them, a permanent under-class in our society such as you will find in the streets of New York City. We're not there yet, but the train is on the track, unless our government and our businesses choose to bring in programs that will lift these people to the situation where they can learn to take part in an advanced-employment society in this country.

These are questions that are absolutely fundamental to the kind of nation we are going to have in the 21st Century. What answers do we give? Warner Troyer said earlier that individuals in this country are powerful and that is true. Each one of us is in a position to push and shove and pressure everyone in the political process in our neighbourhoods, in our communities, in our Cities and particularly the Minister of Education and the Federal Government - our Members of Parliament and our Senators. All of you are in a position to put that kind of pressure on our system to place this issue actively on the Agenda.

You are also in a position to help, and there are so many things you can do. Be a Tutor, write letters to the editor, help in fund-raising, get projects working on your street, start reading circles for children. Those are things that each one of us can do not only to raise the level of basic adult education in this country but also to give our kids a break; to give our kids a chance. I urge you to use that power to force your governments to care and to give you the tools to to do the job.

Questions and Comments from the Audience

Question:
I'm on the board of directors of our local church literacy group and we
have an active, involved board. We have a successful program of
some 28 matches of Tutors and Learners. We have a part-time paid
Coordinator and this whole involvement with literacy has had a
tremendous impact on me.

Here's our problem at the community level. What we have is the
provincial government making announcements on things that they're
going to do - and dollars; we have the federal government making
announcements on dollars - and publicity. It's a good thing to be
concerned about literacy.

Back at the community level of our board of directors, nothing filters
down. What happens is that the dollars are siphoned off two ways.
One goes to the educational establishment, to consultants, to OISE
[Ontario Institute for Studies in Education], and there's also dollars
that go to the bureaucracy in the Ministries of Education and at the
federal level.

How do we get some of that political commitment and some of those
dollars away from those vested establishments to local groups such
as ourselves and to all of the community groups which are basically
starved for funds. It's not getting down there.

John O'Leary:
You're absolutely right; and perhaps Joyce Fairbairn may have
something to say to this as well.

I think now it becomes a political process. A lot of the money is going
towards services and things that, I agree, we perhaps don't need.
Your group knows how to teach the people in your community how
to read. You don't need an extra bunch of research to support that;
you don't need an extra bunch of documents from literacy programs

in the past, and so on.

In Ontario, specifically, we need to keep the heat on. The government has taken the first step by setting up a Fund for Literacy and the context is that going back perhaps three years ago, there was absolutely nothing. So, we have come forward. Now it becomes a political process of keeping the heat on.

Alvin Curling, the Minister, is fighting very hard in cabinet to ensure that that Fund is sustained, and that it grows. I think he needs support from people in our community. I don't have a magic answer for it, except that if we can keep that lobbying effort going, I think the money cannot diminish.

Joyce Fairbairn:
Just one thing that I would like to add. It is true that money that has been announced does not seem to be filtering down and I hear that across the country. I'm from Lethbridge, Alberta, and the Literacy Coordinators there say that they're not seeing a penny of it.

I think one of the things that makes this meeting today so important is that, believe it or not, the place that is an absolute wasteland on this issue is Parliament Hill. Very, very few people on Parliament Hill are putting this on their agenda; are talking about it or are seeing it as an issue that they want to become involved in. It's hidden; you can't see it and so, therefore, it's hard to promote.

This is where pressure is needed on elected Members of Parliament and on Senators to raise the issue of where the money is going. Where *is* the $110 million that the Minister announced going? Get them to get it filtering down below the bureaucracy into the kinds of programs that you have talked about.

Until that happens, it's going to be a very uphill battle. I would hope, my dream would be, to see a very small but active group of Parliamentarians acting as watchdogs to see that that money is being distributed down at the ground level, where the volunteers need it to teach. I'm begging you to lobby.

Question:
What I would like to say is that first I think you have to get the illiterate people to admit and to come forward. We have to remove

130

the stigma that we place upon people who cannot read. No, they are not stupid but they themselves must say, "I need help." And how do you reach them? This, I think, is the first step because I know for a fact someone who could not read or write but would never admit it.

John O'Leary:
We had a student in our program and a couple of years ago we had him matched with a Volunteer Tutor, a University of Toronto student, a young woman. This was a young man who had been recently married. At one of our Tutor meetings, the Volunteer working with this man - we'll call him John - said, "I have a problem; John's wife doesn't know that he cannot read and John is making excuses when we come to meet together; that he's going out to meet some friends, that he's going to go shopping.

I raised this with him. I said, 'Look, John, I'm phoning your house occasionally, and your wife is answering, and I'm leaving my name. And you know, your wife might think we're having an affair or something.'" John apparently went completely white and said, "No, no. We can't tell her. I'd rather she thought I was having an affair than that I couldn't read, because if she thought I was stupid she could never love me."

Now, that's an extreme case but it's an example. You're right: It's a stigma and I go back to my earlier point; I have never heard an adult say "I am illiterate" - ever. It's a horrid term.

Most of our students come to us by word of mouth and by referral from social agencies. As the issue becomes more prominent, I think the stigma that we attach to it will diminish but you're right. At the moment that's a very serious problem. In the Southam Survey they pointed out that most people who we would label illiterate do not see themselves that way and are grossly insulted by the label.

Question:
We've heard about all of the evils of illiteracy but what we haven't heard is the basic cause of illiteracy. All illiterates in Canada have gone to our public schools. They have all been educated. The illiteracy exploded as a national question about 1985, so it's extremely recent. We still have not had people stating clearly the cause of illiteracy.

The cause of illiteracy in Canada, and in all anglophonic countries, is the English language. It is too irrational to teach. We find a large number of very highly educated people - especially in the scientific field: engineers, scientists - who have trouble spelling, because they think rationally and the language is irrational. The solution is the reformation of our language. People become attached to things whether they're rational or irrational; so a lot of people like the language even though it's irrational.

My question to the Panel is would they be prepared to begin to discuss the English language structure? Notice how I worded it. I'm assuming, if their reaction is the reaction I've met all over the place, that they're not prepared to say, "We are willing now to chop up the English language and rebuild it so it makes sense." They're not willing, unless they're different from people I know, to say that.

John O'Leary:
I'm definitely in favour of plain English. To give an example, the real enemies of literacy in our country are not teachers and educators; they're lawyers. The Southam Survey points out that the basic document governing our civil rights is the Charter of Rights and Freedoms. It's absolutely impenetrable for most Canadians to read, partly because of the problem our Questioner is pointing out. Southam found out that over 40 per cent, almost half of us, are not able to read and understand the Canadian Charter of Rights and Freedoms.

That's just an example of how not being able to read well can exclude a person from fully participating in our society. As for the reformation of the English language, it's not really in our governance. My business right now is to try and help people who have immediate needs to deal with them.

Joyce Fairbairn: I'm not sure I would tear apart our English language but I would certainly agree that it has to be used in communications in a way that people can understand or there's no point in communicating.

That was part of the difficulty in the Trade issue. I think this is where each one of us can be a watchdog, in keeping an eye on what we receive from governments at whatever level. If you can't understand it, then chances are people with reading problems can't understand it at all. Then get out there, again, and pressure the people who are producing this language, to do so in a way that people can understand and learn from.

Photo: John Rowlands

Tourists love our restaurants on the Danforth where they are served cuisine from all over the world. The restaurants provide jobs in our area, especially for young people. Women entrepreneurs like Kim Wong, who runs one of the finest Vietnamese restaurants in Canada, are playing an increasing part in our business community.

Section Five:
Multiculturalism

Strength in Diversity

Dennis Mills
Rocco Rossi

*Rocco Rossi was born in Toronto and edu-
cated at McGill and Princeton. He has
worked as a freelance writer for the "mainstream" and "ethnic" press, and contributed
to books such as* Canada Not For Sale *and*
Mass Media and Popular Culture. *While
still writing, Rocco also helps to run the
family business.*

It is sad to think that almost twenty years after Prime Minister
Trudeau introduced his policy of Multiculturalism Within a Bilingual Framework, we would still be reading articles like McKenzie
Porter's on February 6, 1989 in the Toronto Sun. Most of you have
no doubt already read it, so please forgive a brief summary of the
arguments - such as they are!

Drawing on an article by Elaine Dewar in Toronto Life, Porter says
how depressed he is by the way certain nomination contests were
fought: "the political methods some Italians now employ at riding
nomination meetings...are...most distasteful". Why are they distasteful to Porter? It is because "organizers engage in ethnic practices aimed at replacing the traditional British standards of Canadian government with others more akin to those of Latin Europe".

And what does Porter want us to do about all this? His solution is
that from now on "no Canadian citizen born outside Canada, save the
children of citizens working or vacationing abroad, should be allowed to become a candidate, or to vote, in any municipal, provincial
or federal election". If we adopt those measures, concludes Porter,
we "would preserve and prolong the nation's most noble and historic
heritage".

This is complete nonsense. The only thing Porter's plan would preserve is an exclusionary politics that smacks of racism. Interestingly enough, if Porter's proposed conditions had been in effect when Canada was founded, we would have had to do without great Canadians like John A. Macdonald who happened to be born outside of Canada. Place of birth, while important, does not determine one's ability to contribute to the life of one's country - adopted or not.

Let us be clear that these were *Canadian citizens* who were running for office. They were not "Italians" or "Portuguese" or "Greeks" or "Sikhs" but Canadians who happened to be of a different origin to Porter's. If citizenship is to mean anything, it must give *every* citizen the right to participate fully in the political life of the society and when these people participate Canada is the beneficiary.

Many were shocked by the stories of "instant" Liberals and closely fought nomination meetings, but what was often ignored was that these candidates were merely using the existing rules. These were technically correct, if "instant", Liberals nominating candidates. If there are problems with that, the solutions lie in changing the process and constitutions of the political parties and not with sanctions against people's ethnic origins.

Porter, and others who were horrified by the "undemocratic" practice of "packed" nomination meetings, should be asked to explain how the fine "British" tradition of a few high party officials choosing a candidate is more democratic. Moreover, Latin Europe did not invent these so-called "ethnic practices" of packing meetings and to think so is pure ignorance and prejudice. Even the United States, which Porter applauds for having instituted the practice of "American-born-only" Presidents, has a history littered with machine politics in the tradition of Boss Tweed of New York and Mayor Daley of Chicago. America has nothing to teach us about democracy!

The most troubling aspect of Porter's article, and it's certainly not the only one, is that it completely rejects any notion of multiculturalism. Porter maintains that "most of the ethnic children born in Canada ardently seek assimilation. And this is the attitude expected of them, quite reasonably, by the Anglophones and Francophones". What makes this truly disturbing is that there may be too much truth in the first part of that statement, and for that we must all take some responsibility.

Trudeau argued on Friday, October 8, 1971, in the House of Commons that:

National unity, if it is to mean anything in the deeply personal sense, must be founded on confidence in one's own individual identity; out of this can grow respect for that of others and a willingness to share ideas, attitudes and assumptions. A vigorous policy of multiculturalism will help create this initial confidence. It can form the base of a society which is based on fair play for all.

Truer words were never spoken but, unfortunately, between the idea and the reality, much was lost. Some progress was made, led by a few individuals like the Hon. Jim Fleming, but what developed was a three-tiered cultural system that saw the Ministry of Communications, the CBC, the Canada Council, and other institutions dealing primarily with English and French cultural matters, while the Secretary of State dealt with the "Ethnics", and the Ministry of Indian and Northern Affairs dealt with the cultural needs of native Canadians. This apartheid must end. We need *one* Ministry of Culture that represents Canadian culture - which is essentially *multi*culturalism. Canada doesn't need to search for an identity - we have one alive and well in multiculturalism.

Once in place, with the proper mandate, a unified cultural ministry can help to ensure that all government policies and institutions help to forward multiculturalism, not simply as a policy for cultural retention, but for cultural evolution and creation. To survive and offer a model to the world, multiculuralism must be dynamic and growing.

That is what must be put on the Agenda for the 21st Century and beyond and that is what we must start talking about today. Let's make sure that we aren't reading another Porter-like article twenty years from now.

Photo: Chris Fermanis

Photo courtesy of the Roman Catholic Archdiocese of Toronto Archives.

Religion plays an important part in the lives of many Canadians.

Above: The Holy Name Roman Catholic Church recently celebrated its 75th anniversary.

Top left: Rev Len Self of the Westminster Presbyterian Church (second from left) has headed the BIA since it formed three years ago. Here he welcomes East York Mayor Dave Johnson (far left) MP Christine Hart, East York Hydro Commissioner Frank Johnson, and Councillor Steve Mastoras to East York's first Sidewalk Sale.

Bottom left: Bishop Sotirios of the Greek Orthodox Church leads the annual Greek Independence Day parade along the Danforth with (from l to r) Councillor George Vasilopoulos, Frank Faubert MPP, Councillors Helen Kennedy & Marilyn Churley, Greek Consul General Moutsouglou, the Bishop, Dennis Mills MP, Hon Gerry Phillips Minister of Citizenship, Jim Karygiannis MP and President of the Greek Community Dr Anastasios Karantonis

Questions and Comments from the Audience

Kirthie Abeyesekera:

I am the North American correspondent for the Associated Newspapers of Ceylon - that is, Sri Lanka. And like all right-thinking people, I was terribly, terribly annoyed with Porter's voter philosophy. You probably read what the Toronto Sun publisher, Paul Godfrey, had to say about his columnist. What he says adds insult to injury. In the Sun of February 17th he says it's up to McKenzie Porter to decide if he should apologize for the controversial column of February 6th. Godfrey says he is diametrically opposed to the views expressed in the column, and that they "in no way reflect Sun editorial policy". Now, that's the punch line. If what Godfrey says does not reflect editorial policy, why does The Sun have on its payroll columnists who write, regularly, something that is diametrically opposed to Sun policy?

I call upon the Liberal Party to take specific action against The Sun newspaper, because all the time they publish stories like this the publisher gets away with it by making apologies which have no meaning at all, and columnists get away with this type of stuff. In today's Sun there's another column on similar lines where the columnist is supporting some crime statistics which were based on the racial origins of people in the area in which I live, the Jane-and-Finch area, where Staff Inspector Julian Fantino of Police Division 31 prepared some statistics which show that the Black community in that area is responsible for a large percentage of crime.

This is ridiculous. I have been a crime investigative reporter for over 20 years. I have visited many countries in many parts of the world and I have never known the police in any country to prepare crime statistics based on the racial, religious or ethnic background of peope. The public in general and the police in particular might conclude that just because the crime in the North York area of Toronto is committed largely by blacks, you could also conclude that most blacks are criminals. I mean, this is the reaction that some people would make out of statistics that are prepared on the basis of ethnic origin.

These are some of the things that I would like everyone to address their minds to.

Vera Ke-Plawuszczak:
I'm from a Ukrainian newspaper. I'm very appalled that every time we get a new Minister of Multiculturalism, in half an hour he's replaced by somebody else. Another curious thing; every time they are going to have an election, our Prime Minister and other Ministers all have visible minorities as their assistants or assistant-assistants. One is Black; one is Yellow; one is with the long nose, with small nose but as soon as the election is over, there is a big change, and there is Mrs. McThis and Mrs. MacThat and Mr. Smith and Mr. Brown, and every invisible minority just disappears. This is very puzzling.

As far as newspapers are concerned, I think everybody has to write what he thinks. This is a free country and freedom of the press is very dear to our heart. Why shall we be angry when somebody expresses something that we don't like? If there are people who hate us. Well, it's good. It's better that we know about that. So now it's up to us; we have to write our point of view and write it intelligently.

Dennis Mills:
I'd like to react to two points that you made, and I started off at the outset by saying that we are in a process, here, of developing an Agenda for the 21st Century. We are not three years into a mandate, here; we are sixty days after the last election. And one of the reasons why we're having this meeting and one of the reasons why we had our Conference three weeks ago is because I heard, going door to door, exactly what you just said: "You will get elected, and then we won't see you for another four years."

That's not the way we intend to operate here in Broadview-Greenwood and, as the party's Co-Critic for Multiculturalism, I don't intend to wait two or three years to get you all together to hear your views. So, we are beginning the process of listening, and developing some ideas so that we can have a very strong representation in the new fabric that will be our platform for the next time. It doesn't even have to be an election, quite frankly. If we can come up with some good ideas here today, that can be refined over the next six months, then I personally have no problem if the Prime Minister of Canada enacts them immediately; I have no hard feelings that Mr. Mulroney has a few more seats, at this point in time, than the Liberal Party. What's important is that the good ideas become part of our government. And that's where I'm coming from. So I don't want you to think that I'm treating today's meeting as a partisan event. I've got to believe that if we come up with good ideas, he'll buy those ideas as well and he shouldn't reject them just because they came from another party.

Hasanat Ahmad Syed:
I'm Editor of *New Canada* and my paper is the spokesman for the visible minorities, who are not getting a fair deal. That's my impression. So, as a beginning, the initiative taken by Dennis Mills is very good. I also endorse the views expressed by Vera. Although she said it in a light tone, she said a lot of things which are substantially correct.

Canada has certainly a freedom of expression, and whatever McKenzie Porter has written he has represented one school of thought. The way to combat this school of thought is not to attack him, or accuse him of anything. We have to develop a new concept, a new idea, to counter his argument that the foreign-born Canadians should not be allowed to stand as candidates. That's the only way we can logically convince these people. But it reflects a very disturbing trend among the people who have now started realizing that the ethnic people, or ethnic groups will be exercising a lot of influence in the coming elections. In order to forestall that growing influence, such theories as Porter's are now being expounded.

There is one thing which I must say: The Liberal Party was probably the only Party which permitted a number of ethnic candidates to stand and contest the elections. Although the Liberal Party has done a lot, what is still missing is education among the people. Ethnic candidates, if they stand, simply cannot win on the basis of the strength of the ethnic voters. They have to get votes from the people who are not ethnics and that's very important. The Liberal Party has to emphasize that.

I will mention one thing, which is based on my own personal experience. During the elections, the PC headquarters organized a press conference. They invited the ethnic editors too, so that they could explain their policies. That press conference was addressed by Joe Clark and Mr. McMurtry. I happened to be there. During the press conference I rose up and asked Mr. Joe Clark why the Conservative Party is treating the visible minorities like second-class citizens. His face immediately became very red and there was dissention all around. The Globe and Mail and Star carried the news next day with banner headlines. Since that day, the Conservative Party believe that I am their enemy but I actually raised a very pertinent point. Ontario has the largest ethnic population and, if you see the names of the people put up in Ontario by the Conservative Party, during the whole election there was not a single candidate who came from the ethnic group. So what I said was the truth but they were very defensive; they didn't want to accept it.

The Liberal Party did put up a number of candidates but most of them (actually there were four or five) lost the elections because it was their first try and they could not get proper support. What I'm suggesting now is that we should prepare - the Liberal Party and other parties should prepare - to develop a ground whereby the ethnic groups, or ethnic candidates, should be able to get support from the non-ethnic groups.

Dennis Mills:
I want to respond to you on a couple of points. First of all, we are all ethnics and we talk about a new concept in terms of the contribution that people make who come here from all over the world. At the risk of offending some of you journalists out here today, I think that you've done a lousy job (a lot of you; maybe it's not this particular group here but some of the people you work with who are responsible) of promoting your contribution to this country. And I want to give you an example.

About four years ago, I had to go to Tokyo; I was working with a large auto-parts manufacturing firm and I had to go and see Dr. Toyota. I can't speak Japanese, but I found a young Canadian, who was born in Japan, who came here when he was 15 years old, who got his Master of Business from the University of Toronto and he accompanied me on this trip to Japan. From the moment we arrived, he told me everything that people were saying about us and we could communicate to them what our view was. We got together with the Toyotas and there was no strain in terms of our communication because this young M.B.A. was there with his language skills. So

143

what was to be an exploratory mission, with a follow-up six or eight months later, turned out to be a very successful economic mission. We came back with a letter of intent to do business in the millions and millions of dollars, which created all kinds of jobs for young Canadians, which in turn contributes to the health-care system, the pension system, and so on.

I think that multiculturalism, over the next 20 years, is going to give us a trading advantage that no other country in the world will have but you must communicate that strength that you possess in your various communities. So often people think of multiculturalism as people getting together on a weekend to dance or to sing (and that's terrific because culture is a cornerstone) but we don't talk about our entrepreneurs who can trade all over the world. We don't talk about our Doctors who have come here, who are saving lives at Sick Kids and St. Mike's and Toronto General; we don't highlight that contribution. You people have the power to get that message out and, quite frankly, I don't think it's being done very well. But that's just my opinion. I mean, I'm open to reaction to that.

Unidentified Speaker:
Did you invite the main media?

Dennis Mills:
We invited the English press and I must tell you, and I will confess this openly to you, I know a journalist at MTV who bet me dinner and my choice of a bottle of wine that the English media wouldn't show up. I took the bet. I don't differentiate. Is The Toronto Star here? Is the Globe and Mail here? Is The Sun here? Is CFTO? CBC was invited, CFTO - they were all invited. I hope I'm not going to lose my bet. Sometimes they get a little smug and they prance in late and push their cameras around - I've been there before! You must remember, I worked with Mr. Trudeau for four years, and it used to make me sick the way some of these people behaved - that's why he told them all to go to hell at times

Diane Grell:
I'm an East York resident. I've been quite involved with the multi-ethnic media; I have a lot of compatriots here in that area. And I come from, quite literally, a multi-ethnic background: My mother was born in Scotland; she was Scottish-Irish. My father was born in the West Indies. What disturbs me greatly are all these divisions

144

between people that should not exist in a country where we should be proud Canadians, taking pride (an enormous amount of it) in our ethnic heritage. I find that often the people who suffer, if there are divisions, are those of mixed race, mixed ethnicity - especially the children. They're going to be as much part of the future, those children as anybody. They're the ones who are going to be Canadian, and they're going to have to contribute to Canada in the future. We all are part of this.

Therefore, somehow, we have to do something to try to eliminate all the problems that we have and all this upset and misunderstanding. I got involved with multiculturalism because of my ethnic background. I grew up with it. I'm intensely proud of it. When my father came to this country, he was proud to be in Canada and in those days they didn't have multiculturalism. There are probably a lot of people here who remember that time in Canada when you really had to play it by ear. You didn't have a lot of protection. You didn't have any systemic way of getting involved with multiculturalism.

It disturbs me that we now have all the upset that we do. I don't suppose there's any one answer, except thinking in terms of a little more cohesion and liaising with one another. You see, I'm very proud of that Canadian flag - intensely proud - and I think that other people are too. You can be proud of it in conjunction with being intensely proud of your ethnic heritage. It doesn't matter if its mixed.

My husband's daughter-in-law is Italian. I come from a West Indian-Scottish-Irish background. My husband was born in Canada of Scottish extraction but he doesn't consider himself British with everybody else; he regards himself as an ethnic. He uses Gaelic expressions and people who have their own expressions and their own toasts often relate to that. I think we need a little more of that liaising. I hope other people agree with me on this, because I think the differences that exist are most disturbing. We're all ethnic, as Dennis Mills just said, and there should be no sort of hegemony anywhere. You know, we're all in this together; that's my point - we are all on common ground. I feel very emotional about it and I thank you very much for listening.

Dennis Mills:
Common ground; common future. There is another area where we must all get involved. I'm referring to our environment. There's a

145

very important issue where we could all be taking a very strong lead - not just because of our presence here but because of our links abroad. If there was ever an issue that will bind us all together, it's going to be the environment. It's not just Canada that's involved in this issue; it's the world and we're going to be pleading for linkages all over the world to make sure that we galvanize not just national will but international will, to fix up our environment. There is going to be an opportunity for the special feature of our country - our multiculturalism - to play a dominant role. I hope that people here who have this access to the pen or the radio or television jump on this and take the lead.

Unidentified Speaker:
We must stop calling ourselves "visible minorities". We must stop calling ourselves "the ethnic media".

Dennis Mills:
I agree with that. The word here in our Riding is "multiculturalism". That's got to be our national symbol.

Marek Goldyn:
I'm the publisher of *Canadian Political News and Life*. I'm a new immigrant; I'm seven years in Canada. I have run a few businesses, so I have quite good experience. I have some comments about today's meeting and about ethic media. I had a Polish radio programme for four years and was very active. I think what the ethnic media are not doing, they are not writing about Canadian life - what is going on in general and the major political events. Usually we just cover news from the old country, with very little about what's going on in Canada. There is actually a good service by Ben Viccari, who runs *Canadian Scene*. He supplies some materials to ethnic media in their language. So don't blame, for example, The Toronto Star or Globe for not coming here, in a way, because, as ethnic press, we are not representing any kind of power. We are not writing about the political events. It's that simple. If you take a look in our newspapers you would find a lot of greetings from the Prime Minister and other such things. I think this is for the government's purpose. We are not writing about Canadian life and giving our views on the issues.

There is a lot of pressure from the black people to make black people, or visible minorities, invisible. I think that now we are in Canada we are equal; we are all people. So forget about visible or invisible because we are living here and we are free people. Everyone is different, has a different way of thinking, and we have to respect that. That's an advantage that Canada has; so we have to improve it.

I used to run a travel agency and in business you don't make any stupid comments about any customer. I remember very well having a neighbour who was an Arab from Syria, and I didn't know that some Arabs hate each other - how would I know? So I almost said, " your friend from Iraq sent me here". It was good I stopped, because I would probably be killed because they hated each other. But also this is a business. I would lose a customer, so I would lose my money, you know.

Maybe our small world is not interesting for the English media, because they have other problems, you know. We are part of the media, so don't expect someone to write about us. We have our own tools and express our own opinions and we can send copy to this man, Porter.

Dennis Mills:
I just want to clarify a point, because I believe that when we write about an issue that piece shouldn't be restricted to just one or two papers. If it's a piece that is well written, well described, we should exchange these pieces. Genius has no language barriers or boundaries and I think it's a good thing to exchange that talent.

Stanley Ansong:
I am with *The African Letter*. I do agree that we have the right to state our point, and that's what this country's all about. But also, we do have the right to challenge the views of people. This brings us to where we have to think about this so-called ethnic media. I have heard quite a few people discuss the ethnic media and appropriate ways of handling messages within different communities.

I'm not from this constituency; I should say that. But this is the point I would like to make: We live in a system that we could classify as capitalistic, and we love this system. It's good; it works for us. At the same time we should also bear in mind, whilst we're thinking of ethnic papers, that they function on money. Financial strength allows a publication to make a point. It doesn't matter whether it is an ethnic or mainstream paper. There were mainstream papers in the

147

'States who broke the Watergate story and were attacked by the Nixon government. They were going to lose their radio station licenses. That means money. It takes money to run a newspaper.

Most of the ethnic papers, and I like to call them ethnic papers, are ghettoized. They were ghettoized first by the Liberal Party, I'm sorry to say. If the government was going to speak to the press, they were divided into two sections. First, the main section where they talk to the Globe and Mail and give them the statistics and everything; and then the second one being for the ethnics, where everything was toned down to give to the people. Pictures were taken with the Ministers, and things like that.

Now, a paper cannot function without advertising. That is the first thing in our system. You can write everything, anything, but people have to put money in. How do you do it when you don't have advertising money? Nobody's going to print it free for you.

Another thing is that the government - any government, Liberal, Conservative or NDP - has a method of throwing ad money around when it's time to go for election. The ethnic publications get some because everyone wants to get into publication at that time. When it's over, the market is dry. So, the ethnic publications have to go back to their own ethnic groups. If you're from the Ukraine, it means that you have to talk to Ukrainian business people who may really not find it necessary to advertise in your paper but would like to help you out. One of the worst things is trying to put a paper together and you're begging for money, actually. So, therefore, these papers are not strong. So to stand here and say, "Well, let's use them to make our point" ignores this problem.

Our ethnics do not cross borders. Ukrainian papers do not go to the Chinese community; the Chinese community newspapers do not go to the Rumanian community. To be able to read what has been written in Chinese language concerning the great Canadian scene in your own language it must be translated. Somebody needs to translate it but that is his profession and you will have to pay. So I think the main problem here is money. We live in a society where money works, money talks, money sleeps, money's active, we should take a very good look at money acting.

The ethnic community and its newspapers is a very poor group of people trying to make links and, in most cases, they are second-class in circulation. When Mr. Porter writes his article, it goes throughout the nation; it's heard; it vibrates. When any ethnic paper writes anything, even within that ethnic group where the younger ones may not speak the language any more and that paper may be dying, it will reach very few people. So, I think we should take a look at that before we jump to the conclusion that we should be out there giving the news to the ethnic press, and they will be able to make the point. They will make the point, but it will not be as strong as when McKenzie Porter writes or the Globe and Mail writes. They have money to make their system work.

So it comes down to whether business groups or the governments are going to help the ethnic publications to be powerful enough to counter-act people like Porter or whether the ethnic groups should find a way to have a voice within the so-called mainstream publications.

Dennis Mills:
I will respond to a couple of points that you made. First, you should know that I'm not defensive about Mr. Trudeau. We were not per-fect. But I was the Senior Policy Advisor to the Cabinet Committee on Communications for a year and a half, and it used to disturb me the way we handled the allocation of funds for the multicultural media. The problem that we had was how to know who to give the money to. So often we had people from the community come in and I would sit in my office and hear their complaints directly - not through a bureaucrat - and they would say, "Dennis, why did you give that newspaper $5,000.00 when the fellow only publishes once a year, if that? Have you ever asked him for a copy of his newspaper? Did you ever ask him what his circulation was?" That was a problem and so there was a period there when we weren't handling the tax-payer's dollar in the best way possible. Based on that experience I think that there should be some basic criteria in terms of number of times published and amount of circulation before we hand out tax-payers' money - and I'm sure you would all agree with that.

In response to your point about ghettoizing, if we just give someone $1,000.00 for a newspaper ad because we don't want his community upset with us, well then I think we are furthering that process of ghettoization. I think we have to set some basic standards, and people must rise to them.

Now, in getting to those standards, I believe that we are now at a point in time in our community where men and women, who maybe 20 years ago were just beginning their businesses and were preoccupied with building up their equity and their balance sheets, have now made it and they are from communities all over the world. I believe that you should go to those people and you should say, "Listen, we need you to help promote your cultural heritage. And this is one of the instruments." And I think they, in turn, could use some of their leverage on some of the people that they buy product from.

Let's follow this through. Imagine that someone was a backer of this newspaper. You wouldn't just want them to buy an ad; you would go to them and say, "You buy millions of dollars worth of Coke a year; you buy millions of dollars worth of Tide; you buy millions of dollars of whatever for your business. Can you use your marketing guy, your buyer, to maybe make a few calls to some of your suppliers, and maybe they could put a few little ads in our newspaper?" And that's how it works. I really believe you have to tap into that. Did that answer that a little bit for you? Because I believe what you say. You need the money to get to a standard that makes it respectable.

Richard Chambers:
I'm not with the press and I don't have your facility with words. I've found that Mr. Porter seems to represent certain vested interests. His interest seems to be in polarization - divide and conquer - which has been a traditional approach in any society that had a small minority that wanted to hold on to power. It's been very effective and, to date, it's worked very well. So, I'd ask you, when you look at future articles like this, to ask, "What purpose is this serving, and who is it serving?" I think that's something we should all do - especially the press - and try and answer the points in those articles to our own audiences. Mr. Porter's view is that we live in a closed society; as a Liberal, I see myself living in a very open society. Mr. Porter is representing a very small and narrow focus, while we tend to look and see things in a much broader spectrum. I think Mr. Porter believes the clock should be turned back - turned back 50 years, 100 years, whatever but we can't go back. Mr. Reagan tried it in the United States, and we see the price of Reaganomics. We see an economy that's in shambles and an American dollar that's gone to hell. I think that our message to Mr. Porter should be, "I'm sorry. It's too late. The clock can't be turned back."

Dennis Mills:
Thank you. That was insightful.

Unidentified Speaker:
I am from the Estonian community. I belong to an ethnic community but I would like to point out that, at the present time, too much emphasis has been put on multilingualism and multiculturalism in Canada. It makes polarizations. I hope in the next century, the sons and grandsons of the people who are now here, will be the ones to get into the Canadian Parliament and legislatures.

I found it astonishing you were surprised that Star, Globe and Mail and Sun were not represented here. I understand they are the big papers. You should have asked the representatives of the English and French communities to come here. Then we could talk about all the new ethnic groups with their languages and with their culture who can come in and make connection with the culture and language of the founding nations. They are still the majority and we, the ethnic groups, should respect them. They have brought Canada to where it is at the present time. As a person elected to the Parliament, you should absolutely respect them too. We cannot cut them out and speak just about minorities and ethnic groups and their demands. It is too much. We are, of course, pleased with the money you give the ethnic groups and so on. Our ethnic group has received some and we appreciate this understanding. But we should be, first, Canadians and talk and live together with the other groups. The East Asians are brilliant boys, and they should be recognized. In sports, the black people are the brilliant ones. Nobody will say that there should not be so many black people in sports. They are there; they're the best ones.

Dennis Mills:
I want to make one clarification. When I say "we are all ethnics" I mean English and French as well. And when I speak as a parliamentarian, I speak for Canada; I don't just speak for a few groups. I just wanted to make sure that there was no misunderstanding on that point.

Ben Viccari:
I am Editor of *Canadian Scene*, which as most of you know is a multilingual news service serving 200 ethnic publications and about 120 radio and television programs. I thought I detected a note of

pessimism, in one or two remarks, about the inability of various cultural groups to get on with the others. Now, in the three years that I've been editing *Canadian Scene,* I have increased the number of success stories; stories with a positive ring, about any particular cultural group that I can get my hands on and which reflect positively on our multicultural society. I notice that, for example, the Italian and Greek publications carried a lot of my material on all other cultures. If I do something for, say, Mr Altermann of the *Deutsche Press* about native Canadian culture or Italians, he'll run it. And so on and so forth. There is a great cause for optimism because I think our communities are beginning to show an interest in one another, and not just at Caravan time. I'd like to salute the people who are doing this.

Dennis Mills:
That was a point well made.

Dick Altermann:
I'm the Editor-in-Chief of the *Deutsche Press,* which is the German-speaking newspaper. I would like to address this to the Government. As my esteemed colleague pointed out, it's a dollars and cents sort of operation. Most of the ethnic newspapers, whatever we call them, operate on a shoestring. Isn't that true? Money is something which is very hard to come by, but you need money to pay people. A lot of information comes out of the Government - press releases, communiques - and it's terrific but it's all in English. You can't print that if you're an ethnic newspaper and print in one ethnic language. Ben Viccari goes ahead and translates everything he does so its no problem; we give this to the typesetter and he typesets it and it goes in the paper. What can we do about the English stuff that we get from the Government? We don't have the money to translate it; it's as simple as that. So, if you can make some arrangements for some of those larger ethnic groups to have these communications translated into their language, they'll go into the paper. Otherwise, they'll go into File 13 - sorry.

Dennis Mills:
I think you've made a valid point. I don't think that we should restrict information. I think that we should look into seeing if translations are being done on these issues. We should probably have a secretariat for that service.

George Mallia:
I'm the Editor of the Maltese publication *L-Ahbar.* I'd like to look at something from a business point of view. I don't think there was better advertising for the new book that was published in England a little while ago by the name of *Satanic Verses* than somebody going out to demonstrate against it. There was no better advertising for the movie that came out last year called *The Last Temptation of Christ* when people demonstrated against it. So, with somebody like McKenzie Porter - who somebody said is living in the last century, and I know what kind of British system that he is trying to push because I come from a country that was dominated by the British for 160 years - the worst thing that we can do is publicize it. If you don't like what you hear from a certain publication, don't buy it. When lots of you don't buy it, not only are all your 30 cents lost to them, but also the numbers. When the numbers go down, the advertising goes down. And we're talking about mainstream newspaper now, not our little 2,000-edition papers. We do that for the love of our culture and our language, and most of us are doing it out of our own pockets. When you don't demonstrate, but you just totally ignore the paper, you don't buy it, and the numbers go down, then the publishers will get the message that we don't want to hear and we don't want to read about that garbage.

Linda Lynch:
I'm probably known to a lot of you as an environmentalist in Metro Toronto. But I am also a free-lance journalist and I write for several community newspapers. One of the things that really bothers me is the comment that was made about "the big white press" not being here. I think that you're being overly sensitive when you say that because, when we've had press conferences on environmental issues, it isn't a question then of racial discrimination if they don't come, it's that we're not big enough and we're not important enough. So, I don't want you to think that it's an ethnic situation when the large news-papers don't come out to cover you because I've experienced it in terms of environmental issues.

What bothers me more than anything is that we're not asking our-selves why the article was written. What made him write such an article? I think it's fear, fear of the unknown, and I think it comes from a failure on the part of ethnic groups to integrate. I say that also with the thought that the government needs to do more. I think that we need language centres. We also have to integrate our cultures.

I know that when I went to Mexico and spent eight months there I had a choice. I could have read the Canadian newspaper that was published in Acapulco and along the coast, and I could have stayed with Canadians. Instead, during the eight months, I travelled through the jungle areas and I went native; I learned to speak the language and that enabled me to communicate. And I came away totally enriched.

So, I have some questions for the ethnic press. Are you not walking a very fine line? Isn't it dangerous? If you protect and promote your language and your culture without an equal mandate to integrate that culture into the multiculturalism of an emerging, new and exciting Canadian identity, have you not defeated the very thing that you set out to do? I believe that the ethnic community and its press has a responsibility for outreach. In your editorial boards and staffing, you have to reach out and encourage your readers to participate outside of that small, introverted community; that could be the danger, if you don't have an equal mandate to reach out into the mainstream of society. It's very discouraging for me when, for example, I'm trying to lobby on an environmental issue and I can't talk to the Chinese community, or the Italian community, or the Greek community. I have a message that I want to give to every single person that's a matter of our health and our future. You know, Metro Toronto is not a white majority. I've heard figures ranging from 64 to 78 per cent in terms of ethnic mix in Metropolitan Toronto. What a wonderful opportunity that could give us. I believe that being able to talk to one another is the first and most important step.

Dennis Mills:
You know, I guess one of the real frustrations of our Francophone friends is the fact that they were founding partners in the country, and for so long their freedom of expression was restricted to only one part of this country. So, you can just imagine the frustration that a young Francophone had when Canada was his country, and he would go to Winnipeg and apply for a job, but because he didn't speak English, he probably wasn't considered. All of us who have had the experience of living in a community where, initially, we didn't understand that language, and couldn't really get to first base in terms of opportunity, I think should be able to sympathize with some of that frustration.

I agree with you about environmental issues and I think that was the point that I was trying to make earlier. When we do our Summit on the Environment, that is an issue that every newspaper, every radio station, every television station should be encouraging and making sure that every member of every community takes an activist role. If most people don't understand what it's all about then, you know, that's why sometimes you end up with a small, select group of people getting involved in these things.

Alexander Pruszinski:
I publish a Polish paper. I think too many of us and too many people in the Peterson Government are over-reacting to the issue of the French-language press at the expense of the ethnics, or non-English/non-French. There is a free-distribution French-language paper in Toronto which is almost totally supported by the federal and provincial governments. It's getting ads which we never can. Air Canada is not advertising in ethnic papers; it's not advertising in my paper. Okay, I'm small fry. But how about the Italian paper which is bigger? There is a much bigger community of Italians in Toronto - ten times bigger than the French. So I have had enough of French. Yes, I think there were some cases where the French were not treated equally. But right now in Canada, ten of the biggest corporations in this country are headed by French-Canadians. So let's not pretend that the French are getting a bad deal. How much is it costing us to make everything bilingual in this Province? I think it's about time we look at the price because everyone here's paying for it. Equal does not mean super-equal.

The issue which brought us all here was that people not born in Canada should not be running for Parliament. The distinguished gentleman who wrote that column saw the issue; the issue was that some ethnic people have been packing pre-election meetings and were getting nominated by the fact that they went around, giving $6 or $8 to people and buying their votes. The same people were signing up for the Liberals, Conservatives and NDPs. I am not talking theoretical; I'm talking from experience. I stood for the Conservative nomination in Mississauga East and I didn't have a few thousand dollars so I lost it. In England, if you're not a member of the Conservative or Liberal Party for six months or a year, you're not allowed to vote at a nomination meeting. So if our laws are stupid, people will take advantages.

So I think this gentleman who wrote that column hit the wrong stick.

155

People of all origins are using these laws for their own benefit. I think this is the major issue. Something has to be done about it because it is crooked. Let's face it: people who have money can get those votes. I would like you to pass a strong message to Mr. Peterson and Mr. Turner. And in the Conservative Party it is the same issue. We should all say, "if you are not a member of the party six months, or nine months, or whatever, sorry fellow you can't take part in the nomination."

Dennis Mills:
I can only presume that I missed making the point earlier. The fact is those nomination meetings were wrong, not because of anyone's origin but because the process and the constitution of the party, whether it be P.C. or Liberal or New Democratic, allowed it to happen. I have very strong views that we should change our nomination process because I think it's absolutely ridiculous that people can come in at the eleventh hour (when other people have been working sometimes for two and three years building party policy) and vote without even knowing what they're voting for. I don't think that's the way to build a healthy foundation in any party, and I don't just say it as a Liberal; I think most parties would agree.

I disagree with you on the issue of our relationship with Quebec. I have strong views that the French language should be promoted and developed from one coast to the other, not in a way that it's going to be fiscally irresponsible but so that Francophones, in and out of Quebec can be served in their language; just as I want that same right when I go to Quebec City. If I have to take my daughter to a hospital, I want to make sure that that service exists. And I think it's great that you cited the ten leading corporations in Canada who are now being run by Francophones. For 15 years, we went through all kinds of difficulty in this country, where people were almost racist in their attitude towards the French. And now that we have Francophones leading in every walk of life, and they're participating in the mainstream, and they're captains of industry from coast to coast, I think it would be absolutely ridiculous to ghettoize Quebec.

Terry Brackett:
My husband and I are, I guess, new kids on the block as we started *The Leslieville Newspaper* about six months ago. In this month's issue, I have a teenager who writes for us. He has interviewed skin heads. And I was absolutely sickened, as a mother of teenagers in

the community, that the skin heads that told him they were out for a pure white supremacy in this area. They don't want anybody else. I also attended a meeting, recently, about a new development that was going in at Queen and Leslie. I was really just heartbroken to hear some very racial statements afterwards about the gentleman, who was of Asian background, saying that they didn't think that his kind of money was welcome in Canada. I was really upset with this, and after attending something like the Mosaic Conference, what I'd like to ask is if you could recommend something proactive being done in our communities. I think one thing would be cross-cultural training within our schools; starting with our young people and, as you say, not just showing peoples' dancing and food, but also explaining each person's different culture.

Dennis Mills:
Well, you know that I will support that. I think that's fundamental, and not just in terms of cultural heritage, but also for economic soundness. What we can also do is get together in three weeks' time for some feedback. I'd also like to put on the agenda the Summit on the Environment, which is taking place in the Don Valley in September. I believe that this is an area where everyone in this room can play a major role. Let's face it, most people go for results; they measure results. If people can see your contribution, your activism, and your ability to motivate others to get involved and make contributions, you have a much better chance when you go and ask for further participation, whatever the issue may be. I am willing to work with you and with your ideas to make sure that we can try and create a new sense of contribution and a new sense of marketing force for the multicultural press of this community.

Famous sculptor E B Cox is a resident of Broadview-Greenwood.

Section Six:
Communications, Culture and Change

Adjusting to Change in the Workplace

Karen Fraser

Karen Fraser was the first Canadian to teach adaptation skills for the eighties and beyond and she is always at the edge of innovative training. Her company, Women Like Me, assists both employers and employees to adapt to present and future roles in the emerging corporate culture.

It is my job to teach courses on the future. I have done so now for twelve years. During the first ten years everyone laughed at me but each year, as changes happened, they would have me back and I'd get paid a second time while they laughed. My mother wishes I would get a real job but, in the last two years, people have stopped laughing and started asking serious questions - particularly since last October after our mini-crash in the stock market.

You've heard a lot of subjects today that deal with the future - a lot of them upsetting, a lot of them very motivating. So, what I am going to do is give you a positive framework for what's happening because it's easier to deal with things if you have some idea where you're going.

We've always had a future but what's different about this one is the speed of its arrival. We have never had a future hit us as quickly as this. Now, the speed wouldn't matter if human beings liked change; but we don't. We would rather stick with things that we're used to, even that we hate, than try something new that might be better. It's just human nature.

So, what are the changes that are coming this time? Well the main one is that we're leaving the great era known as the Industrial

Revolution. What does that mean for all of us tomorrow? It means that everything we thought of as being normal is shifting to the side.

In the world of the '50s, the great era of the Industrial Revolution, that we were all raised in, everything was a ladder. The economy was the corporate ladder; homes looked like the economy. Schools looked very much like our factories; we sat in rows and did dull, monotonous work that got us ready to grow up and do dull, monotonous work in the '50s.

The ladder for men started at the bottom, in the mail room and then they were supposed to work for ten years in complete boredom until they got to management. Now that was what your dad told you was "paying your dues", "showing you had the right stuff", "pulling yourself up by your bootstraps" - I'm sure you all got this speech from your parents when you went to work. So, when you got to management, the fight was on and, in the end, the best guy with the right-est stuff would get to be president.

Women also had a corporate ladder, only ours was rather small - it only had two steps - and you fell off our corporate ladder the day you got married, and you went home and waited for the husband to bring home the money. And we bought things in the '50s - like couches from Eatons - and put them in rec rooms. And that was the world. We had expressions for it. We had values that covered it. We were "saving up"; we were "waiting until". Everything was step by step. There were rules and the rules were what made it work; they were very black and white. I was raised that the right way was my mother's way; everything else was wrong. My grandmother told me that beef was meat "and the rest is what foreigners have" and that was the end of it; no questions asked. Very black and white. This is what's changing.

If you can picture it, our ladder is turning sideways. Instead of the full spectrum from failure to president - with room for everyone - we are very quickly moving into a new economy where you're either *in* or you're *out*, with very little in between - and it isn't just local, it's global. It isn't black and white any more; it's shifting areas of gray. What was in this year might be out the next. Now if you're hearts are already starting to pound at the sound of all this, you know that you don't like change but hang on; it does get better.

We are going to live in a different economy. Basically, the agreement we had in Canada in the '50s was that we would give all of our time, all of our effort, and we would get money, security, a gold watch and a pension. What's happening now is that the giving and getting is re-arranging and there's a lot of confusion about what workers should give and what they should get in return.

In the new world we're all going to have six to eight careers, and many jobs within those careers. Before you panic, remember that most of us will develop a skill bank that we will take with us from career to career.

In the '50s, a man with the right stuff was known because he had one job per lifetime. My Uncle Jack didn't have the right stuff. He quit at Eatons when he was 40! Now that's 30 years ago but, whenever something goes wrong in Jack's part of the family, people still say, "Well, you know Jack, he quit at Eatons." The older people believe that makes poor Uncle Jack a flake. The younger kids have no idea what people are talking about.

In the present world of work that type of worker, Mr. Right Stuff, who Uncle Jack never managed to be, is a liability. If he ever gets fired from Eatons, he'll probably never be employed again. People wonder why he hasn't got more initiative. "Why hasn't he had more than one career?"

Most people in the future will not be on staff from nine to five; they'll be working out of their homes. Now, most wives, the day their husband retires, do the right thing; they get a full-time job. Because they know what will happen if the two of them are in the house day-in and day-out.

The rest of us will be going to school most of our lives. A friend of mine who's in computers once told me he didn't want any more training. He felt that what he got at Queens, half-drunk, at 18 would last him till he's 80 in the computer field. Recently, he's decided to take more training because the computer languages he learned at Queens are now nearly obsolete.

There'll be fewer children - at the moment, women are still having them, but who knows - and we will not be retiring at age 65.

Photo: John Rowlands

Service industries are already well established in our community. John has been cutting hair in Broadview-Greenwood for over twenty years.

So you can see, it's going to be a different world; a different balance, a different giving and getting. Now, if your heart's still pounding, you realize you really *don't* like change one bit. Personally, I love change, as long as I like what's going on. If I don't, the lower lip goes out like a manhole cover. But does life care that you don't like the changes? No, it'll run right over your lip and keep right on going.

So, how do we react to change? Well, first, we're terrified. "Don't like it. What's going on? Everything was fine. Why back in World War II, the world was perfect and..." No it wasn't!

Now, when we're frightened, we become angry; it's a lot more fun to be mad than frightened, anyway. There is a lot of undercover anxiety in Toronto now. People are upset, but they don't know what to do about it. You'll find out about it if you bump their cart in Loblaws. They threaten to take your spine out, from the front.

But you know what they're upset about? They need someone to blame and if it's you who bumped their cart you'll do just fine! So finding someone to blame is the next reaction to change.

And lastly, we have a tendency to want to go back. "Let's not listen to Dennis. We'll just turn on the TV and it'll be fine. Why it'll go back to the '50s; this is just a little glitch in the system." No it isn't; it's a new era.

That's how we react, and that's what we're going to see in people in the next few years as they struggle with change. But it is going to be, I think, the best working and living economy we've ever had. Yes, the black-and-white rules did work but it wasn't perfect; a lot of people were not happy in that system. My father put out a tremendous amount of effort in his job; I don't think he ever liked it. The term "job satisfaction" would be completely foreign to him.

Now, I have the pleasure of enjoying my career and, in the future, when people work by assignment, they'll be able to pick and choose. They're going to be very confident, highly skilled people and that means that if companies want the best, they will have to create work environments that are safe and environmentally satisfying to the workers or they simply won't work there; and there are signs of that already.

Are our *companies* reacting well to the future? Not really. They react just like people. When they're frightened and angry, they tend to become more 1955 than they were in 1955. When they realize that they're 20 years behind the rest of the world, instead of being creative and adapting, they try to cover their assets by buying somebody else's. We've had several examples in the last two weeks. This is just the old corporate dinosaurs' one last desperate fight before they're forced to adapt because, when they just merge and take over, they don't find new solutions. They don't create jobs; people lose them. We can't allow this to go on. Yes, it's a transition, but it's going to be too painful.

So, what kind of people will succeed? Now that your hearts are pounding, you think perhaps you should have shot yourself in the washroom at lunch. Don't panic. The rules are actually quite simple for the future.

Number one, you have to be very flexible. For '50s people, that's probably the most difficult one. We were raised with "that's the way it should be and that's the way it is." People in the '90s will learn not to accept clichés about complex issues, to give every side a fair chance.

Secondly, people with a good general background will do extremely well in the '90s. All those over-educated bums of the '60s are finally going to have their chance; and I think the MBAs are in big trouble.

You'll need a very good image - that means physical image - because the competition is going to be stiff. Remember, you're either in or you're out! And if you're dressed like 1972, they'll think that's when your brain stopped. So, your vocabulary has to be up to date. If you can learn to say "double-sided, double-density" - you don't have to understand it; they probably don't either - it sounds great. And, your awareness must be up to date. That's the kind of image that companies want.

That goes with the next rule; you must have excellent communication skills. Companies want to hear from people within the system what is changing in what department. They want the information to go up to the top, quickly, unlike the '50s, where the policy came down. In the '90s it will be heading up.

Next, we must be good time managers. In a time of change, when the rules are breaking down, you can do whatever you want, and become totally exhausted running in circles.

The successful people of the '90s will set their own career and personal paths (because the government and the companies will not be able to do it for them) and then they will stick to their own plan. And even if there are things that interest them, they will put them aside at least for a few more years.

Also, we'll need very strong values that we can dump at a moment's notice. I have no idea how we do that.

We will need to have an excellent network, and that's one reason Dennis has brought us here today. Information is the new key to success in the '90s - how to get it quickly and know the right people to put it in place as soon as possible, before it becomes obsolete. Networking allows what you know and who you know to interact and to make certain you get the future that you want.

Another rule is that we must be active in our own life. Now, that sounds very silly, but where are all your friends who said they were going to come here today then, at the last second, didn't quite make it? They're still living in 1955. You have to be active.

When Dennis calls for ideas, plans, suggestions - that's exactly the key. Governments, corporations, haven't any more idea of what's going on than we do. When I travel around the country, people say: "Where do you get all your theories and your ideas? Where do you learn all of this?" I say, "It comes from the people in the seminars; they tell me." If it comes to a battle of the experts, the people that I meet, the people living it, have a much better idea of what's going on. So be active, participate.

Lastly, work together. We must because there's too much at stake. And, every time you feel yourself saying, "That's not the way it should be" stop and think that perhaps you're making a mistake; you're looking back. Forget "the way it should be". Take a clear, informed look at the way it "could be" and then work together to make sure that we get the future the way we want it to be.

Thinking Beyond Revolution

BW Powe

B W Powe was born in Ottawa but has lived most of his life in Toronto. He is the author of A Climate Charged *and* The Solitary Outlaw. *His new book called* Outage: In Electric-City *is to be published by Random House.*

Photo: Andrew Danson

The other night, I was watching television. I flipped stations with my remote-control, creating a collage of commercials, talk shows, old movies and test patterns. I scanned the TV without registering content when, suddenly, the screen flashed:

The Revolution is Here

The graphics dissolved into the image of a sleek new car rolling up to the edge of a screen. A voice intoned about "revolutionary change" and "re-tire your old wheels". Then the tires, somehow disconnected from the rest of the car, rolled off the screen. The message was repeated:

A Revolution in Travel

I took off my glasses and slumped back on the couch.

Revolution! A word that makes us cringe with embarrassment. No other word has become so stuck in the cycles of cliché, yet our whole age is revolutionary; innovation, upheaval, and modernization are the very grounds of our society. Consume. Create. Re-cycle. Renew. There are more breakthroughs in technology per minute, scientists tell us, than at any other time in history. Revolutions in nanotechnology, taxpayers' revolts and fundamentalist revolutions... we are revolutionized to the core. But the paradox is the more innovations there are per minute, the more productive and consuming society becomes, the more static and resistant our thinking seems to be. Nothing stays still. The result, no progress of understanding. So, the wheels of invention spin and we feel our spirits worn down because of the accelerating pace; while under the surface of this revolutionary drive is the thwarted desire to imagine alternatives to what we are and what we do. Somewhere within us a rebellion thrives.

After the revolution, history says, comes the reaction. The great political revolutions in 1789, 1917, 1870, which were based in ideology, came back full circle to state control and terrorism and dictatorship. The original rage in the streets was battered back by fear, murder, control of the body, closure of the spirit, a manacling of the mind.

In Canada, our revolutionary society is not ideologically based; it is centered in technology and the need we've felt to communicate over huge distances. In our time, "change" has become another token word, one that reveals how our own milieu is in motion. Yet, as we experience doubts, and as we ponder questions about our world today, we encounter a problem with language. In 1989, "revolutionary change" all too often means a fascination with gadgetry, a faith that machines will solve all.

And us, here, now? We are the speed of light generation who live on livid nerves. Those of us raised on TV, rock'n'roll, telephones and computers know and feel the cross-currents of constant upheaval. The speed of light generation has had unprecedented privilege, affluence, and access to information. Yet it is we who have often turned out to be the most cautious, the most cynical, the most materialist, the most prone to playing "Let's Make A Deal".

Our revolution wasn't one of ideology but of sensibility. In North America, we have moved from a culture of books to a culture of TV to a culture of computers, all in the space of thirty years. I take Black Monday, the Stock Market Crash of 1987, as the first global sign that the computer revolution truly informs our whole environment.

But sometimes we find the only way we can cope with convulsion is through numbing. The reaction speaks when we hear people say, "too much", "stop", and "I'm over-stressed". The fundamentalists (with their abiding dislike of intellect) are an outgrowth of so many revolutions per minute. They too shout "enough" and speak of censorship, the past and restriction. Reaction in revolutionary societies is found in those who confront chemical dependence (with drugs, toxins, the mainlines in our wired whirl), and demand more surveillance, larger police forces, more machines. Reaction sets in when borderlines collapse, and we feel that limits to social contact have been erased. Reaction occurs when there's an overflow of news, and we recoil, turn inward, form exclusive clubs, and build walls around ourselves. Again we find a paradox: how many times have those in the speed of light generation, for whom motion is all, found themselves slumped in consumerism, indifference, and exhaustion?

Now we speed on to the turn of our century, the finale to an apocalypse-haunted time. Those in a millennial mood tend to be possessed by dreams of utopia and nightmares. History creates flash points - sometimes arbitrarily. Moments, myths - like Black Monday or the Storming of the Bastille. Our mood, however, is restless, confused, alarmed, and ecstatic, and it is all of these things at the same time.

Why then do I say go beyond revolution and reaction?

Because I believe the conventional bonds of our thinking haven't sufficed. We don't have a terminology to describe our yearning. We've felt the results of revolution, reaction, and revelation, and we see in our leaders and institutions a philosophy of deal-making - an exhaustion that suggests an inability to sift through the signals. Somehow, our old ways of thinking about these processes haven't worked. We are without many helpful guides. Specialization, the fragmenting of ideas into boxes, has created a sense of disconnection. Our thinking is scattered, dislocated; yet we feel the urgency to break out of the hold of the old, so that we don't stop ourselves from feeling what it means to venture out and explore.

* * *

In the streets, here, I look at Toronto and I see the redesign of corners and buildings. I see the obsession with size, with self-reflecting mirrors in bank towers, with competition and the North American *mythos* of money. I look at my home and see how far the philosophy of accommodation has taken us.

But I look at Toronto, and I see possibility. The possibility of this city is the possibility of a country. Multi-lingual; affluent enough to be generous; with a need to be just; a willingness to re-build. This is a place where we can listen to the currents and where we can question the *status quo* - whether that *status quo* be government, media, corporation, police, academe, or our own beliefs.

Then I look at the mega-world and its corporate cities, where revolutionary technology is the ground. There we can see a killing of the earth, a loss of beauty, light and air, and the extinction of silence.

I see Canada in the grip of the same spirit that possesses the world. The suburbs of Agincourt have the same look as the suburbs around Houston, Florence and Leningrad. The sameness means we share something in common. It also means our imaginations are not being stirred. And out of that sameness, that absence of love for variety and beauty, surely our souls search for energies that will galvanize us and not repeat these cycles of revolution and reaction.

With our opportunity and our wealth, our challenge is to crack the systems that confine a vital restlessness. I cite G K Chesterton, who said, in reference to the blind jingoism of England in his time:

We are the children of light and it is we who sit in darkness. If we are judged, it will not be for the merely intellectual transgression of failing to appreciate other nations, but for the supreme spiritual transgression of failing to appreciate ourselves.

So, on this day we should be asking questions.

What will we do with the toxins we allow to seep into ourselves and into our landscape? Is it the crack on the streets or the crack in our hearts that we must first heal? Is the issue of political nationalism and nation states finished, and should we be looking instead at world confederation and global citizenship? Is inward-turned nationalism, whether in Toronto, in Quebec City, or in Edmonton, a thing of the past? Should we not begin to re-think economic justice, and what over-consumption means? Do we have the will to break the sword, and so develop ideas that are not merely about peace, but which express a passion for peace? Are we ready to overcome the fear of strangers and the obsession with self-security?

If borderlines and structures are altering at a rapid pace, then we must soon become adept at handling multiple connections, wires and strands, a myriad of information, many channels at once.

For the future will surely depend on our dialogue, and not on monologue.

*   *   *

I'd like to end by honoring the spirit of energy. 1989 is the 200th Anniversary of the French Revolution. On July 14th, 1789, the Bastille was attacked and sacked. Though I've said we must not hug history like a protective blanket, the 18th Century does have relevance to the present. I am not recalling the bestial delirium of The Terror or Robespierre's dictatorship. Recall, rather, the destruction of feudalism, the Declaration of the Rights of Man, the sudden surge that spilled out into the boulevards in defiance of suppression. The 18th Century attends us in movies and books because it was when a corrupt regime gasped, liberalism took root, and citizens wrenched themselves out of alienation and into engagement. The ideals of social justice, the protection of the weak, the belief in individual possibility and community, the faith in education, all made up the colour of enlightenment. Recall what that energy was when we try to go beyond TV ads that only talk of change. A witness at the Place de Bastille saw history fly open, in a spectacle of risk, an instant before the vision fell back into darkness. It was a witness who spoke out of a hope for human ability and for all people who abhor jails, snares and boxes. In his Journal, this witness wrote:

The air ignites. We started with words and ideas, whirling debates in salons and cellars. Now it is they who pull down the currents and catch up the fire. The element of air is upon us; the season of the charge is here. Franklin made the sky break and bend to his kites and keys in America, and these bodies have picked up that key, which is their prayer to the current, their call to contact. They will bring down the walls; bring down the old power; shatter the compacts made without their choice; bring down the prisons of mind as well as of flesh; and ignite the air.

170

Communications and Culture: The Bonds That Unite Us

Jerry Grafstein

Jerry Grafstein is one of Canada's leading broadcasting lawyers and one of the founding members of Multilingual TV, City TV and CKORadio. He was appointed to the Senate in 1984.

Albert Camus, the great French author, once wrote that "great ideas", great thoughts, arise on the public scene in disguised form. They caress the public agenda as quietly and "softly as the wings of a dove in flight." There is nothing quiet about this Conference. The ideas and the debates here are loud and contagious.

My topic is Communications and Culture. Let me start with a truism. You cannot have a culture without the ability to communicate that culture. Communications without substance or content (culture) attracts no net worth. So we have in Canada, at this very dynamic point in our time, an unusual convergence between Culture and Communications - a natural phenomenon that unites us. Canada, we tend to forget, is quite a distinct society in many, many ways. We are very self-effacing and modest about what we've constructed in this country. Constructing bonds of unity lies at the heart of our national idea.

All of us know the historic analogy. We all recall our text book history as the country linked together, east and west, by the railroad. And today in Canada we find ourselves even more closely linked together in a way that's different and distinctive in the world. We are more cabled than any other country in the world. The subscriber cost of our cable is probably the lowest in the world; we have more people,

171

Photos: John Rowlands

Above: Louis sells thirty different newspapers from all over the world and serves two thousand customers a week.

Below: Mary Shih and her family operate a drug and herbal medicine store on Gerrard. They always have a prescription for you no matter what your ailment and Mary's predictions for the future have a good track record.

in relative terms, connected to this giant cable grid in all parts of this country. Cable's reach is more pervasive than in any other single nation in the world.

We have welded telecommunications links and telephone links that are more extensive than any in the world. Do you know that we speak on the telephone, daily, more per capita than any other country? We love to communicate. And we are tied-in, from Charlottetown to Victoria, from the North to the South, by these voice, broadcast and data links. We spend - and have spent - more than any other country in the world per individual, per citizen, to organize and to bond ourselves together so we can easily communicate with each other. We have more published poets per capita than anywhere in the world. Why? We've done this almost unconsciously as part of our natural Canadian value system. We have collapsed our geographic separation by communications. Nobody much broods or notices the fact but what we love to do in our daily life is communicate with each other.

Let's talk about hyper communications in Toronto for a moment. Those of you from the rest of the country will forgive me because I'm proud to live here and proud to describe this exploding communications phenomenon. We have more information available to us on a daily basis in Toronto than almost any other place in the world. We've got more radio; we've got more TV; we've got more news - we've got four lively daily newspapers, even though I don't always agree with their editorials. We've got more magazines. We have more daily packaged information at our fingertips. We have weekly newspapers and periodicals, TV and radio in over 24 languages.

Now, that's not to say that we all watch all the displays of this information, or listen to them or read them, but they are here, available and in abundance. It's a quite fantastic measure of the sheer amount of culture in all its multiple forms that we are exposed to on an hourly basis. Almost like the pulse of our nation, the communication mills across Canada never rest.

When we turn to live theatre, we have that too in Toronto in abundance. On a per capita basis, we see and have available to us more live theatre than anywhere else in the western world save New York or London. We have daily print, radio and TV in all the major languages of the world. Our streets teem with lifestyles and languages from every corner of the globe.

What does this tell us about communications and culture - in our official and other languages? And what does this tell us about Canada? We are very serious, as Canadians, about communications and culture. All the major battles that fester today are less about economics than about language - communications. Our civil wars are wars of words - wars about language. Canadians love to fight about communication. It is an intrinsic part of the Canadian lifestyle.

How can we modernize for the next decade? How can we move together toward the next century?' Let me turn to 1967, when, by osmosis, we created a new cultural structure in this country that was quite unusual. In 1967, we celebrated our Centennial and Expo '67. From Charlottetown to Victoria we built public theatres, public auditoriums. Now in Canada, 20 years later, we have in virtually every region of the country, first-class live theatre facilities. Yet we haven'ot utilized those, as Canadians, as best we could.

So, where do we go from here? What's crowding us? We've got the Canada-U.S. Free Trade Agreement. I think we'll overcome its difficulties because I think we're stronger and better than some of us give ourselves credit for.

In 1992, an even greater global event will occur. The European market is about to come together as one market - much bigger and stronger than the North American marketplace. Gorbachev - the interesting and fascinating Mikhail Gorbachev - has put forward an even greater idea for Europe. He argues that by the year 2000, what should be envisaged is a united Europe from the Urals to the Atlantic; in other words, that the East and West should join together in Europe and unite in one common marketplace.

This is not idle political talk. At the last EC meeting in Brussels and at the last round of GATT in Montreal, for the first time we had on the global trade stage China, Russia, Estonia, Czechoslovakia - all lusting to be part of the global trading network, the GATT. How can we deal with these traumatic events? Deal we must or be shunted aside by these global changes. New communication giants are being fashioned to meet this new international environment

Well, I've got three simple ideas. In Canada, we must start to reorganize our communications and cultural organisations.

The first involves live theatre. I know the lively arts may seem an insignificant place to start but we must bring the country together as a vibrant unified nation to energize our ability to survive and thrive in this new age. We must first learn to communicate more about ourselves as a people. We must give our writers and composers a chance to dream with us about this Canada

I'd like to see our live theatre built into an active network where we present Canadian musicals, Canadian drama, with Canadian artists, singing Canadian songs. I want to see touring across this country, not a musical called *Oklahoma* but a musical called *Alberta*. I don't want to see *42nd Street* at the O'Keefe Centre; I want to see a musical about *Kensington Avenue*. Now that's something that we can do by building regional workshops and creating a grand, nationwide live theatre network made in Canada by Canadians. Canadians have something to sing about!

Secondly, I'd like to see us break up and restructure Bell Canada and build three competing fiber-optic networks across the country so there would be infinite channels and infinite capacity with lower costs and increased accessibility to all Canadians. We can interact with each other without surrogates - and our children will show us the way.

Third, and most important, I want to bring Ottawa closer to the people. Why can't we put Parliament on a train? Why can't we insist, as a constitutional resolution, that Parliament cannot be Parliament unless it holds sessions in every region of the nation once a year. Why can't we put Parliament on a train so that it spends at least a week of the year in Alberta, a week of the year in Prince Edward Island, a week of the year in Newfoundland? We can do this by train, and by our communications links and satellites. We can neutralize our geography and banish the alienation that segregates us as a nation.

I think if we do some of these things, things we can do easily, we will demonstrate to ourselves and the world that the Canada-U.S. Trade Agreement, the ECC, isn't going to damage or arrest us, because in Canada our vibrancy, our value structures, our freedom, our ability to communicate will be greater and better than ever before. Canadians love challenges in life. We are quietly dauntless - that is our national character.

Canada is a distinct unified society, with lessons for all. That's the challenge we should demand of ourselves because it's a challenge every Canadian can meet and would love to meet. Canadians are optimists! The best is yet to come!

Photo; JM Carisse

Dennis Mills introducing Québec artist Richard Séguin at Barrymore's in Ottawa.

Questions and Comments from the Audience

Question:
I'm a little nervous here but I think I've decided to be active and participate a little, for a change. It sounds like the future's going to be full of changes. And from what I've been told by various people in my lifetime, the Conservative Party of Canada is dead set against changes of any kind, traditionally. However, I've heard it said many times that the Liberal Party is for the common man. It sounds to me that with the Liberal Party in the lead, that we'll have a greater chance for the future, because it sounds like they're a little more flexible, with their traditional leaning towards the common man. I'd like to say that I've had some problems with employment, and so this subject is of great interest to me. I just wanted to tell you that a friend of mine told me the other day that I should really consider being, and working, with people who I communicate with. I liked that idea, because the idea of communication, to me, gets rid of a lot of other things - for instance, prejudice which I've seen in the news recently - and it doesn't make me feel quite so guilty about things. I like the idea of being able to work with people who I communicate with. I think that overrides a lot of other invisible enemies who can create problems.

Dennis Mills:
I think that the point you've made is precisely where we have to go. In other words, we must create an environment where everybody can get involved this time because, if you're not involved, the environment and the community is not going to work.

Karen Fraser:
I think, also, one of the great joys of the new era will be that when people realize that we need creativity, they'll have to accept it from anyone who has it; they will find that prejudice is a luxury we can't afford any more. It doesn't matter the racial background, the sexual background, the interests of the person involved; you're after their ideas, their energy and their enthusiasm. That should be the only

177

qualification for the job. The companies who feel they're a gentleman's club and want to stay that way are going to be the companies that we'll see disappearing; and that's fine with me. I think Canada has a chance to be the leader in the information industry and the environmental industry in the next two decades; and we have no time for gentleman's clubs in my view.

Question:
I brought with me today, because I thought it was timely, a piece out of The Toronto Star. It's an article about a worker who feels that he may he laid-off by Molsons and a couple of quotes from the article relate to what Tom Hockin essentially said earlier this week about looking in the paper for another job:

Beer worker John Gill has some news for federal Cabinet Minister Tom Hockin 'Watering plants doesn't pay anywhere near $40,000.00 a year.' So Gill, a 17-year veteran of Molsons Toronto plant, combed the Classified Ads yesterday for work that matched his skills. And he earned $18.05 an hour, or $40,000.00 annually. 'If I were a qualified stock broker,' he says, 'I could work for twelve fifty an hour.' And he scoffed at that: 'That would only be a $5.00-cut in pay.'

I think this is an excellent example of what you talked about earlier, Karen, when you said that we're going to have to be educating ourselves all our lives. It's no longer possible for people who have, over the last 20 to 30 years, existed in industries that were protected by legislation, tariffs, import quotas, unions or whatever, to continue to exist under this global economy. And, if there's a message I could leave with Dennis, essentially it is to convince the people at the federal level - even though you are in opposition - that continued training and re-training throughout a lifetime is a positive and a rewarding way of spending time; and that, not only should people be assisted with training when they're young, but throughout their lives. Special programs and various other means and alternative methods of training - right up to the age 65, or perhaps 75, which we might end up working to - should be considered by federal and even provincial governments.

Karen Fraser:
All your points are very well made. I think the key is: If you see your industry in trouble, don't bury your head in the sand. In the industries that I've worked with where there were going to be massive lay-

offs, the people who saw it coming didn't like it but prepared for it and did very well; the ones who waited till the last second and then said, "we had no idea it was coming" were the ones who had the trouble. I saw that with the teachers in North York and I taught with the staff at many of the psychiatrist hospitals in Ontario that were closed. The ones that left early, well prepared, made it; the others didn't. So, you might not like some of the future, but always be ready for it and take it a little bit at a time. Read about things you don't understand. Don't let the whole thing come up and hit you in the forehead; it'll overwhelm you. And some people, I'm afraid, just aren't going to make it. They're not even going to be in or out; they're just going to fall in between - but that's not going to be anybody here, not in this Riding, right.

Question:
It's all very well to have a concept of the future when you suggest the follies of the past - say in the '50s, if we can look back that way. In what you said, Karen, the past seemed to hold a bit more virtue, a bit more of a hard-working attitude than maybe the future will in some people's view. But I wonder, in the face of things like Free Trade and a global economic community, if the phrase "work harder" isn't something of a cop-out? When you say "there is a lot at stake", and "we have to work harder; we don't have to look back" and what you've just said now "people may not be in or out; they may just fall flat on their face." Why does the economic system have to work that way? Why don't we have assurances? Why don't we have Employment Adjustment Programs in the face of Free Trade? We've been talking about attitudes towards work, and we've been exhorting the worker who is faced with losing his job under this Free-Trade Agreement, who is faced with a lot of pressures, to worker harder. Simply working harder in a system that doesn't protect the worker, that doesn't provide him with things, won't work. You can't just work harder; there has to be some sort of basis or structure to work from.

Dennis Mills:
I think that that's a great point. And I think that governance is about creating a blueprint to provide that kind of hope for people, and this government hasn't done that. So, let's develop some ideas here, and put them to the government to react to.

Karen Fraser:
I think there's been a tendency to hope that it'll be someone else's

problem, because the changing of an era is a massive problem for anyone to try to handle. The Japanese do it differently (and I am not saying we should have Japanese management because there are many aspects that simply wouldn't fit in our culture) but they do believe in being responsible, and that's a word that we've heard many times today.

I think there has been a lot of profit and too little responsibility. I don't think we just have a financial deficit from the '50s and '60s, I think we have a moral deficit too. The time has come to react and I really think we'll do it. That is one nice thing about the rules breaking down; you do get to start again. I think we'll do it well; Canadians always have. We're quiet and modest, but we're really effective once we get going.

We need the blueprint. It's going to be difficult. And many of the pieces, we haven't a clue what they are yet; so there will be some fumbling. But I believe we're trying here to say that we need the blueprint and to put the pieces together, but it's going to take a while. We need a new expression for the responsibilities now, a new vision.

Question:
I'm very encouraged by what I'm hearing. I'm encouraged by your themes, Karen, of adapting to change and Dennis, I think your concept of a basic national emphasis on environment is absolutely what we need - not an emphasis on militarism. I want simply to point out, for your comment, a recent article in *Saturday Night* about Sweden. If there's one nation that has adapted itself so well to the dual needs of social structure and employment, it's Sweden. If you see that article, you'll read that what they have been most adept at is managing change. They do not keep old industries alive; they let them close, but they re-train the workers so that they can go into other industrial sectors. Unfortunately, in Canada we haven't seen the political Sisco Steel in Cape Breton die, and come up with more productive ways of employing those people. I wonder if we'll ever see that political will. Are you feeling very optimistic about that? Is it happening? I'm hearing about it more and more and, again, I'm encouraged.

Dennis Mills:
I think part of our responsibility is to develop ideas which will put the gun to the head of government. What we need now are ideas, and

that's the purpose of today: to begin that process of creating ideas where the government will have no choice but to react.

Question:
I'm getting tired of hearing about Japan or Sweden all the time. Those people have the same language, same heritage; they are small countries and Sweden is a very large arms manufacturer, the third largest in the world. Everybody serves in the armed forces; therefore they have a low unemployment. In Japan, not everyone serves in the armed forces, but they were given a great deal of help by the Western Alliance after World War II to get back on their feet; and they haven't been giving much back to us - except in the way of technology. I'd like to know where you see unions playing a role in the future?

Karen Fraser:
The unions are part of a confrontation system that resulted from the abuses of the early Industrial Revolution; they certainly have a role to play in the future. I think some of the unions will be wise, and adapt their methods and their ideas to what we need for the '90s; from some I still hear the 1962 rhetoric and I think they're going to lose ground. That would be a shame because, with friends, you argue both sides.

I've worked with companies where there are unions and there are problems; I've worked with companies where there are no unions, and there are problems. I think we need new management and new union styles for the '90s, and I think we're beginning to get it. They're beginning to change their way of doing things - with some notable exceptions.

Dennis Mills:
I share that view. In other words, if unions don't start investigating systems of equity participation and profit sharing as part of their basic formula, then as far as I'm concerned, they're heading in the wrong direction and they won't survive.

Question:
Karen, ten years ago I took your course *Women Like Me* and, inspired by that course, I started my own business. It slowly grew and became quite successful, so we were able to move from our 800 square feet into 3,000 square feet where we've been for the past three years. I'm presently moving from 3,000 square feet into 1,700 square feet

because I cannot find staff. Listening to you reading your speech earlier on, it sounds as though we have a job shortage rather than a labour shortage. We have a chronic labour shortage in Toronto; in fact, we have 120,000 jobs going begging. Meanwhile, we've got 60,000 people collecting UIC. And how many more collecting Welfare? Meanwhile my business is dying; I'm very upset about it. I cannot get any help from anybody.

Karen Fraser:
All small business is having this difficulty. If I was here another day, I could do my other subject called "The Terror of the Mediocre". A lot of the people that we have - and it's not just young people - are people who are not '50s people, but they've rejected the work ethic of the time. They're not '90s people; they're not confident or skilled. What they are is demanding, arrogant transition people who are driving small business crazy. Their idea of a give-and-get balance is get, get, get and give nothing. Also, they're rather a peculiar bunch. They seem to have absolutely no understanding of how work functions. For example, I hear stories all the time of people in offices going out for lunch and simply not coming back, and they've got the bank deposit book with them. And when they finally return several days later, and the boss tries to be upset, they'll say, "Well, dock my pay; I was busy, okay?" It's not laziness; they're not that malicious. It's just a different value system; and I think they're going to be the people who fall through the cracks. And that doesn't help you one bit.

Many big companies do not have to put up with it - particularly if they're glamorous - because they get the cream of the crop; they're getting the *ins*. Small business needs your average good worker and we can't get them. What most of us have done - and I've done the same thing - we've down-sized our businesses and we've purchased technology so that we don't have to hire staff. So it isn't machinery that causes unemployment for some people; it's people who cause it. And it's sad, because small business in Canada employs more new employees per year than the corporations do, and we're the ones who can't get people, can't train them. And we're deciding that all the fun is going out of our business because of our staff, and we're firing them all. And it's a terrible problem.

Our partial solution - and I don't know if it would help with your business; we could talk after - is hiring other entrepreneurs, even if they have no idea how to run my business. If they have a sense of creativity, enthusiasm and responsibility - if I can get that kind of person, I can teach them anything. An MBA with a bad attitude is completely useless to me and anyone else. My sympathies are with you.

Question:
Canada Council has a lot to do with the vibrancy of the arts in Canada, but it probably won't last very much longer. Fifty per cent of its budget goes to support seven institutions in this country - seven institutions which bring us dead playwrights' plays to Stratford, German ballets to Winnipeg, Italian opera to Toronto. And the problem is, that's a lot of money that isn't going to artists. But what do artists have to have? You know, besides a paint brush, they need a source of income to let them paint. Painting costs a lot of money, particularly in a city like Toronto where young artists cannot even afford a studio.

When will the government - or when will people, advocates such as yourselves - push for things like tax breaks for individual artists? So that Canada Council's budget will not have to increase but that artists will have an opportunity to make a living by selling their art or at least getting their own acts off the ground - so that people don't have to do anything for them; they can do it for themselves.

Jerry Grafstein:
I have a controversial idea. I'm not against bigness when better things happen from that bigness. At the CRTC, if you're a large communications company and you want to get more, the Commission won't throw you out; they'll say to you, "You must, in fact, demonstrate that you're going to make a significant contribution above and beyond the cost of the particular purchase or sale that you're entering into." That's almost a tax, if you will, to get bigger. Now, I don't know why we should not say to the government, "If you want to make these major mega-firms bigger, why don't we have a take-over tax - a Canadian culture tax? So that, if companies like Molsons and O'Keefe get together, one of the benefits will be an increase in Canadian culture by putting a transfer tax on those mega-transfers that will immediately go into increasing the funding for Canadian artists, and for Canadian culture. That, to my mind, would be taking business and making a demand on business and spreading the benefits on the Canadian side. Now I think we can do that, and there's no reason why we shouldn't. Both those companies could afford it.

Photo courtesy of Doug Dales, Cinevillage

Above: The motion picture industry is an important part of our local economy. Nick Mirkopoulous and his family are an example of Canadian entrepreneurship at its best. They have recently converted an old warehouse complex into a thriving new movie studio. This complex, Cinecity and its neighbour, Cinevillage house the largest movie studio complex in Canada and employ 3,000 people including craftsmen such as lens grinders as well as actors, writers and producers.

Right: Richard Séguin, a Québec rock star, is as talented as any of his counterparts in North America. This Canadian star is not heard on English radio stations outside Québec yet French stations in Québec will play Corey Hart. This is typical of the frustrations Québec artists must face in Canada. There truly is a need for English stations to start showcasing Québec talent. This is not to say that government should dictate consumers' tastes in music, but there should be more initiative shown which taps into this other musical dimension and allows listeners to be the judge.

CARISSE PHOTO

B.W. Powe:
The Canada Council itself is not really the answer; it's done wonderful work and most writers in the country have benefited from it in one way or another. But I would also say that the future would have to lie in more incentives to business, as you are suggesting. Allow artists to have a different kind of tax form - they had that at one time - something that would allow some of the breaks, as you were suggesting. Beyond that I would say, too, that perhaps something like a complete tax write-off for individuals holding artistic, creative, intellectual talk circles in their own homes would be an interesting way to get people out of the institutions as well, and talking to people directly.

Question:
There are two things I'd like to say while we're on the subject of artists. I'd like to see something for the people who do ballroom-type dancing; there's nothing. You know, there's people who have the talent, but everything is just against them, you know, unless they get a break. But talking about '67 at Expo, I'd like to say one thing and that is about the Cinesphere or whatever they called it that Bell put on. I have travelled a lot of places and I saw a lot of them, even in the States, that couldn't touch the one in Canada. When I saw it I just felt so proud of being a Canadian; it was just beautiful, and I've never seen anything like it anywhere.

Question:
It seems to me that Canada's greatest challenge for the 21st Century is to finally put an end to talking about multiculturalism, to giving small cultural sops to various non-mainstream ethnic groups in the country, and to finally make a commitment to having a single cultural entity that takes multiculturalism seriously. We have to put an end, once and for all, to having Canada Council for English - and French-speaking people, and the Secretary of State for Multiculturalism or even this new Ministry of Multiculturalism for Canadians of non-French and non-English origin. I think it's cultural apartheid with a smile, and it has to be put to death once and for all.

Jerry Grafstein:
Are you saying that because the balance in the cultural institutions tends to be divided between Anglophone and Francophone granting, that somehow the third force is being left out? Or what?

Question:
I don't believe in having special treatment for anyone. I think if we have cultural institutions, they should be for all, regardless. And you shouldn't have a special organization to deal with ethnic cultural needs or native cultural needs.

Senator Grafstein:
Well, you won't have any quarrel with me. What you're saying is that the greater the freedom of expression and the greater the removal of institutional barriers to help freedom of expression, the greater the freedom and the greater the democracy we have. If that's your point, I agree with you.

Denise Chong:
I think you do raise a valid point. When the Multiculturalism Act was passed just before the last election was called, it got snowed-under in a flurry of other news. And you're quite right, that debate about its merits didn't get a chance to be aired.

Question:
I wanted to direct a question to Mr. Powe. I just want to invite you to talk some more about what you would have us do specifically towards peace and justice. If we're the children of light, what in fact, would you have us do specifically?

B.W. Powe:
Well, I think that that's really the purpose of this Conference, to allow ourselves to ask questions. At this point, I'm not entirely sure we even know how to put the questions and that was part of the thrust of what I was trying to say; that there's something perhaps even wrong with the language itself. If I were to offer policy initiatives, then that would be giving you a dishonest answer - which is that I have a lot of answers at this point. What I would prefer to say, and to suggest to this group, is that perhaps we need more groups like this more often in Toronto; more seminars or discussions in which we do begin to ask the questions seriously, even of ourselves. Why certain things seem to erupt at different times? Why these various policies are not being addressed directly? Why this particular federal government seems so obsessed with trade, economic deals, and seems to be ignoring so many other kinds of things? I wish I could give you easier answers to those questions, but perhaps the real answer is to let us at least begin to ask the right questions. And

then we can begin to ask what the initiatives could be after that.

Question:

I believe it was Mr. Grafstein who mentioned about having Canadian musicals. I would like a reaction, or a comment from the panel in general, but maybe the Senator in particular, about doing a bit more to promote some very talented Canadian opera singers. I think it's marvellous to have visiting opera stars with the Canadian Opera, and I'm sure we enjoy their performances very much but there are some extremely talented Canadians who could be starred - such as Theresa Strogosis, for example. And ironically enough, she became a star by going to the Met, you know, several years ago; she just packs them in there. Canadian-born. Of course, years ago we had Edward Johnson; we had Dame M.L. Bani. I think there are quite a few who are certainly in that category, or potentially in that category, who could be promoted through the Canadian Opera Company.

Jerry Grafstein:

I think you make a very valid point. What happens in Canada is that we tend to say to ourselves that unless you've made it some place else, you really couldn't make it in Canada. So Theresa and Victor Braun, and others that you mentioned, had to make their mark elsewhere for them to be recognized in Canada. But I think that's changing. I really believe that if you take a look at the Canadian Opera Company, the number of people that are taking primary roles and primary supporting roles is certainly changing quite dramatically. Not changing fast enough - I agree with you - but it is changing. Did you know that the Canadian government, in effect, funded the first computer in North America and, because they couldn't get additional funding, they went down to the United States and got it down there. That funding led to the creation of IBM; but it was here in Canada, at the Census Bureau, that the first idea of building a massive computer got started. We started it, but it had to go somewhere else to get exploited. That's almost the Canadian way! But I think it's changing; I really believe it's changing.

Section Seven:
The Meech Lake Accord

Photo: Jerry Hobbs

The Decentralization of Canada

Timothy Danson

Timothy Danson is a constitutional and corporate/commercial litigation lawyer. He is a member of the Executive Board of The Canadian Coalition on the Constitution, which is a broadly-based group of Canadians and organizations from all provinces who are concerned with the direct effects of the Meech Lake Constitutional Accord.

On May 2nd, 1988, the Canadian Coalition on the Constitution launched a lawsuit against the Prime Minister and the Government of Canada. Morris Manning, Edward Greenspan and myself are representing the Coalition in this lawsuit. In essence, the Coalition says that the Meech Lake Accord undermines the integrity of Canada as a federal state. In time, we submit, Canada will evolve from a federal state into a confederacy. That is, we will have ten strong provinces which are held in a loose federation called Canada. [A copy of the Coalition's Statement of Claim is included in the Appendix]

If you believe in a decentralised Canada, Meech Lake may be attractive to you. If you believe in a balkanized Canada, a Canada which in essence is nothing more than a community of communities, without a national spirit or a national will, Meech Lake is likely a move in the right direction.

However, if you share the feelings of the Coalition; if you believe in a strong national government with strong provinces, where we look to our differences as a source of opportunity rather than an excuse for division, then Meech Lake is a document which you should find disturbing. Meech Lake plays to our weaknesses rather than to our strengths.

189

On September 27th, 1988, the Trial Division of the Federal Court of Canada agreed with the federal government that our action was both premature and speculative because Meech Lake had not been ratified and therefore was not law. Yet the Prime Minister of Canada repeatedly states that Meech Lake is a done deal, and indeed makes Senate appointments in accordance with Meech Lake as if it were ratified, and further 8 out of 10 provinces have ratified the Accord. With all due respect, the issue is not whether we are premature but rather whether we are too late.

The case is now before the Federal Court of Appeal and hopefully will be heard sometime in June, 1989. We hope we will be successful. We want the opportunity to go to trial and cross-examine those people who are responsible for the Meech Lake Constitutional Accord. A cross-examination will undoubtedly reveal that those who signed the Accord are not of one mind; they all have a different understanding and interpretation. In order for a constitutional agreement to be affirmed there has to be consensus *ad idem*; that is, all parties to the agreement have to agree to the essential elements of the Accord. For this reason, the government must keep us out of court because they fear that our cross-examination will expose the truth.

Perhaps the first question we should be asking about Meech Lake is "What is it?". The answer is simple: it is a constitutional document which defines and shapes Canada as a nation. It sets the parameters within which we, as Canadians, see ourselves and how we interact with one another. When we speak to the issue of Meech Lake, we are speaking of a vision for Canada; it deals with the soul of our nation. So, who are these people who dare allow Meech Lake to be ratified, notwithstanding their own acknowledgement that it contains many fundamental flaws? And flaws that are unnecessary when the solutions are so simple. Equally alarming is the fact that according to public opinion polls a large majority of Canadians do not realise the implications of the Accord. Of those people who do understand it, a large majority are opposed. When polls consistently show that a majority of Canadians do not understand the Accord, one would think it time to stop and take a further look before we irrevocably change the face of Canada.

The issues that most people are preoccupied with are the "Distinct Society" clause and the federal government's spending power. I will leave these critical issues to the other speakers. I would like to address some other problems that I feel many people have over-looked.

One serious problem relates to the Supreme Court of Canada. There are two preliminary points which should be understood. Firstly, under Meech Lake, the process under which judges are appointed to the Supreme Court of Canada has been changed in that the federal government has given up its exclusive right to appoint judges to that Court. Now the federal government can only make appointments from a list of candidates submitted by the provinces. Secondly, under the Accord, three judges from the province of Québec must, as a matter of constitutional law, sit on the Supreme Court of Canada, and therefore these judges come from lists submitted by the government of Québec.

I would ask you to consider the following scenario. Between 1976 and 1985, the federal government appointed two judges to the Supreme Court of Canada from the province of Québec. Between 1976 and 1985, René Levesque and the Parti Québecois were in power. What would have happened had Meech Lake been the law of the land during this time and the appointments could only be made from a list provided by the Parti Québecois? What would a provincial government committed to the dismemberment of Canada have done?

I believe René Levesque would have done one of two things. Firstly he could have done nothing. After all, the Parti Québecois does not believe in Canada and therefore the worse the federal state looks, the better for them. Had M. Levesque followed this course of action and put no names forward, we would not have been able to fulfil the constitutional requirement of having three judges from the province of Québec sitting on the Supreme Court of Canada. Alternatively, M. Levesque could have put forward a list of known separatists which would not have been acceptable to the federal government. In either case, we would have had a stalemate and the question would then have arisen of how to solve it.

Well, I am sorry to tell you that there is absolutely no mechanism within the Meech Lake Accord for resolving this problem. Under our scenario, there would not have been three judges from Québec on the Supreme Court of Canada and, as a result, the Court itself would have become unconstitutional. So, we have within the Meech Lake Accord all the ingredients to call into question the very constitutional existence of the country's highest court.

At all the constitutional hearings, leading constitutional experts told the politicians that this is a very serious problem and one that must be resolved before ratification of the Accord. At a minimum there must be a mechanism to resolve any stalemate. Yet those who support Meech Lake and want it ratified immediately argue that they will deal with this problem another time. The problem, however, is that changes to the Supreme Court of Canada require unanimity and, once Meech Lake becomes law, changes will effectively be impossible. The province creating the crisis is not about to resolve it by agreeing to the unanimity provisions of the Accord.

A further problem with the Accord is the way it deals with the issue of Senate reform. Most Canadians do not appreciate that under our present constitution and under Meech Lake, the Senate has the identical constitutional powers as the elected House of Commons. The only difference between the Senate and the House of Commons, as a matter of constitutional law, is that money bills must originate in the Commons. Moreover, the Senate does not have a veto over constitutional amendments. In all other regards, the two Houses of Parliament have identical constitutional power.

Just prior to the last federal election, the media and the politicians made a big fuss over John Turner's decision to use the Senate to obstruct the Free Trade Agreement until after the matter was decided by the people of Canada in that election. At that time, Brian Mulroney, Ed Broadbent and others said that that was undemocratic; it was constitutional but undemocratic. Well, I think it offensive to have a constitution that is undemocratic or has substantive provisions that are undemocratic. If people were concerned that an appointed body like the Senate had the constitutional power to veto matters over which the federal government has exclusive jurisdiction, I can tell you that under Meech Lake that would become permanent. At least under the present constitution we can achieve constitutional amendments with the support of 7 provinces representing 50% of the population. Under Meech Lake, Senate reform would require unanimity. Under Meech Lake, the Senators would be appointed from lists submitted by the provinces.

Over time, as Senators retire and new Senators are appointed from lists provided by the provinces, the Senate will evolve into a "House of the Provinces" with its orientation and loyalties to provincial interests. This new provincial Senate will have absolute veto power over matters of exclusive federal jurisdiction. This is a serious affront to the democratic process and Canadians should be shocked to know that the Meech Lake Accord entrenches this into our constitution. How would we resolve a constitutional crisis where the *appointed* Senate was obstructing the *elected* House of Commons? Under our present constitution there is a flexible and workable amending formula, but under Meech Lake amendments require unanimity.

Canada exists as a federal state by operation of a division of powers between the federal and provincial governments. Under section 91 of our constitution there is a list of powers over which the federal government has exclusive jurisdiction. It is important to appreciate that the Senate is a *federal* institution. Under Meech Lake, not only has the federal government transferred significant powers to the provinces but Parliament will no longer be composed of two federal institutions but only of one - the elected House of Commons. The Senate will, over time, evolve into a *provincial* body, yet retain its veto power over matters of exclusive federal jusrisdiction. Accordingly, the elected House of Commons will no longer have absolute jurisdiction over matters for which Canadians elected its members.

At a minimum, by way of a compromise or stop gap measure, we can do one of two things. Either we restrict the power of the Senate so that it does not have absolute veto power over matters of exclusive federal jurisdiction, or we curtail its power to that of a review body able to hold up legislation for up to six months. This would at least provide a mechanism whereby, in the end, the democratically elected politicians would have the final say. Under Meech Lake, the provinces will retain their powers over matters of exclusive provincial jurisdiction yet gain the advantage of a provincially oriented Senate with veto power over the House of Commons. Provincial power is further augmented by a potentially provincially oriented Supreme Court of Canada, which will be called upon to determine legal disputes between the provinces and the federal government. It will no longer be the same type of national insitution.

These are the two areas that, I believe, are not getting sufficient exposure, yet they are very, very serious. When they are combined with the other provisions of the Accord such as the Distinct Society clause, with the impact on Charter rights and the federal govern-

193

ment's spending power, we see a new vision of Canada which most Canadians would not find acceptable. These two areas threaten the core of our constitutional existence as a federal state. What Meech Lake does is fundamentally transfer powers from the federal government to the provinces; powers which are indispensable to the federal government's ability to govern as a national government. This will have the effect of decentralizing Canada; it will balkanize Canada; and in time we will simply be a community of communities; we will be a confederacy. It will be an admission as Canadians that we are incapable of achieving the grandeur which lies within our grasp; incapable of transcending geographical boundaries and cultural diversities.

I hope that many of you share the concerns of the Coalition and will do everything that is necessary to stop the Meech Lake Accord.

A Dual Society

George Radwanski

George Radwanski holds degrees in law, political science and philosophy from McGill University. In his extensive career as a journalist he has worked for Time Canada, *the* Montreal Gazette, *the* Financial Times *and the* Toronto Star. *He is a best selling author and has been a special advisor to the Peterson government in Ontario.*

I wish we had more time to talk about Meech Lake because it's fair to say that all the other items on the Agenda that refer to our future become irrelevant if we don't have a country to do them for and with. The great risk of Meech Lake, without exaggeration, is that Canada as we know it could cease to exist.

Why do I say that? Well, essentially, the Accord changes in a fundamental and irrevocable way the whole nature of our nation. It would change us from a nation based on pan-Canadianism - ten essentially equal, if different, provinces bound under a national government that represents the greater good of the whole - into a kind of a dualism: a French Canada on one side, Québec; the rest of Canada, English, on the other; and nothing more than a weak kind of secretariat at the centre trying somehow to hold it all together.

It would turn us from a nation where it means essentially the same thing to be a Canadian from coast to coast, in terms of basic rights and assumptions about the nature of Canada, into one where what it means to be a Canadian would vary fundamentally, depending on where we live. It is, ultimately, a prescription for our national disintegration.

195

The distinct-society provision is one of the worst elements of the Accord, although every single part of the Accord is, to me, profoundly and almost unfixably flawed. What does the distinct-society clause mean? If you listen to the Premiers of Ontario or the other primarily English-speaking provinces, it means very little; it's just a recognition that Québec, after all, is different. If you listen to Premier Bourassa, however, it means something very different.

According to the Premier of Québec, on June 18, 1987:

The entire Constitution, including the Charter of Rights and Freedoms, will be interpreted and applied in the light of the section on the distinct society. The exercise of legislative authority is included and we will thus be able to consolidate existing positions and make new gains.

In other words, the distinct society, in the view of Québec, gives that province dramatic new powers. And, in fact, if distinct society (in the Constitution and as an article of interpretation) means anything, that is what it has to mean.

Every part of Canada, every province, is in some way distinct. A citizen of Newfoundland going to Alberta, say, would find himself or herself in a very distinct society; an Ontarian moving to British Columbia would tell you that he or she is now in a place quite distinct. That is why we have Sections 91 and 92 of our existing Constitution (the division of powers) that give the provinces jurisdiction over areas like education, aspects of social policy, internal trade and commerce, and so on; all those things that can be relevant to making and preserving the distinctness within the province. It is also why we have a great many other powers that are given to the national government in the name of preserving a whole that is greater than its parts; saying essentially that every part of Canada is distinct, but we are bound by common will and common purpose; and therefore, there are things that we must do together.

Now, if our new Constitution under Meech Lake is to say that only Québec is a distinct society, what does that mean? That Québec is more distinct that any other part of Canada and the Constitution is to be interpreted that way? That means, surely, that Québec is to wield powers that other provinces don't have. What powers? Could they open their own embassies? Perhaps. Could they pass their own criminal laws under this Accord? Perhaps. Could a Québec government use the distinct-society provision to try to restrict the passage of Canadians from other provinces across its borders, or restrict the right of Canadians from other provinces to settle in Québec? I don't know; perhaps.

Now, it's easy enough to say that won't happen; that that's not the purpose of this kind of constitutional amendment. But who will decide? Funny you should ask that because it will be the Supreme Court of Canada who will decide. Here we come to another provision of the Accord, which is that the provinces will effectively control the selection of the Supreme Court.

Now, why are the provinces being given that power? Why is it that this kind of benefit, from the provincial point of view, is being conferred? Do the provincial governments and provincial premiers really feel concerned that, unless *they* make the choice, judges of the Supreme Court won't make the right kind of decisions in criminal law?

The one instance where Supreme Court appointments would be of benefit to provincial governments is if they want to ensure that the judges named to the court from now on have a de-centralizing view of Canada; that where there is a dispute between the central government and the provincial governments or one provincial government, it is the provincial view that will have a more sympathetic hearing; a preferred access.

On top of that, when you consider that Québec alone is guaranteed three of the nine Justices on The Supreme Court, it's not hard to extrapolate what would happen with that kind of an arrangement once we had a fully province-selected Supreme Court. We would end up with a Court on which three Justices were from Québec and surely chosen for their de-centralist views; it would take only two more of the remaining Justices of the Court to concur with that view and "distinct society" would mean a great deal indeed; it would mean, essentially, anything a Québec government chose it to mean.

Then, of course, we have the provisions regarding the Senate, which would effectively put the federal government, our national government, under provincial trusteeship because there would not be a decision that our national government could make on behalf of the national interest if the provinces objected.

Say goodbye to the principle of parliamentary government in terms of a cabinet responsible to the elected House of Commons. Say goodbye to any vision of Canada being able to act in a way that sets the broad national interest ahead of narrower, self-serving, provincial or regional interests when they arise.

Why are we doing all this? Well, we're told we're doing it to bring Québec into the Constitution. Well, Québec already is in the Constitution, both politically, legally and morally. The Supreme Court ruled that Québec was bound by the current Constitution. Seventy-two out of 75 duly elected Members of Parliament from Québec endorsed the current Constitution in 1982 and only approximately 30 per cent of the population of Québec agreed with the separatist Premier René Levesque's refusal to sign that Constitution. So in every sense, Québec is in that Constitution.

If there is a reason to claim that Québec needs to be brought into the Constitution - that it's not already part of the Constitution - then how, I ask, could the Bourassa Government be currently using the "notwithstanding" clause of the 1982 Constitution to justify its current language policies?

The reality is, you can't bring Québec into the Constitution by destroying the Constitution. The further reality which must be emphasized is that we can't resolve these issues with side-deals by the premiers regarding Senate reform; we can't resolve these problems with a bit of tinkering at the margins to deal with minority language rights in Québec; and we can't resolve it by saying that we will pass this, flawed as it is, and then fix it later. If Québec will not agree to changes now, when the whole passage of this deal is at stake, why would we expect it to later when it has a veto.

I believe we have to recognize this as a flawed deal; it's a botched deal. It represents, yet again, a failure by the Mulroney Government to act coherently and intelligently. It is essentially the same thing with Meech Lake as with Free Trade. The Free Trade deal left the most fundamental aspect, the definition of what constitutes an "unfair" trade subsidy, to be negotiated later after the deal had been signed. The Meech Lake Accord leaves one of the most important aspects, understanding the meaning of the "distinct-society" clause, to be worked out later by others, or by the courts, after the deal becomes law. I don't believe we can run the nation that way.

I believe it is fundamental to our future as Canadians that this Accord not become our new Constitution. I congratulate people like Dennis Mills and others of good conscience, who are doing everything in their power to make sure that, in fact, the kind of Canada that we want will continue to be our Canada for the long term and for the future.

Photo: J M Carisse

The Right Hon John Turner and the Hon Herb Grey introduce the new member for York North, Maurizio Bevilacqua, to the House of Commons in Ottawa, watched by fellow members of the Official Opposition, April 3, 1989.

Competing Visions

Gordon Crann

Gordon Crann is a holder of the Laskin Prize in Consitutional Law from the University of Toronto. A former alderman for East York, he has also been an Ontario New Democratic Party candidate and a political columnist with the Toronto Star. *He is currently a public affairs consultant.*

Photo: Ashley and Crippen

I agree that the Meech Lake Accord leads to a decentralized Canada where the provinces have more power, and that the power to govern effectively is taken from the national government, but I want to take a different tack and look at the competing visions of constitutionalism and of Canada that are involved in Meech Lake.

When you look at the history of constitutional law in Canada, there have been two main visions of constitutionalism. One that goes back to 1867 and the British North America Act deals with *federalism* and the division of powers. Who is going to be able to do what? Are the provincial governments going to have the power or is the federal government going to have the power?

Since the Second World War, there's been another competing vision of constitutionalism in this country; and that has been the vision of *rights,* of individual and group rights. It's not to do with which government has the power, but rather how rights protect individuals and groups from government interventions into their lives. Although this started to evolve in Canada around the time of the Second World War, it came to a head in the early 1980s when Pierre Trudeau and his government pushed forward, over provincial opposition, with the Canadian Charter of Rights and Freedoms.

202

Now what Meech Lake does, in many ways, is encapsulate one of these visions. Meech Lake deals with federalism, and it forgets about the vision of individual and group rights in this country. What Meech Lake talks about is how to divide up various powers. When you compare that to what happened under the Charter you see that the two visions come up with two different types of constitutions.

What you had in the old British North America Act and what you have in the Meech Lake Accord is what Alan Cairns calls a *governments' constitution*. This is something that the governments think is theirs, and no one else can tamper with, even though it indirectly affects everyone, because what various governments do affects all of us.

But there's a competing way of looking at a constitution. A constitution can be what Alan Cairns has termed a *citizens' constitution*. That's essentially what the Charter of Rights and Freedoms that Pierre Trudeau brought us was - a citizens' constitution. Various groups who had been marginalized and did not have political power before - people like women, native Canadians, multicultural groups, the handicapped - all of a sudden had a constitutional identity; their status was entrenched in the Constitution and protected against government interference.

Meech Lake is solely a governments' constitution. It forgets and ignores people's rights and yet it has a profound effect upon them. When you realize *that,* it suggests alternatives to Meech Lake. What we have to do is reconcile these two competing visions of constitutionalism in Canada. We have to make sure that anything that happens takes into account people's rights; that the citizens aren't on the sidelines having no say in what the Constitution means.

There are various proposals being put forward. One that may show a way of going beyond Meech Lake is the idea of a *companion resolution* that various Métis associations and Aboriginal groups across the country have been putting forward. I prefer to talk about a *companion and parallel constitutional amendment* that can undo some of the things that Meech Lake has done and that can provide a citizens' constitution - a "people's package" - to counteract and counterbalance some of the various provisions that the provinces and the federal government have put into the Meech Lake Accord.

203

It is clear what some things in that package should be. For instance, it should make sure that the closed process of Meech Lake never happens again. When eleven men from across the country can get together and decide on their own what the Constitution of this country is going to be and then say that it's a *fait accompli* without any consultative process that involves the people of Canada, we are headed for trouble. We have to open up the process. We have to make sure that citizens of this country have a say in constitutional reform. Let the citizens help set the Agenda for the 21st Century of constitutionalism in Canada.

Another issue that has to be addressed in any companion constitutional amendment is the "notwithstanding" clause. As we've seen in Québec with the use of English on commercial signs, as long as the notwithstanding clause is in the Constitution none of our rights are really protected. Governments can always say that they are going to override legislatively whatever the courts have decided. So it's clear that one of the things that has to be done in any companion constitutional amendment is to abolish or severely restrict any use of the notwithstanding clause.

Personally, I favour abolishment of the clause but, if that's not possible, then one thing that we should look at is providing a further check on the use of the notwithstanding clause, so that one province, alone, could not pass a piece of legislation which said that notwithstanding what the courts say are our constitutional rights, we are going to do this anyway.

If a Supreme Court of Canada decision is going to be overridden, let's at least have the province concerned *and* the federal government involved, so that everyone in the country would have the chance for their representative to say whether or not it should happen. Even better, why not require *all* governments to agree if the notwithstanding clause is going to be used?

The most important thing is to let the citizens of this country decide what the constitutional Agenda for the 21st Century is going to be. Let's not allow the First Ministers (meeting in private, dealing just among themselves, and protecting only their own interests) to do so without our participation. Make sure that Meech Lake is the last opportunity they have to put forward constitutional amendments in which the citizens have no say.

Questions and Comments from the Audience

Question:
I want to congratulate and thank the Panel for their leadership in opposing the Meech Lake Accord. As an anglophone from Québec, I am strongly opposed to the distinct-society provision. As you know, the anglophones in Québec have lost some freedom of expression. My relatives and anglophone friends in Québec are organizing an appeal, not to the Québec National Assembly, not to the Parliament of Canada, but to the United Nations to try and get some restoration of their basic freedom of expression. I think this is a tragedy for Canada, that we have an oppressed minority in Québec who cannot get redress in Canada. We believe in one Canada that's distinct, bilingual coast to coast, and multicultural.

The question for the Panel is how do we stop this Meech Lake deal? How do we turn Premier Frank McKenna and Sharon Carstairs, perhaps, into Canadian folk heroes who will save Canada from Meech Lake? What ideas and suggestions would you have for us?

George Radwanski:
The first thing I'd like to remark on is, while I share your concerns about what's been done and share you concerns about the language law in Québec (clearly, it's simply a stupid law, and there's no other way to characterize it), I think we have to be careful not to be maneouvered into the position of saying that we don't want the Meech Lake Accord to go forward simply because of concerns about minority language rights in Québec.

Speaking for myself, I don't want the Meech Lake Accord to go forward because it is flawed and wrong in every one of its provisions and would, quite simply, wreck the country. So, it's very important that it not be turned into something that could be characterized, at least in Québec, as some kind of an English-language backlash. I believe the Accord is bad for Québec, as well as for the rest of Canada.

As to how we stop it? Well, in every imaginable way. A forum like this is one of the ways. Simply giving more people an opportunity to talk and think about it and, when it's broadcast on cable, for more people to see the arguments.

In terms of the provincial governments that have not ratified and where it might yet be stopped, I think it's important for people everywhere in Canada to make their views known. Write to Premier McKenna - send him a telegram or whatever - and tell him now, strongly, that you support his views that the Accord can't go forward, and encourage him to hold firm. Do likewise in terms of Manitoba; write letters to the editors of the media in Manitoba expressing your view as Canadians about the importance of this not going forward.

Above all, I think we have to be very careful to discourage tinkering at the margins. You know, it's not by the Premiers getting together and simply adding some phrase that protects minority language rights in Québec a little more, or that protects the rights of women a little better, or does something about native rights, or throws in some paragraph about the Senate. All of that might correct some of the more blatant flaws, but it wouldn't change the fact that the whole thing from start to finish is a botch.

We need to go back to the drawing board and decide what kind of changes, if any, to the present Constitution are desirable, not because that's the way for a bunch of premiers to sit down and get a deal, but because each of those changes will, in some demonstrable way, make Canada a better, fairer, more governable, more successful, more just nation, and any change that cannot be defended or justified on that basis should not become part of our fundamental law.

Question:
I've spent the better part of the last decade in Montreal, although 18 months ago I happened to find myself working in Ottawa. I resigned so that I could speak out publicly against the Meech Lake Accord. I feel strongly about this issue. I think the point has been made that the Meech Lake Accord reinforces an idea of Canada that has been supported by a number of people throughout our history; not the ones that I tend to identify with, but those who have always seen Canada as fundamentally an English-speaking country with a French-speaking minority that one had to tolerate.

That is the vision of Canada that is fundamentally given even greater credence in the Meech Lake Accord, where it speaks openly about "an English-speaking Canada" and "two Canadas, an English-speaking and a French-speaking Canada." It makes some small reference to the fact that "this fundamental characteristic must be reinforced."

We know that the predominant interpretation of this vision of Canada, as expressed by Mr. Divine in Saskatchewan and Mr. Bourassa in Québec, is one where English Canada will become increasingly English-speaking and French Canada will become increasingly French-speaking.

That is a vision of Canada that, of course, goes against everything that people from Laurier to Henri Bourassa and Pierre Elliott Trudeau stood and continue to stand for. I think that the Meech Lake Accord is so widely supported in Québec because it is seen by Québeckers as one of the first times in Canadian history where Québec has been able to negotiate a settlement with the rest of Canada on the basis of an agenda put forward by Québec.

I believe that the Meech Lake Accord must be scuttled but those who are fighting against the Meech Lake Accord must show their tremendous sensitivity to French Canada, and must show the kind of good faith that has not always been the case; that certainly is not shown by Mr. Fillman and Mr. Divine, and Mr. Getty in Alberta, who are trampling on French-speaking rights in their provinces. In fact, any parallel resolution to Meech Lake has to put forward a very, very determined, progressive agenda with respect to the realization of an increasingly bilingual, multicultural Canada. David Peterson has to be made to recognize that Ontario must become constitutionally bilingual. There have to be no buts about it - Ontario has to become constitutionally bilingual.

The Northwest Territories Act has to become part of the Constitution, making Alberta and Saskatchewan constitutionally bilingual. French-language rights in the rest of English-speaking Canada have to be respected and then we will have Québec respect the Supreme Court judgment.

Timothy Danson:
We agree.

Gordon Crann:
Yes. I think we agree and I think the point that was made, which is very important, is that we don't want to be seen as anti-Québec.

Timothy Danson:
Absolutely not.

Gordon Crann:
That what we want to put forward are positive suggestions for a better Canada, not just be negative.

Question:
I'm not a constitutional expert, but then again I don't think the eleven men who made the Meech Lake Accord are constitutional experts either. I don't think they know a lot about constitutions; I think they know very little. Unfortunately, these eleven men have set the Agenda for the 21st Century and beyond for the Canada that you and I and our children are going to live in.

They have a fundamentally flawed document that they are trying to make into a Constitution; it's basically going to have the effect of poisoning the roots of Canada and the great tree that is Canada is likely going to tumble. I could go on for hours, point by point, on the Meech Lake Accord, showing all the flaws and how it is doomed to tear this country apart, but I think that most of us are agreed that one of the major, fundamental effects that Meech Lake will have is to weaken the east-west bonds that tie all these distinct regions into one country and that have taken over a century to grow. The Meech Lake Accord is giving powers to the premiers and giving powers to the regions and setting them apart and against each other.

Now, the comment I'd like to make (and I'd like a comment from the Panel if they share this or if they have further comments) is that now, with the passing of the Free-Trade Agreement into the law of this land, a north-south bond with the US that we've fought against for years, for a century, is now becoming stronger and stronger. At the same time, it's weakening the east-west bonds. So we're faced with breaking apart on a double front in this country, by both Agreements. Could the Panel comment on this aspect: How the Free Trade Agreement impacts on Meech Lake and, I guess, the untying of the bonds of Canada?

George Radwanski:
I agree. I don't know that there's much that needs to be added to your point. It's very much the case that the combined effect of the Trade Deal and the Meech Lake Accord stands to be even worse than the individual effect of either - each of which is horrendous on its own.

Question:
Someone gave a statistic that 69 per cent of Canadians don't know what Meech Lake is about. The people in this room, many of them, probably do have an inkling of what Meech Lake is about. So, what are you up against in trying to educate the broader Canadian public in this kind of race against time, as the Accord gets ratified across the country?

Timothy Danson:
Well, certainly from the perspective of The Canadian Coalition on the Constitution, the way we address the issue (apart from attending public hearings and putting our position forward in briefs and speeches and forums such as this) is the law suit that we have brought. The most fundamental aspect of the law suit (that has been launched against the federal government and which Edward Greenspan, Morris Manning and I have taken on behalf of the Coalition) is that we want an opportunity to be in court, where the main players to this Agreement will be forced to come forward - subpoenaed if necessary - and subject themselves to what I would think would be vigorous cross-examination to explain what on earth they're doing. It is the hope of the Coalition that, during that process, the trial will be covered carefully by the media, and that Canadians will see for themselves that these people really don't know what they have done.

It's very easy for them to put themselves into a situation where they are talking to the media in short spurts, so that they don't have to address the serious issues. However, when these main players are on a witness stand, they will not have that luxury and we're hoping through that process that the Canadians who do not understand Meech Lake will come to understand it. Obviously, you have to get to the media because they're the ones who have the mechanism to spread the message across the country, and that's one mechanism which we are planning to use.

Question:
It appears that the focus is on the eleven Premiers who have prosti-

209

tuted the interests of Canada, and I say that very seriously. I think in '82 when the Charter of Rights came, we had the hope of a country where all people are respected and part of a truly democratic society. Recently, in the Philippines they got a democracy; a young democracy. They got a Constitution through the democratic process, not through back-room deals of Premiers. Now, why can't we get on with a process like that in Canada? We are supposedly a mature democracy and we should be able to initiate a process like that.

Why can't the people get up and do something about it, and get a *people's* constitution for the first time in Canada. Not the Queen's, not the Premiers', but the people's. It's about time we get on that track. How can you help to do that or is that what The Coalition for the Constitution is trying to do?

George Radwanski:
Well, I think an obvious difficulty, when you get right down to basics, is that when you have representative government you have to trust that your representative will protect you against consequences that are harmful, and that's where the process really broke down. I don't think we can all break off into little groups of our own and start writing a Canadian Constitution.

First, the Meech Lake Accord, as it stands, has to be stopped; and I don't think we should become diverted with companion resolutions or trying to fix something that is built on such a bad foundation that although you can improve it at the margins you can't solve the fundamental problems; first we have to get rid of that.

Secondly, to the degree that there is to be further Constitutional change, let's not kid ourselves, we already have a Constitution. We do not have an emergency or a crisis such that we have to slap some further changes together without time to debate and reflect carefully on what we are doing. To the degree that we're going to have further changes (and obviously a Constitution is a living document that has to evolve and change) any change should be defendable on its substantive merits.

For instance, Québec obviously has a legitimate concern about being able to preserve the characteristics that make it distinct (it's French language, and so forth) but if there are to be changes in that regard, rather than an umbrella phrase like "distinct society" that nobody knows the meaning of, let's have the courage to debate and discuss

210

and negotiate specifically what additional powers, if any, it needs in order to be able to maintain its internal distinctness and its linguistic character. It will take some demonstrating to convince many people that there are a great many additional powers that are needed if you look at what the Québec government is able to accomplish as it stands but let's negotiate that; let's debate that. Let's negotiate any other changes on the basis of their individual merits.

I would argue that far-reaching constitutional changes in this country, once they have been negotiated, should be subject to some kind of a national referendum process, the mechanics of which could be worked out. This should make sure that never again can a group of eleven people, or even a number of governments having majorities, try to hijack our Constitution and change our nation in a way that a majority of Canadian people don't want to happen.

Question:
It's rather unfortunate that this kind of debate on the Constitution Amendment - call it Meech Lake - is getting its hearing after the fact. However, it's still not too late. One of the questions I'd like the Panel to answer is, is it conceivable that, if Meech Lake goes through, that we could not amend the Constitution again - based on the idea that we have to have consensus to amend the Constitution.

Timothy Danson:
The problem is that once Meech Lake becomes law, there are key provisions that go right to the core of Canada as a federal state and these can only be changed through a process of unanimity. I think that we will become the only free nation in the world that can only change and amend its Constitution in material respects through a process of unanimity. Now, it's one thing to be a country with imagination and to lead other nations but, perhaps on this point, we should look at why other free nations of the world don't have a provision that requires unanimity.

One of the great dangers of unanimity (that it's perhaps presumptuous and arrogant of us to ignore) is what right do we have, in 1989, to impose our vision of Canada in a permanent sense on people 20, 30, 40 years from now? When a crisis does happen (and whether it's the Supreme Court of Canada or the Senate, it's just a question of time before it does) all the people of Canada, at that time will have to resolve this problem and they will be confronted with the fact that,

211

in 1989, we decided to impose our vision of the future on them. I think that's a dangerous, dangerous mechanism which we are entrenching into our Constitution, and I hope that we can reverse what we're doing, so we will not be the first country in the world to have such a restrictive amending formula.

Question:

I feel I owe it to the other people who also had questions, to say on their behalf that there is so much interest that maybe more time should be allotted at a Conference like this on another occasion. I want to say that if we're developing an Agenda for the 21st Century, surely it should be based on intelligent discussion. I heard George Radwanski say that we must have the courage to discuss things. Surely the Fall of 1988 and the federal election showed us how dangerous it is to deal in over-simplifications and myths.

We were looking at lack of information on the Trade Agreement and it has been, for many of us I think, a very disappointing and frustrating experience that we didn't communicate effectively with our fellow citizens how complex the issue really was. We started to, during the election, but we hadn't taken in just how complex it was. I'd like to express my disappointment that of the three speakers, there was no one there representing the positive side of why some of these eleven Premiers (who I believe acted in good faith) made the decision that they did.

Denise Chong:

I agree with your point; a debate is several sides and I am extremely sorry that we are out of time. We have only two minutes before the next session. At least what has happened here is that the seeds of more debate have been planted and the debate can continue beyond this short session.

Editor's Note: *In response to the very valid concern of the last speaker, we are taking the opportunity of including in the Appendix of this book a pro-Meech Lake Accord position. It is taken from the main text of the presentation made by Yves Fortier, our recently appointed Ambassador to the United Nations, to the Speyer Committee on the Constitution.*

Broadview-Greenwood resident Denise Chong, economist and author, acted as our main moderator for the Conference on Developing an Agenda for the 21st Century.

Photo: G Manos

Ethel Blondin, the first native woman elected to the Federal Parliament, addresses the Conference watched by (from left to right) Françoise Ducros from Québec, Mary Clancy from Nova Scotia, Dan Hayes from Alberta, Roger Simmons from Newfoundland and Moderator Jim Coutts.

Section Eight:
Regional Perspectives

Introduction

Jim Coutts

Jim Coutts was born and educated in Alberta and holds a law degree from the University of Alberta and an MBA from Harvard School of Business. He has served two former Prime Ministers of Canada, as Secretary to Lester Pearson and Principal Secretary to Pierre Trudeau. He is currently Chairman of CIC Canadian Investment Capital Ltd.

I started out in a small town in Alberta called Nanton. We didn't think very much of the people in High River, a town 15 miles north, because we thought High River received more attention, more grants, and more support from government than we did. Later, I discovered that in High River, they didn't like the people in Calgary for the same reasons, and Calgary had a rather fierce rivalry with Edmonton - people in each town thought the other received more support, more attention, and special privileges. The only thing that would ever unite southern and northern Alberta was an intense dislike of the east, whether the east was Québec or Toronto. East-bashing will always pull Abertans together.

In the final analysis, one discovers that our Alberta dislikes and rivalries are no different from the way Cape Bretoners sometimes feel about Halifax, people in the interior of British Columbia feel about Vancouver, or northern Ontarians feel about southern Ontarians. The force that pulls things apart - the force of strong regionalism - is a very powerful force in Canada. Regional leaders spring up naturally and it is quite easy for them to be strong advocates of local issues. It's just natural to try to convince people that others are to blame for the region's failures. "They", the outsiders, are the reason there isn't the growth and development there should be in the home district.

Dividing Canada and pulling it apart has been natural in this country from its very beginning. But there has also been another kind of force in the country - a national force, a sense of country. And national leaders have tried to foster this sense of nationhood. A positive feeling for one's country has been a much more difficult force to create; it's been a much less natural force to try to work with, but at times it has succeeded extremely well.

One reason pan-Canadianism succeeds is because there are national leaders, people who work at the business of nationhood, people who happen to know their regions and the sense of local grievance, but who also understand what a nation is. We are fortunate in that some of those who are national leaders as well as regional representatives are speaking out. Their views are represented in the following pages.

A View from Newfoundland

Roger Simmons

Roger Simmons was born in Lewisporte, Newfoundland. Following a career in teaching, he was elected Member of Parliament for Burin St Georges in 1979. He has also served as interim Leader of the Opposition in the Newfoundland Legislature. He was re-elected to the House of Commons in 1988.

Newfoundlanders are born jokers and supreme optimists - and both for an eminently good reason. Our laughter and our hopes have their genesis in the selfsame wellspring as do negro spirituals; they help us to endure the present while contemplating and planning for a better future.

The present in Newfoundland is clearly something to be endured. A jobless rate more than twice the national average; an abundantly rich fish resource being criminally pillaged by the French, with the dastardly acquiescence of the federal government; a provincial treasury being savagely looted by politicians like Peckford - determined to put two cucumbers on every plate, no matter what the cost; a national agenda whose maniacal stampede to the American bosom tramples underfoot our regional aspirations and our hopes, not to mention our social programs.

Certainly, the current reality in Newfoundland and Labrador is not pretty but it's not without unwitting humour. An old fisherman said to me, during the recent election campaign, "That fellow Peckford wants us all to start eating cucumbers. He must be out of his skull. I'd rather devour a full bottle of pickles."

Nor is our current reality in Newfoundland and Labrador without some hope. As a Newfoundlander, I'm confident that Newfoundland and Labrador stand on the very threshold, on the very brink of a dramatic and unprecedented economic upturn - the dual corner-stones of which will be the fishery and the off-shore oil development, and the results of which will be a substantially improved lot for all of our people.

I've told you how I feel as a Newfoundlander in terms of the years down the road. As a Canadian, I must confess to you that I have less reason to be optimistic for our continuance into the 21st Century as an independent political entity. Meech Lake, notwithstanding its very laudable objective, and the Free-Trade Agreement dangle ominously as the twin wrecking balls of the Canadian Confederation, as we've come to know and cherish it. I don't want to live in a country where might is right. I cannot understand the precept that teaches that the protection and the enhancement of majority rights must depend for their success on the diminution of minority rights - whether those rights be regional or linguistic.

Having said all that, let me not betray the Newfoundlander that I am; one whose tools in trade include an intrepid and incurable optimism. I believe it is possible for things to turn out less dismally for this country than I have so far suggested.

In conclusion, therefore, I want to suggest to you that the national agenda - certainly the Liberal agenda - for the years ahead as we enter the 21st Century, must focus on several specifics; among them:

* *Retrieving the tools of national sovereignty pawned away to the Americans by the Mulroney Government;*

* *Restoring a strong central government whose capacity to protect the poor and / or the less populated parts of this country is not stalemated by provincial greed and empire building;*

* *Focussing on the restoration of our proud and, until recently, our eminently successful crusade as the relentless defenders of minority rights, and as the practitioners of fairness for all Canadians, whether here in Broadview-Greenwood or in the geographic extremities of this country.*

218

A View from Alberta

Dan Hays

Dan Hays was born in Calgary and has History, English and Law degrees from the Universities of Alberta and Toronto. He was summoned to the Senate in 1984 where he has served as Chairman of the Senate Committee on Agriculture and Forestry and on the Committee on Energy and Natural Resources. He also farms in Alberta.

I would like to try and set a stage for you which will, hopefully, provoke you a bit and lead you to conclude, as I have, that there are a couple of very important items that should be on our Agenda for the 21st Century.

I will present this perspective in as objective a way as I can - being a Liberal from a province that has not elected a Liberal Member of Parliament in 20 years or a Liberal incumbent for more than 30 years. That may seem a complaint but I am going to try my best not to characterize what I have to say as such but rather as a set of circumstances that we must bear in mind, now, if we are to enter the 21st Century still a successful country.

The stage is set, as well as anything, by quotes from two items in today's paper which might have been found in any paper any day of the week. The first says that "the General Agreement on Tariffs and Trade is dead," according to Lester Thurow. He made this comment at a thinkers' conference in Davos, Switzerland, and he told the group that "the current trend is away from liberal trade; the trend is to a more managed trade between trading blocs."

The second, on the same page, has to do with the US dependence on foreign oil. It says: "The United States' dependence on foreign oil is likely to reach historic peaks in the 1990s as consumption grows and production slides. They are at their highest dependence on imported oil since 1957" and "In the case of natural gas, there is no active exploration for that commodity and it is expected that they will become more dependent on imported natural gas." Those imports will, of course, come from Canada.

These two statements are related and I will demonstrate that relationship to you and how it affects two items of great importance that must be on our 21st Century Agenda.

I will remind you, although I am sure you already know, that Alberta accounts for about two-thirds of all of primary Canadian energy production in a year. Ontario accounts for about five per cent and consumes about 33 per cent; Québec accounts for about 5 per cent of production and consumes about 20 per cent. This has led us to have certain policies in the past that are trade-related within our own country, and which have been very unpopular in Alberta and the West, and very misunderstood, I believe, in Canada generally.

I'm suggesting to you, therefore, that we must ensure that we have on our agenda the development of a policy which takes into account the friction that can result from not satisfactorily resolving the different interests of *producing* Canadians and *consuming* Canadians. And we must now be mindful of the fact that it is no longer a Canadian problem, but that it is a continental problem. We have now, in effect, pooled our energy with the United States,

Whether we know it or not - and I regret that it wasn't more of an issue during the election - we are now (tempered by the inertia of transportation systems that were created at an earlier time to move energy east) on our way to a continental market in energy. Which means that, while we are a net exporter of some billions of dollars of energy a year to the United States, we are highly dependent on imported oil in Eastern Canada.

People in Eastern Canada will become dependent on imported oil to an even greater degree, because the natural transportation patterns that will result from the Free Trade Agreement that we've entered into with the United States, will naturally flow along north-south lines.

220

So, we are going to have to do something about that; we will have to devise, or fashion a policy in the most difficult of circumstances - that of strong regional feelings. We're going to have to develop a policy that suits both *producing* and *consuming* Canadians, and this will be of the utmost importance.

As an Albertan I would like to introduce to you a second item of importance. I feel obliged to say that in my region - and it's true to a lesser degree of the other Western Provinces and, I think, of Atlantic Canada as well - we feel very strongly that parliamentary reform must proceed. Meech Lake is an impediment to that. Executive federalism is an extremely bad practice, which is not conducive to good parliamentary reform. A vital reform, according to my fellow Albertans, revolves around a different kind of Senate and I would, myself, add to that, a different kind of Parliament. These reforms are needed because we have to give power to a legislative body that will ensure adequate regional inputs into the federal legislation-making process. That must also be on our Agenda.

A View from Nova Scotia

Mary Clancy

Mary Clancy was born in Halifax, Nova Scotia and holds Law degrees from the Universities of Dalhousie and London (England). She has been a practising lawyer, actress and broadcaster. She was elected Member of Parliament for Halifax in 1988.

We Haligonians love coming to Toronto, because it's the only place in the country that's hated worse than we are. Just a joke! In Halifax - which in case you didn't know, is the most urban Riding east of Montreal - we tend to reflect national issues and to share in national perspectives but lurking always near to the surface is the reality of being the slightly more prosperous centre of what is, essentially, a have-not area.

Consequently, Halifax has urban-specific concerns - notably the environment, particularly in light of our desperately polluted harbour; an escalating crime rate, which is directly related to the escalating drug trade in our city; a severe housing crisis which is directly related to the urban poor; the ever-present problems of youth unemployment and poverty; and the specific questions of urban alienation.

The increase of uncertainty with respect to defence policy regarding NATO, in what is still a Navy town, is also something that preoccupies most Haligonians and most Nova Scotians. Nova Scotia, and Halifax in particular, has always tended to fare better economically than the other Maritime Provinces. So the residents do tend to have a vested interest in national concerns.

The Mulroney Trade Deal has, in a sense, awakened Maritimers as nothing else, including the Meech Lake Accord, could do. A very real concern now exists about the nation's future; a worry about whether truly Canadian qualities can survive. Under that heading, the most pressing worries relate to the survival of regional subsidies, the future of the fishery, and an almost all-pervasive fear of losing our sovereignty - whether we're talking cultural, economic or political - to our southern mega-neighbour.

During the recent election campaign, I was frequently accused of turning this into an emotional issue. Well, I guess I have to plead guilty to that. It *is* an emotional issue; it's a passionate issue and I don't think that there is any need to apologise for being passionate about the future of our country.

These fears have been exacerbated by Premier Bourassa's use of the notwithstanding clause. Nova Scotians, as I'm sure many of you know, have had their deficiencies in the area of minority rights slammed home to them by the Marshall Commission which is investigating, among other things, Nova Scotia's judicial treatment of minority groups. Consequently, there is a higher level of awareness of equality issues, and a real sense of puzzlement that is asking "What is happening to Canada?" and "What is Canada to be?"

If minority rights are so important in Nova Scotia - and we've spent somewhere around $8,000,000 on the Marshall Inquiry to prove it - why are they less so in Québec? Why should language rights be different from legal rights? Why should it be different to be a Canadian in Québec than a Canadian in Nova Scotia?

My reading of the mind-set of Nova Scotians is one of trepidation. We have to address these fears and establish a vision for Canada - a vision of Canada that will rekindle a spirit of hope and endeavour that is truly home-grown and not made in the USA.

A View from The North West Territories

Ethel Blondin

Ethel Blondin was born in Fort Norman, educated in the Northwest Territories and Alberta and has taught at the University of Calgary and Arctic College. She was Assistant Deputy Minister of Culture & Communications in Yellowknife and is now Member of Parliament for the Western Arctic.

I was speaking to someone and they asked me how I felt about being in Toronto. I want to tell you that I find Toronto to be very exciting and I make no apologies for being one of those Canadians who likes Toronto as a city. I like the people and I like what's happening in Toronto. I particularly like what is happening today in Broadview-Greenwood.

I would like to take the time to give you an idea what the Northwest Territories is like. We cover a land mass of 1.3 million square miles, and we're on what's called a formula funding arrangement with the Federal Government. We get $800,000,000 a year to administer and deliver programs and services. We are, I guess, what you would consider a non-constitutional entity. We are not a province. We do not have party politics; we have a consensus government. Our legislators are elected; a majority of those legislators are native; they're aboriginals.

The North is broken up into two constituencies, two Ridings. My Riding is the Western Arctic (thirty-one communities fall in my constituency); the other Riding is the Nunatsiaq, which encompasses the Eastern Arctic.

We have 53,000 people; 15,000 of those people are Dene and Metis.

They are are in the throes of negotiating final stages of a land-claim settlement. They will be beneficiaries of a claim that will result in them becoming the largest landowners in Canada - 70,000 square miles - with a cash settlement of $450,000,000. The settlement of the land claim is very critical in the North, in that it opens doors not just for the native people but for the other people who want to proceed with their agendas for the 21st Century.

The North relies heavily on the mining industry, and that particular industry is set back until the land claim settlement is achieved. We also have initiatives in tourism; we have a vast territory; we have many resources. We have the open space; we have parks. We have the people that want to deliver the service.

We also have impediments. We lack an adequate infrastructure. We don't have the highways that many, many of the provinces take for granted; we don't have direct, linked transportation to many of the thirty-one communities. Much of the travel that I've done in my campaign was done by air, and much of my constituency work is done by air transportation. The responsibilities for roads and highways and for airport transportation and airports still lies with the federal government. We're in the throes of negotiating these two very, very expensive items - very expensive. Roads have to be upgraded before the responsibility is handed over to the government of the Northwest Territories.

Being also a non-constitutional entity, we are generally sidelined when it comes to such events as the Meech Lake Accord; our leaders were not allowed to participate. Neither the Yukon's nor the Northwest Territories' government leaders were included in the First Ministers' Conference negotiations on the Meech Lake Accord.

We are currently negotiating what's called the Northern Accord, which includes the management of resources and the sharing of revenues. This will be a very, very heavy item to negotiate.

Our main industry, I guess we've said for years and years and years, is the potential that we have and it is a *vast* potential; we are resource rich. We produce approximately 25,000 barrels of oil a day that are piped to Alberta through the pipeline; none of the revenues come to the North. So if we get $800,000,000 a year from the federal government to administer programs and services and we don't share in the revenues of the oil and gas that are piped to the South, then I think we basically have a system of accommodation. That has to be resolved.

The North is not a stand-alone economy. We're not heavily into industry. I stated in my maiden speech on Free Trade that, really, Free Trade will not result in any direct benefits for the North at this point in time. We don't have the critical mass; we don't have the people who have the skills to deliver the research, the expertise, to run a lot of the specialized industries that are needed to have an economy that stands on its own. We need an infrastructure that will cut back on costs; we don't have that yet.

I guess basically what I'm saying is that we have a number of items to work out before we can even consider becoming a province but what we would like to do is have the opportunity to participate, in negotiating an economic and political agenda for the 21st Century. We occupy one-third of the land mass of Canada and we should have an opportunity to participate. Sovereignty is another issue in the North. People are the best reflection of who holds ownership to the land. Residents are the best claimants to land.

As consumers, our prices are in some areas 26 to 37 per cent higher than Edmonton. In some other areas, they're 60 to 70 per cent higher. That doesn't even include produce; those items are inaccessible. We don't have access to them. This has implications for nutrition and health - very, very bare essentials that many Southern communities take for granted.

We have an emergence, or a re-emergence, of the military in the North. We're basically a strategic area, a listening-post for detection. And there are many things happening in the North that Northerners can become involved in.

These are the things that we concern ourselves with and, at the same time, we are juggling with a number of other items - constitutional development, economic growth, the environment. I am pleased to have had the opportunity to bring a few of our concerns, a few of our political agendas, a few of our economic problems to your attention. I am pleased to have been here with you. I'd like you to know that I find it exciting that we've bridged the gap.

A View from Québec

Françoise Ducros

Françoise Ducros studied History and Law at the Universities of Ottawa and McGill. She has worked for Justice Rejean Paul studying the implementation of the James Bay Agreement and the problems facing the native communities of Northern Québec. Most recently she worked for Lucie Pépin, former MP for Outremont.

There's a very, very sad and scary situation going on right now in Québec. I have been sheltered from it in the last nine months, because I had the honour to work for a strong, passionate federalist - and a Québecoise all the way - who was concerned about the whole of Canada from the East to the West, from the North to the South - Lucie Pépin.

What's going on in Québec, the provincial government's use of the notwithstanding clause, is heart-breaking to me. I grew up in a completely bilingual setting; I grew up with the confidence of the French Canadians who had learned to be a part of the Canadian political process through great men like Pierre Trudeau. I grew up in a situation where there was a growing tolerance and mutual understanding between the English and the French.

Then I went to Ottawa, and I was reinforced in my belief that strange voting patterns exist in Québec. Québeckers like a strong, nationalist, provincial government; and they like strong, centralist federal governments. They vote for René Levesque and they vote for Trudeau, and then they watch things unfold.

There is this push and pull at the provincial-federal level because

227

there's no question that Québec does feel threatened by the rest of Canada. Eventually, perhaps, it won't feel that way but right now it does; Québeckers speak a different language and they're afraid but they also feel a part of Canada. How else do you explain the Trudeau years?

Occasionally, when the provincial government removes rights and the press condones it, and no one speaks up for Canada, Canadians in Québec become confused and anxious - which is what's happening right now. But I'd just like to assure everybody that, as passionate and as vocal and as radical as the minority in Québec might be, I and others like me are just as passionate.

There is another point to be considered as we pilot ourselves towards the 21st Century - multiculturalism. It is especially relevant to Montréal, where I come from, because by the year 2000, three out of five Montréalers will be of ethnic origin. I think that it is absolutely crucial for the future of Canada that we ensure that individuals from all our ethnic communities are included in the political process; that we bring back meetings like today - the equivalent of town-hall meetings - so that everyone understands each other and everyone keeps talking.

Questions and Comments from the Audience

Question:
I want to pose a question on energy policy. I understand the needs of Newfoundlanders and the off-shore, and the needs of Alberta, but what I heard being proposed was the old style of energy policy, which was large-scale, centralized, foreign-owned; where the profits tend to leave the region; which is environmentally damaging and where fossil fuels contribute to the greenhouse effect. What I want to hear comments on and which I think should be our Agenda for the 21st Century, is an energy policy where energy production is decentralized to the regions, where it's appropriate technology, where it's labour-intensive instead of capital-intensive, and where it's renewable because I would think both Alberta (who could produce gasohol from grains) and certainly Newfoundland could produce liquid energy from renewable sources, where the profits stay in the community.

I don't feel that we can continue to subsidize off-shore; I don't think the economics are going to be there in the future, frankly, and that's what I was disappointed in. I would like to hear some comments on what I think would be a new energy policy for Canada that would be appropriate to the regions, and satisfy all these regional aspirations, while still keeping a strong Canada.

Dan Hays:
That's a very difficult question to deal with briefly, but I'll try. I may not have pointed out that in Canada we are currently producing about a million and a half barrels a day; we consume about half of that here and we export the rest. We are, as of '87, about 73 per cent self-sufficient in crude oil; the rest of it we import. So we should, as part of our energy policy, be very concerned about the degree to which we use our own energy to supply our own market.

The policy of the Government of Canada today, and the Government of the United States, is that market forces will govern what happens to price and transportation patterns for energy. That will mean a

229

very dramatic change in the North American energy picture, unless Canada is aware of the need to satisfy its own need with its own supplies so that, in the event of a short supply or in the event - as inevitably is going to be the case - of low-cost energy becoming scarce, we will have put in place transportation systems and the means to take full advantage of our rich energy resource.

The Trade Agreement is a major impediment to this, and we're not sure just yet how great an impediment. The United States, on its way to 50 per cent dependence for its crude oil energy needs from imported markets, and Canada being the United States' greatest supplier, and Canada holding a grand total of one per cent of the world's conventional crude oil reserves, it's obvious to me that the United States entered into this Agreement looking at energy as a strategic commodity where they had to make special arrangements with Canada to satisfy their strategic needs, while Canadians looked at it as a commodity that was plentiful, like all other commodities.

So, the development of a future energy policy for Canada - the one we have now being completely and totally inadequate - means that we, as Canadians, have to look at energy as a strategic good. We consume more per capita than any country in the world; energy is our lifeblood. We can't look at it as a commodity, like other commodities. You referred to methanol, presumably bio-mass of some sort being used to generate that methanol. That's about the only job-intensive area that I can see for future energy development.

As for the off-shore. You're right. Hibernia is expensive but bringing Hibernia on - and I'm critical of the details of the Hibernia Agreement - would satisfy some security-of-supply concerns, because it would satisfy the energy requirement in Atlantic Canada that is currently being satisfied totally by imported oil.

So we need to develop policies that will ensure that, to some considerable degree, we supply our own requirement even if not a hundred per cent of it. A case in point is the issue between the producing part of Canada and the consuming part of Canada over long-term contracting for natural gas needs. At the current time, natural gas is cheap. The consumers of Ontario want to buy that cheap, short-term gas. Consumers in California, I can tell you, are contracting gas for 20 years. We currently have over a third of our 72 trillion cubic feet of gas in Canada under contract to the US at this point in time.

I don't know whether you read the financial pages closely or not, but more and more and more of that is being committed to the U.S. market. That's the cheapest natural gas we'll ever find. So it just puzzles me as to why the government of Ontario would resist that approach for Ontario yet they are resisting it.

It seems to me that a national concern comes into play here and that the federal government has a role in encouraging consuming Canadians to remember about the strategic nature of energy. I'll leave it at that.

Question:
Luckily or unluckily, we have a Prime Minister who is what I call a former branch-plant manager. And he has - with the one wrecking ball moving towards us from the south - converted Ottawa into another branch plant of Washington. It's unfortunate that today, we don't have anybody from Manitoba or New Brunswick. I would really like to have the regional perspectives on what is happening in those regions and, if nothing is happening, why nothing is happening to help Manitoba and New Brunswick stop Meech Lake.

Mary Clancy:
The reason that nothing is happening in Nova Scotia is that John Buchanan and his gang ratified it; they forced it through the Legislature in the province of Nova Scotia. However, if you have been following the public hearings in New Brunswick, the statements from all the groups appearing before the provincial committee to hear briefs on Meech Lake have, as far as I understand, been unanimously against. I think New Brunswick is handling the matter really quite well on its own.

At this time, certainly from the point of view of the province of Nova Scotia, they're not going to get any help from the government. But Vince MacLean, who is the Leader of the Opposition, has made his opposition to the Agreement - particularly as it relates to the fishery - very strong, and he has been saying that since the beginning of the debate. Beyond that, I'm not quite sure what you would suggest the other provinces could do to assist. But as I say, with the Conservative government in power in Nova Scotia, it's a problem.

Roger Simmons:
First of all, I want to say to the Questioner that insofar as the lan-

guage issue in Québec is concerned, I'm having a very great deal of difficulty explaining it to my people in Burin-St. Georges, a Riding that takes in pretty well the whole of the south coast of the island of Newfoundland and a bit of the west coast, one hundred and fifty-eight separate communities and villages. People just don't understand why, in order to protect and enhance the rights of one group, you've got to trample on the rights of another. It's a live issue there and I'm critical of those around me, that we haven't been more vocal on this. The last Speaker alluded to this: there was a silence, an absence of voice on the issue. Somebody ought to have spoken up and I guess I'm as guilty as anybody. Somebody ought to have spoken up more for the minority in Québec or else we're going to have a patchwork situation where, to be a Canadian in one part of the country, is different to being a Canadian in another part of the country.

That brings me to the other point that the Questioner raised, the one relating to Meech Lake. At the time that the signatures were put to Meech Lake, I was in the Newfoundland House of Assembly as Leader of the Opposition and, in that capacity, I had the obligation and the opportunity to respond to Mr. Peckford's introduction of the Meech Lake legislation. I feel the objective of the Meech Lake initiative was laudable, but that the price was far too high and part of the very high price is mixing up the levels of government - this nonsense about having provincial governments having a say in the Supreme Court, and particularly in the appointment of Senators, just for example.

The most elementary principal of federalism is that the levels of government are autonomous within their areas of jurisdiction; they're quite separate. If we're going to have provincial governments appointing a watchdog on the federal government, why don't we become completely ludicrous and advocate that the federal government also ought to appoint a Senate for each province to keep an eye on them?

Ethel Blondin:
On the issue of Meech Lake, within the Territories we've just had two of our legislators go to the New Brunswick hearings and, basically, plead for representation. We've had our Government Leader in a series of discussions with the Prime Minister, as well as Senator Murray, essentially begging to represent the North at the First Ministers' conferences; to represent the North and to be able to negotiate and have some input into the amendments that were put

forward on the appointment of Senators, the appointment of judges, the unanimity clause, and also with regards to the boundary issue - the great deal of concern that Northerners have about boundary encroachment into the Territories by the neighbouring provinces.

Really, all we have on our agenda right now is to try and secure some kind of representation. Our sole representative on Meech Lake was the Prime Minister. You, as provinces, have two representatives: You have your Premier and you have the Prime Minister; we have one representative and that is the Prime Minister. We would like our Government Leader to represent us at the negotiations but we see no shining light in terms of securing that representation.

As the Member of Parliament for the Northwest Territories, I have written a letter to Lowell Murray asking for an explanation of why the North is not to be represented; why we are not being granted an equal right for representation; why can we not secure this represen- tation that's afforded to everyone else. Both the Yukon and the Northwest Territories should, at the very least, be heard but I've yet to receive a response.

So, basically, what we're doing right now is not even extending our work on Meech Lake in terms of the amendments; all we would like to do is secure some kind of representation. And that in itself is a problem. There really has been no reasonable explanation given. There's been a lot of double talk; there's been a lot of, "We'll wait and see." There have been other invitations made to speak outside of the realms of the actual official negotiations but we feel that if it is ratified, there really will not be an opportunity to have the kind of input we want.

Françoise Ducros:
I just think that all the things we've said about Meech Lake today I agree with completely. One point that we haven't touched upon, though, which is odd, is this whole idea of opting out of federal programs. We've talked about the environment, and it's a national and its a global issue. By the same token, we're faced with this political system where we're telling the provinces that they provide clean air too and that they can do it independently of what everyone else is doing. I think that all the other issues are fundamentally important, but we shouldn't forget this last one, because it's more innocuous. It involves spending power.

Question:
Last year, at the provincial annual meeting for the Liberal Party, Meech Lake was almost brought up again before the MPs to re-study and re-assess where they were, but that was defeated because party hacks and paid workers had to show up downstairs to cast their vote for the Meech Lake Accord. One of the things that astonished David Peterson was when he went into the Francophone suites and discovered that the Francophones were completely, one hundred per cent against the Meech Lake Accord. I would like to ask if something is being done to reach out to these people and to help them to continue their work in helping to defeat this two-pronged attack on Canadian sovereignty (Free Trade being the other) because, essentially, one is eviscerating our government and the other is turning it over to American interests.

Roger Simmons:
When I was 16, I worked at Danforth and Pape in Colgate-Palmolive. Does that qualify me as being from Ontario? Keep in mind that in operative terms, the people holding the cards now are the Manitoba Legislature and in the New Bruswick Legislature and their governments. I'm sure you've gathered that in the federal Liberal caucus there is a divergence of opinion on this issue but that at the federal level it's an academic exercise at the moment in terms of the capacity to effect change, if that is the desired objective.

The legislation has passed the House, and it has been ratified by eight of the other ten Legislatures. It all hinges now, as you well know, on what happens in New Brunswick and Manitoba. So, first of all, it's a matter of wait and see. But secondly, of course, if you want a more productive wait and see, my advice to you is to make known your moral support or outrage to Sharon Carstairs and Frank McKenna.

Dan Hays:
I'd like to comment on the rider the Questioner put, which has to do with the Canada-U.S. Free-Trade Agreement, and acknowledge that I agree with the thrust of his question, that it is going to have a profound effect on the nature of Canada by bringing the United States to the table when we must deal with regional problems.

When the Agreement was first signed, the Attorney General of Ontario, Ian Scott, made a great deal of the fact that it was in and of itself a *de facto* constitutional change because it would change the way in which the federal government's powers were viewed by the courts. I recall at the time the Attorney General of my province disagreed. I think he was wrong and that the Attorney General of Ontario was right.

What we're likely to see - and energy is another example of where this may arise - is a request by the United States for a Panel, under Article 18, to rule on Canada's attempts to deal with its energy needs; and to bring the proportional access provision of the Agreement, Article 904, to bear and to say that it really isn't a Canadian decision any more, but rather a decision the United States is involved in. Because of 904, we have committed to proportional access. So, to the extent that we are now supplying that market, we must continue to do so. And further, that a market-based policy is in the spirit of and part of the object of the Agreement, and that we can't change that. This is one of the serious impediments that we must face, and deal with, in developing future energy policy.

Jim Coutts:
I would like to make three comments. One comes from a book written some time ago by Northrop Frye called *The Bush Garden* which was really a critique of culture. He tried to distinguish between "identity" and "unity" and he pointed out that the idea of identity (which is essentially regional) is easier because it has to do with what you can see and touch and smell and understand and experience; where you are. He thought that the question of unity is a much tougher question because it is more cerebral and it revolves around the world of ideas and politics more than the world of feelings.

It seems to me, therefore, that the task of those who care about nation building in addition to region building is the much tougher job, and that it has both succeeded and failed at times in the past; and it is somewhat weak at this time. It depends on all of us understanding what is going on in the regions - that's why panels like today are so important. It depends upon an enormous amount of recruiting of people who will look at the cerebral questions and deal with the ideas of what a nation really is.

That's a lot tougher work, and we've got an enormous amount of it in front of us. We owe a great deal to Dennis, because he has organized a symposium where we are looking at the question of national unity, not just at the emotions of regions. Not that regional emotion is bad, but the question of unity and of pulling together and of operating as a nation is a much tougher thing to do. Dennis has had a big problem in life. He has been known as an *organizer*. Now, he can't help that; he just does it so well. People say if you want something done in the middle of the night anywhere in the nation Dennis can organize it and so he's got stuck with that label. What people didn't know is that Dennis has a lot of ideas. Now what he's going to get stuck with is the label of the best organizer of ideas in Canada. He can draw people together; he can make them think; he can pull their ideas out of them and get them talking to each other and communicating about ideas.

I think I speak for him when I say that the basic thing about an agenda is that it's a long list of question marks. You keep raising new questions about the future and what Canada will be like and how it can evolve. If we didn't solve it all today we certainly raised a list of question marks for the next Decade and the next Century.

Students from Westwood Junior School in Ottawa learning how Parliament works.

Students: Bobby Antoniadis, Gus Aloumanis, Tom Bartsiokas, Joanne Benakis, Lolita Beredo, Jennifer Brady, Frank Chan, Steve Dariotis, Chris Dinadis, Stephanie Gallos, Gina & Jim Georgopoulos, Greg Goutis, So-kit Kwan, Uwe Lord, Mike Mazarakis, Sean McCulloch, Donna Olgeraio, Helen Pagratis, Sheila Pak, Eva Pardalis, Tony Pethakas, Nicky Pinellis, Troy Singh, Donna Sioklis, Mary Ann So, Chris Stavrianos, Tyhimba Sullivan, Alex Tran, Nicky Tsafatinos, Chris Tsementzis, Peter Tzakas, Laura Varjacic, Peter Vlahos, Anastasia Vlassopoulos, Sia Xilias.

Staff: Mr P Jones and Mr D Mowatt.

Postscript

From Vision to Reality

Dennis Mills

The turn of a century presents us with a dramatic and rare opportunity to begin not just a new chronological era but also a new economic, social and political reality.

If we are to achieve that by the year 2000, we must decide what sort of reality we want and take action now to ensure its materialization. We have a decade to clarify our visions, identify our problems, declare our aims, outline our strategy and decide on our tactics.

Having listened carefully to the speakers at this conference, to my constituents in Broadview-Greenwood and to many others all over Canada, I would like to outline a possible agenda for the 21st century. I want to make it clear that this agenda will require more input from other people and it will need some refining, but it is a beginning.

I personally have a vision for Canada that I am increasingly confident is shared by many Canadians. I want to see a healthy Canada which cares equally for its physical and social environment; a prosperous but compassionate Canada with all Canadians sharing in the prosperity; a nationally united but internationally conscious Canada where diversity is seen as a cause for celebration not conflict; and an honourable Canada which operates on a value system that accommodates the best of all our multicultural values.

I hope you share that vision and believe with me that we can bring it into being. If so, our first task is to clarify its component parts. What do we actually mean by a "healthy physical and social environment", what constitutes "prosperous but compassionate", how do we define "national unity" or "international consciousness", what "value system" are we talking about?

Let me tell you what I think these mean to most Canadians. We see a healthy physical environment being one of balance. This involves treating the planet we live on as a closed system that we cannot afford to abuse. We need to take a global view because what we do in any one corner of the world sooner or later affects every other part. Any costs associated with environmental sensitivity are much less than those that result from environmental mistreatment, which may have been hidden from view in the past but are increasingly obvious now. So environmental health is a positive, cost-saving way forward.

A healthy social environment is one in which every individual can realise their potential without unnecessary hindrance and with equal chance of success; in which everyone can participate and is equally welcomed; in which differences, whether biological or man-made, are used as an opportunity to enrich the human condition and not as an excuse to demoralise it. Insensitivity and human exploitation also result in very high costs, not just for the individual concerned but also society as a whole. We lose people to addictive drugs, to the embitterment of discrimination and sometimes to the mindlessness of crime. These costs are too high. We should not ask any individual to bear them and neither can society afford them. Canada needs all her people for the 21st century.

As for prosperity with compassion, this seems to be the only sane way forward. How can anyone of conscience enjoy the fruits of their labour, however well-earned, knowing that some of their fellow Canadians, through no fault of their own, are living in poverty with little hope of escape. Many people in the course of their lives suffer financial deprivation for a variety of reasons: ill health, bereavement or desertion, employment dislocation, poor education, limited regional economies, or personal entrepreneurial risk. These people need our moral and sometimes financial support to see them through difficult times so that they too can experience and contribute to the general prosperity.

Being united means having the same rights as a Canadian citizen whether you are in Nanaimo or Goose Bay, in Fort Nelson or Trois Rivieres, in Swift Current or Glace Bay, in Moosonee or Baker Lake; it means having the same rights whether you were born in Canada or any other part of the world; it means having the same rights whether you speak French or English or both or neither. Being united means recognising that, as Canadians, we have a much better chance of achieving our objectives than as British Columbians or Newfoundlanders or Québecois; it means recognising that we are uniquely Canadian because of our differences rather than in spite of them; being united means recognising just how much we all have to offer Canada.

International consciousness builds on all that. If we in Canada, with all our new and historic divisions, can learn to accomodate them and use them as strengths, we can show the world that it is possible to celebrate cultural diversity and use it as a positive force for a tolerant, accommodating and confident society. If we can show compassion to our fellow Canadians in times of adversity, we can use that experience in dealing with the less fortunate nations of the world. Keeping the peace at home will be good training for keeping the peace abroad.

Being uniquely Canadian also implies a commonly shared value system that underpins our social structures and our social processes. We need a set of values of which we can all be proud, to which we can all subscribe and in which we can all trust. In the past we have put much emphasis on "rights". We have embodied them in our constitution and they have played a major role in our development as a nation and in attracting to our shores people of many countries, some of whom have enjoyed few rights in the land of their birth.

We must continue to give emphasis to the rights of Canadians but we must also look at the "janus face" of rights - we must look to our "responsibilities". We need to strike a balance between rights and responsibilities that is every bit as vital to the quality of life as the balance we achieve between economic development and environmental responsibility. We need to temper our basic human rights with basic human responsibilities: caring, concern, approachability, integrity and action.

I think you will by now have a pretty clear idea of what we mean by caring and concern so we should look more closely at what we mean by the other responsibilities. Approachability has a lot to do with listening. So often when we want to put our views across, especially if we are politicians, we tend to do a lot of talking. But we also have a responsibility to listen, to hear other points of view, to learn of other experiences, to give consideration to alternative suggestions. As politicians, bureaucrats, business leaders, neighbours and parents we must make it not just possible but easy for others to talk to us. It could be our loss more than theirs if we do not.

Integrity has everything to do with honesty. The public has made it clear that they are tired of people in public or corporate life who betray the public trust by illegal or unethical behaviour. If those in positions of trust honour it, they will regain the public's respect and will earn the right to ask the same standards of all Canadians.

Action will almost certainly be the most important responsibility of them all. It is no good having visions and values, however noble and far-sighted, if we do not put them into practice. So how do we set about acting on our principles and how easy will the task be? This conference explored some suggestions and I will draw on those and attempt to provide at least some answers to the first part of that question. The answer to the second part of that question is: not at all easy - and for a very good reason.

It is not hard to get people to agree on overall aims but to get them to agree on how to achieve them is quite often a different story. Nobody will stand up and say "I am for a polluted environment" or "I think poverty should be encouraged" or "what we need is more inter-racial tension" because by and large people are intelligent enough to know that these things are bad for everyone and not just for those most closely affected by them. However, if suggested solutions threaten their livelihood, or their religious principles, or their mental or emotional well-being, they will not be easily persuaded of the necessity for taking action - and who can blame them.

So any proposed actions will have to be sensitive to the concerns of those who will be affected by them. That does not mean that we should sit by and do nothing because that too has consequences for people. But we must accept that action needs to involve everyone if it is to be effective and that in today's complex and interdependent world there are no easy answers to our problems.

Our first action in general should be to inform ourselves as much as possible about the problems that we face. We live in an age of information but we are reliant on several factors before we can use that

242

information effectively. We need easy access to information; we need an operational level of reading, mathematics and science that enables us to evaluate that information and we need to be able to exchange information.

Much of the time the majority of us are reliant on the media for our information. This puts a grave responsibility on the members of the press. Canada needs more journalists who are true professionals, who report all sides of an issue objectively and whose main dedication is the truth as far as they are able to determine it. Public figures of integrity have nothing to fear from such professionalism but will have a right to complain of anything less because the public is also ill-served by partial truths and biased reporting. Poor journalism can do much to exacerbate divisions and conflicts within out society and that is a great disservice to Canada.

The other main source of information for the public as well as for politicians at all levels of government is the bureaucracy. We need to re-emphasize the accountability of civil servants to the public - either directly to the people or through their elected representatives. Bureaucrats have a similar responsibility to that of the media and the public should be able to rely on their honour and integrity also.

So, armed with good quality information and aided by our media and bureaucracy, where should we begin? From listening to people at this Conference and from all over Canada, and also from my own experience, I would suggest that there are some obvious problems that need immediate attention.

First in most people's minds is the problem with the environment. Many Canadians are profoundly concerned about the future of this planet and with good reason. For example, the Earth's forests are being destroyed by the area of one football field a second. The size of the Sahara Desert will double and more than half the living species on this planet may disappear within our lifetime. Here in Canada more agricultural land is lost by salinization due to poor farming techniques than by urban sprawl

We are all consumers and together we have enormous power to affect the habits of producers and retailers. We must use our buying power to support environmentally responsible enterprises. We can force a change at the cash register by demanding products whose production, delivery, consumption and disposal will make as little adverse impact on the environment as possible. We can insist that packaging be restricted to the necessary and if possible made re-usable. We should press manufacturers to develop alternatives to hazardous ingredients and, where unavoidable, demand that they are clearly labelled, their use carefully monitored and their disposal rigorously controlled.

We should encourage corporations that are trying to be environmentally responsible, even in cases where their past actions have been less responsible than we would like. Ignorance and carelessness are traits that are found in some individuals as well as some corporations and using energy to apportion past blame may take away from finding solutions to current problems. At the same time we have the right to expect corporations to start taking action immediately to improve their operations in respect to the environment.

We should expect all levels of government and all political parties to work together with industry, labour, environmentalists and consumers to reverse the trend towards environmentally irresponsible growth. It is now clear that responsibility to the environment can itself create economic and employment opportunities. We must explore these and support them where necessary by government regulations and fiscal policies. Prosperity does not have to be at the expense of our children's environmental birthright. And on the subject of our children, we should make sure that environmental studies is a compulsory part of the school curriculum.

On a local level we can select a problem that needs attention (in Broadview-Greenwood it is the pollution of the Don River), work together to find solutions to it and keep working until the problem is solved. Just think of the results we achieve when all these local initiatives are added together! We should not be daunted by the magnitude of the task. If we only succeed in preventing the problem from getting any worse we will have achieved something worthwhile, but the chances are that when lots of us work together the problems become more manageable and the goal more attainable.

My suggestion for national action centres on the opportunities that environmental responsibility will provide. This responsibility has great potential for new enterprise and employment. It can involve everyone including seniors and youth and those who perhaps had previously turned their faces away from corporate Canada.

For those of you interested in learning more about these opportunities we are holding an international summit on the environment in September. It will bring together people from all over the world to discuss environmental problems and solutions, to disseminate vital information, to showcase new technology and consumer choices in environmentally responsible products and services.

This conference has been sponsored by Loblaws, a Canadian company which, like a growing number of other companies, now has environmental responsibility as a key element in its corporate philosophy. This new enlightenment on the part of corporations is to be welcomed and encouraged along with the positive actions that Canadian companies are beginning to take. In some cases these actions are as sensitive to the social environment as they are to the physical environment and this is a positive sign for the new prosperity with integrity.

This brings us to the second area that is demanding our attention: our social environment. We need to remember at all times that the environment also includes people and some people are in need of our help. Poor educational and social skills of individuals plus intolerance and prejudice in our society are some of the reasons why too many Canadians now live at the margins and have become alienated or indifferent to the values that most of us believe in.

Some are forced into poverty which is difficult to escape, some take refuge in drugs, some live a life on the streets or in sub-standard housing. Some of these people are easier to help than others. Those whose level of functional literacy is too low for their economic well-being may be the easiest to help. We know how to teach them. Agencies such as Frontier College have a track record of success. They simply need more resources and that includes people. Here is a chance for those of you with literacy skills to pass them on to others.

Those on drugs or on the streets may be more resistant to our help. We certainly have a responsibility to learn as much as we can about drug abuse and physical and sexual abuse, and our communities should support education, treatment and rehabilitation services provided by the police and other social agencies. These initiatives need public and government support.

245

Public support may be best realised through a change in attitudes. If our intolerance or indifference is pushing people into finding acceptance in dubious groups whose values we do not approve of, we should acknowledge that we are contributing to the problem. Showing caring in the form of tolerance may encourage people to seek help and eventually learn the social skills they need to particpate fully in Canadian life. Government support for such practical educational programs needs to be forthcoming.

Lack of affordable housing is also a problem for many Canadians, especially in the big cities like Toronto and Vancouver. Housing is a provincial responsibility and, even if you are not personally in need of it, you should support initiatives in your province that seek to increase the stock of affordable housing. If you are a parent your children will need homes of their own in the future; if you are an employer your employees will also need housing they can afford.

A third concern is to ensure that all Canadians benefit from the prosperity they help to create. Two important trends are shaping Canada's economy: the increasing integration of world markets and the continued rapid introduction of technology. On the plus side, we are well-placed to take advantage of world markets because we have such a multicultural population. We have Canadians who, because of their ethnic backgrounds, have invaluable knowledge of the customs, language and preferences of the countries of the world that are actual or potential markets for Canadian goods and services.

Competition in world markets also requires us to keep up with new technology. New technologies have led to significant gains in productivity and offer new opportunities for industry but they also demand more sophisticated skills of the workforce. Those workers without them could be seriously disadvantaged. In order to move confidently into the 21st century we will need to pay greater attention to all forms of education, training and re-training and this requires *national* programs. I emphasize national because all Canadians have the right to equal opportunities for prosperity, and while provincial initiatives are welcome they could increase the regional differences that sometimes run counter to Canadian unity.

Ensuring that Canadian workers have continued access to the skills they need to enter the workforce is a vital first step. Once in the

246

workforce their full participation and commitment becomes essential. Employers and companies who take action to encourage this will benefit from increased employee loyalty and effort. Measures which take family commitments into account such as child care services and pay equity will allow both men and women to take an active and fulfilling part in the economy.

If workers are providing this degree of commitment they deserve to share in the financial success of their company. Equity participation provides both a tangible reward for effort and sense of belonging to the enterprise. Measures like this which increase the stake of all participants should be actively encouraged, perhaps through fiscal policy which provides a tax break for companies adopting profit sharing or equity participation. Unions are sometimes suspicious of direct equity participation and have initiated alternative mechanisms. Whatever the mechanism, both business and labour can benefit - it is a win-win scenario that should be the way of the future.

The fourth area in need of our attention and which is much in the headlines at the moment revolves around questions of national identity and national unity. Perhaps it was the signing of the Free Trade deal with the US which brought worries about our cultural identity to the fore once again. This reawakened concerns about regional and other divisions - east-west, anglophone-francophone, new Canadians-old Canadians. Those with doubts about the Meech Lake Accord felt compelled to make them public. We are now having to look once again at constitutional issues and once again Québec feels threatened.

We can choose to see all this as negative but I would prefer to look at it as a chance to face all the issues honestly, openly and in a cooperative spirit, recognising that everyone's concerns are genuinely felt and need to be addressed. My own concern is for a strong national government that can provide equal rights for all Canadians and I believe the majority of Canadians would agree with me. But national unity and national identity are not things you can force on anyone or you destroy the very essence of what you are hoping to achieve. We will need a great deal of sensitivity to each other to overcome our differences and suspicions.

For example, we have to reassure Québec that she is an essential part of our Canadian identity. One way forward is to encourage

247

talented Québec artists to perform outside of Québec. The living and exciting French language would no longer be "ghettoized" in Québec or confined to relatively small francophone pockets or immersion French classes in anglophone Canada. English speaking audiences would benefit not only from the exposure to the talent that Québec has to offer but also from exposure to a language that is very much part of the Europe that we need to trade with and which becomes even more important in 1992. Promoting Québec artists may be only one step but it is a start and great things can come from small beginnings.

We also need to remember that there are many Canadians other than those of French or English origins. Our native people and our new immigrants from many other nations are also part of the current Canadian identity and they too have vital contributions to make. Native Canadians, who have traditionally lived more in harmony with nature than any other Canadians, have much to teach us about respect for the environment. New Canadians also have many cultural values that fit very well with our traditional Canadian ones and perhaps even some which would add to them.

So we are back to the basic foundation of any nation - its value system. Whatever our actions, they should be clearly based on the values that we all agree are essential to us as a people. I sense very strongly that ethical considerations will play an increasingly important role in our destiny in the 21st century. The momentum has already begun. "Ethical" investment funds, corporate environmental responsibility, tightened conflict of interest rules are all straws in the wind. It is a movement that I and many other Canadians welcome wholeheartedly. We are more than happy to have it as the basis for all our actions.

As individuals our actions will almost certainly begin in our local neighbourhoods. As we come to grips with the problems in our local communities, solutions can be shared with our neighbours; ideas and experiences will spread and eventually we could galvanize the will of the entire nation. The benefits to be gained are enormous. We can achieve prosperity without damage to the planet or its people. We can live in harmony and earn global respect. I am sure this vision can be made reality and I am confident that Canadians will rise to the challenge. There is no doubt in my mind that Canadians have a great deal to offer each other and the world in the 21st century.

Appendices

Appendix 1

This argument in support of the Meech Lake Accord is taken from the main text of a presentation by Yves Fortier to the Speyer Committee on the Constitution. Yves Fortier, a distinguished scholar and lawyer, is currently Canada's Ambassador to the United Nations.

At the outset, I would like to say without any hesitation that I enthusiastically support the 1987 Constitutional Accord. I consider it a political tour de force that delights me as a Canadian Quebecker and a lawyer. Let me now explain my position.

As a lawyer, I see 1982 as a key date in Canada's constitutional history. That is when our Constitution was patriated, an amending formula adopted and, particularly, the Canadian Charter of Rights and Freedoms enshrined in our constitution. Despite their importance, the achievements of 1982 are so far incomplete because my province, Québec, is not part of the new constitutional order. From a strictly legal point of view, of course, the 1982 Constitution Act applies to Québec. But in this area, as in many others, lawyers must show some modesty. The fact is that politically, and even morally, the 1982 Constitution Act does not apply to Québec. Those who claim it does are guilty of constitutional heresy.

The reason I am going over these well-known historical facts is that I believe that the 1987 Constitutional Accord must be analysed in light of its essential objective of bringing Québec back into the Canadian constitutional family. I had an opportunity to comment on the agreement in principle concluded at Meech Lake in April 1987, in Québec City in May. At the time, my comments focussed chiefly on the recognition of the fact that Québec constitutes a distinct society within Canada. I would like to say a few words about this.

In my opinion, the principle of this recognition is absolutely irrefutable, if only because of the majority language of Québec, its civil law and its culture. Québec is different from its other partners in the

Canadian federation. In this regard, clause 2 enshrines a fact that was already obvious to both politicians and the courts. Does clause 2 distort reality? I do not think so, because Québec society within Canada is not defined solely by the characteristics of the franco-phone majority, and clause 2 states this specifically. Québec's distinct society is composed of English-speaking Canadians, French-speaking Canadians, native people and people from ethnic groups.

As we all know, the drafters of the Accord decided that the way this distinct society would be translated into reality should be a rule of interpretation. Therefore, it in no way alters the distribution of powers or the rights and freedoms guaranteed in the charter. This rule will be one of a number to be used in the legal interpretation of our Constitution.

One of the main concerns raised in the course of the parliamentary committee hearings in Québec City was the fact that the distinct society was not defined in the April 30 accord. In their meeting in the Langevin Block, the First Ministers did not feel it was appropriate to introduce a definition. I actually maintained that had they done so, they would have made our Constitution unnecessarily rigid. I would like to repeat that opinion here today.

This rule of interpretation that the Langevin accord proposes to insert in Clause 2 of the 1967 constitutional act underwent amendments between April 30 and June 3. I would like to briefly comment on those changes and make certain comments about the concerns raised by Clause 16 of the Langevin accord.

First, the change introduced in Clause 2.1(a) is a vast improvement over the text of the Meech Lake accord. Canadian duality is far better described by a reference to French-speaking Canadians and English-speaking Canadians who coexist rather than a reference to a French Canada or an English Canada. Subparagraph 4 now describes with utmost clarity the maintenance of powers, rights and privileges of the federal and provincial governments.

I am not convinced that the addition of that subparagraph was necessary in legal terms. Be that as it may, there is no further possibility of ambiguity. The interpretive rule that is intended to be entrenched in Clause 2 does not have the effect of affecting the sharing of powers between the two levels of government. And their respective jurisdictions concerning language legislation are reaffirmed.

Clause 16 of the agreement seems to be a source of concern for some groups that appeared before you and, unless I am mistaken, for certain members of your committee. They are concerned that because of the specific mention of Clauses 25 and 27 of the Canadian Charter of Rights and Freedoms, other provisions of the charter might be subordinated to promoting Québec's distinct character provided for in Clause 2. And that fear was expressed quite vigorously concerning particularly Clauses 15 and 28 of the Canadian Charter of Rights and freedoms.

With respect, I believe those fears are totally groundless. And if it were not for the seriousness of those organizations that expressed those views, I would simply say we are dealing with a smokescreen. In my opinion, there is a fundamental distinction to be made between Clauses 25 and 27 of the Charter and 35 of the 1982 Constitution Act on the one hand, and Clauses 15 and 28 of the Charter on the other. The former expresses a safeguard clause and an interpretive rule, as in Clause 2 of the Langevin Accord, whereas the latter have clear substantive content.

Clause 15 of the charter proclaims rights to equality both in the content and in the implementation of legislation. To that protection, which contains a prohibition of discrimination based on sex, is added that of Clause 28 which proclaims an equal guarantee of rights for persons of both sexes. Now, Clause 28 is reinforced by a preliminary proposition giving it effect and I quote:

Notwithstanding anything else in this charter...

which means that this provision does not fall under the notwithstanding in Clause 33.

Now, Clause 25 and 27 of the Charter are totally different in nature. Clause 25 proclaims the subsistence of the rights and liberties that the native peoples enjoyed at the coming into force of the charter. Whereas Clause 27, in terms that are quite similar to those we find in paragraph 4 of the clause on the distinct society, proclaims the maintenance and improvement of the Canadian multicultural heritage. I do not at all see how the interpretive rule that is being proposed for entrenchment in Clause 2 of the Constitution could have precedence over the substantive provisions of the Charter, including clauses 15 and 28.

The critics who are crying wolf forget that, in comparison with Canada as a whole, Québec has scarcely been behindhand in promoting the equality of the sexes. Actually people seem to be forgetting, within the context of this debate, the very existence of the Québec Charter of Human Rights and Freedoms. The Québec Charter prohibits any distinction, exclusion or preference based, amongst other things, on race, colour, sex, civil status, social condition, pregnancy or language; to this prohibition is added a preponderance over any Québec law, even those passed after the Charter, unless there figures therein a notwithstanding clause.

In my opinion, it is easy to understand why Clause 16 was put into the Langevin accord. Legally speaking, it was not what I would term essential, but it was justifiable to establish and specify that the interpretive rule in Clause 2, which refers to the two most important linguistic communities in the country, had the same standing as the other interpretive rules specified elsewhere in the Constitution and which recognize the existence and rights of natives as well as the riches of the Canadian multicultural heritage.

Such a provision is acceptable insofar as it refers to provisions of the same nature as the one that you want to circumscribe using the escape clause. I am afraid, however, that if we add to Clause 16 of the Langevin accord a reference to certain substantive provisions of the Charter we will be opening a Pandora's box the effect of which will be to create new and quite considerable uncertainty.

On the other hand, if it were decided to exempt the whole of the Charter from the effect of the distinct society clause, including Clause 1 of the Charter, then that would mean the death of the Meech Lake Accord, period.

As for the Supreme Court and the Senate, I think that I am expressing the opinion of all Canadians when I applaud the entrenchment of the highest tribunal of our country in the Canadian Constitution. Besides being a general appeals court for all of Canada, since 1949 the Supreme Court has been playing the crucial role of ultimate referee concerning the sharing of legislative jurisdictions set out in Clauses 91 and 92 of the 1867 act. As we all know, in 1982 it was also given the responsibility to judge the compatibility of federal and provincial laws with those rights and freedoms guaranteed by the Charter.

I would summarize the important responsibilities of that tribunal simply by pointing out that its authority as guardian of our Constitution is not bestowed upon it by either federal or provincial governments but rather, now, by the text that governs both levels. That is why the double federal-provincial veto provided for the appointment of judges to the Supreme Court of Canada appears to me to be a formula that is the faithful reflection of the Canadian federalist compromise and one that bears witness to the maturity of our political leaders.

I would like to express my most rigorous disagreement with those who maintain that the participation of the provinces in the appointment process of judges to the Supreme Court might tend to compromise that quality and impartiality of those who, in future, will be called upon to assume that lofty responsibility. Their fear shows how little they know about the bench and is based upon the premise of future provincial governments showing ill will towards the federal-provincial covenant. Actually, I would make the same comment on the participation of the provinces in the appointment process for senators.

As for the spending power, I think that the provisions of the Langevin Accord seem to be the most eloquent demonstration of the realism and pragmatism of the signatories of the 1987 constitutional agreement. Federalism, in Canada, is based on recognition of the full autonomy of both levels of government in their respective areas of jurisdiction. In itself, recognizing federal spending power when its exercise encroaches on areas of exclusive provincial jurisdiction constitutes a breach of that principle. In what circumstances should such a breach be allowed? Historically, it has been permitted when the federal government has proposed jointly financed programs in the pursuit of national objectives shared by a majority of Canadian men and women. In practical terms, some of those programs included a right of withdrawal exercised by certain provinces without harm to national objectives.

Having made those preliminary comments, I then examine the

255

provisions being proposed for entrenchment in Clause 106A of our Constitution. I arrive at the conclusion that when a federal initiative does not meet any one of the five conditions identified in the Langevin Accord, the federal spending power remains intact. The federal government can therefore spend, as payments or otherwise, for the benefit of individuals, governments or even entire regions of the country in federal or provincial areas. The only limit to its power is inherent in the federalist principle and has existed since 1867: the federal government cannot use the spending power to invade and regulate areas that fall under exclusive jurisdiction.

On spending power then, the Langevin Accord appears to me to be quite in conformity with the federalist principle as well as compatible with Canadian practice since the Second World War.

Just like some others, I have certain reservations concerning the Langevin Accord. I deplore, for example, the fact that the Yukon and the Northwest Territories are not granted the right to propose candidates for the Supreme Court of Canada and the Senate. A simple oversight? Would that have been a stumbling block? I do not know. My uneasiness in that respect, as well as in respect of other points, does not require immediate amendments to the Langevin Accord. The dynamics that led to the 1987 Accord must not be compromised. Our political leaders should be given your endorsement. With the annual constitutional conferences, there is now a forum for future amendments.

Besides, concerning those annual constitutional conferences, I would have set a timeframe of five or ten years. After that period, it would have seemed sufficient to me to have one every five or ten years. As you know, a constitution is not a document that requires or lends itself to numerous changes. Its authority stems from its permanence and the evolving interpretation developed through jurisprudence.

In conclusion, then, all agree on the imperative necessity of bringing Québec back into the Canadian constitutional family. The concern of some Canadians is whether the conditions of the 1987 agreement compromise those principles that characterize our federation. My opinion is they do not.

And I would also like to add, in terms familiar to the members of my profession, that the burden of proof falls upon the shoulders of those who maintain the contrary. Should the terms of the Accord referred to this committee for examination be amended? Legally speaking I see no necessity for that, and politically speaking I apprehend certain risks in so doing.

An editorialist has said of the Langevin Accord that it is a victory for intelligence, compromise and the sense of the moment. I share that opinion. I believe that the 11 First Ministers have worded an agreement that will at last lead to 1982's unfinished business being completed. With respect for the foundations of our federation, they have finally brought together all partners without pre-empting the future. The task is not finished, no, but there are now mechanisms in place to meet the challenges that are still there, especially the reform of our upper chamber, which so many Canadians would like to see.

I have the firm conviction that the 1987 constitutional agreement is a historic landmark in our country's constitutional evolution. I believe that all Canadian women and men should be grateful to its authors, and I deeply hope that this committee will recommend its adoption. Thank you.

Appendix 2

STATEMENT OF CLAIM OF THE CANADIAN COALITION ON THE CONSTITUTION, INC.

This document is the Statement submitted in the case brought by a group of Canadians and organizations from across Canada who are attempting to get the Meech Lake Agreement set aside by the Courts.

Three prominent lawyers, Timothy Danson, Morris Manning and Edward Greenspan are counsel for the Coalition and the article by Timothy Danson earlier discusses this case and its basis.

IN THE FEDERAL COURT OF CANADA
(Trial Division)

B E T W E E N:

CANADIAN COALITION ON THE CONSTITUTION INC.,

Plaintiff,

-and-

HER MAJESTY THE QUEEN, THE RIGHT HONOURABLE PRIME MINISTER OF CANADA and THE ATTORNEY GENERAL OF CANADA

Defendants.

AMENDED STATEMENT OF CLAIM

(Filed this 2nd day of May 1988)

1. The plaintiff, the Canadian Coalition on the Constitution (hereinafter referred to as the "Coalition"), is a non-profit corporation duly incorporated pursuant to the laws of the Province of Ontario. The Coalition is a broadly based group of Canadians and organizations from all provinces of Canada who are concerned with the direct effects of the "1987 Constitutional Accord" (hereinafter referred to as the "Accord") on their interests and rights as Canadians.

2. The defendants are representatives of the Federal Government on all matters relevant to the within action.

3. On or about the 30th day of April, 1987, the Prime Minister of Canada, The Right Honourable Brian Mulroney and the First Minister of all ten provinces of Canada met at Meech Lake, Quebec, to discuss amendments to the Canadian Constitution.

4. At the conclusion of the aforesaid meeting the parties thereto arrived at an agreement to proceed with constitutional amendments in seven areas, to wit:

    i.   Quebec's distinct society;
    ii. Immigration;
    iii. The Supreme Court of Canada;
    iv. The spending power of Parliament;
    v.   The amending formula;
    vi. The Senate;
    vii. First Minister Conferences on the Constitution and the economy.

5. On or about the 3rd day of June, 1987, the Prime Minister of Canada and the First Ministers met in Ottawa to review formal constitutional amendments emanating from the Meech Lake agreement. At the conclusion of this meeting the Accord was signed by all parties, to wit:

    i.   Canada: Brian Mulroney
    ii. Ontario: David Peterson
    iii. Quebec: Robert Bourassa
    iv. Nova Scotia: John Buchanan

   v.   New Brunswick: Richard Hatfield
   vi.   Manitoba: Howard Pawley
  vii.   British Columbia: Bill Vander Zalm
 viii.   Prince Edward Island: Joseph Ghiz
   ix.   Saskatchewan: Grant Devine
    x.   Alberta: Don Getty
   xi.   Newfoundland: Brian Peckford

6.   On or about the 26th day of October, 1987, the Accord was ratified by the House of Commons. This ratification represented the first fundamental step in amending the Constitution of Canada.

7.   The plaintiff states that most of the parties to the Accord have agreed to proceed or are proceeding as if the Accord had been ratified by all ten provinces. The plaintiff states this is contrary to law.

8.   On or about the 30th day of December, 1987, The Right Honourable Brian Mulroney announced the appointment of Gerald Ottenheimer to the Senate of Canada. The appointment was made in accordance with the provisions of the Accord, and thus contrary to law.

9.   On or about the 26th day of September, 1988, The Right Honourable Brian Mulroney announced the appointment of Gerald Beaudoin, Solange Chaput-Rolland, Roch Bolduc and Jean-Marie Poitras to the Senate of Canada. The appointments were made in accordance with the provisions of the Accord, and thus, contrary to law.

10.   The plaintiff states that the Government and Parliament of Canada have exceeded their jurisdiction in signing and ratifying the Accord in that they have undertaken to irrevocably transfer to the provinces powers indispensable to their capacity to exercise their authority as a national government. The plaintiff specifically pleads and relies upon the doctrine of <u>delegatus non potest delegare</u> and states that even the formal constitutional amendment process cannot enable the federal government to delegate to the provinces (by virtue of a provincially selected Senate and Supreme Court) the totality of its powers under section 91 of the <u>Constitution Act, 1867</u>, as hereinafter described.

A] THE SENATE

(i)   Historically, the selection and appointment of Senators has been accomplished by the Governor General, in the Queen's name, by Instrument under the Great Seal of Canada summoning qualified persons to the Senate. Effectively, Senate appointments have been made by the Prime Minister of Canada, and therefore the appointees have been individuals selected for their compatibility with the Canadian national interests as perceived by the government then in power.

(ii)   The aforesaid appointment system leaves intact the powers of the federal government under section 91 of the <u>Constitution Act, 1867.</u>

(iii)   Clause 25 of the Accord fundamentally transforms the Senate from a federally oriented body to a confederatively oriented one by allowing the Provinces to select the Senators and thereby control the Senate's orientation.

(iv)   Representatives of the Government of Canada have stated that the changes to the Senate, as evidenced by clause 25 of the accord, are intended to provide for an activist provincial body that will have substantive power in areas over which the national government has exclusive jurisdiction.

(v)   At the same time, the newly constituted Senate, having been provincially selected will retain its current power of absolute veto over legislation passed by the elected House of Commons.

(vi)   Notwithstanding their acknowledgment of the aforesaid, representatives of the government of Canada have also stated that nothing in the Accord diminishes its powers on matters over which it has exclusive jurisdiction.

(vii)   Clause 9 of the Accord (section 41(b) of the <u>Constitution Act, 1867</u>) states an amendment to the Constitution of Canada in relation to the power of the Senate and the method of selecting Senators can only be effected through the unanimous consent of the Parliament of Canada and the legislative assembly of each province.

(viii)   The Accord makes the provincially selected Senate a permanent feature of the Constitution by requiring unanimity for future Senate reform thereby irrevocably entrenching the veto power of a provincially selected body over a federally elected body in areas of exclusive federal jurisdiction.

(ix)   Notwithstanding the requirement for unanimity, representatives of the Government of Canada have stated that Senate reform in the Accord is merely "transitional" and therefore in no way affects its exclusive powers under section 91 of the <u>Constitution Act, 1867</u>.

(x)   Representatives of the Government of Canada have stated that the Senate reform created in the Accord would be dangerous to the federal government if it becomes permanent rather than transitional.

(xi)   Historically, voting patterns in the Senate demonstrate that the source of the appointment is determinative of how the Senator will vote.

(xii)   The effect of the aforesaid is a Senate that will evolve into a "house of the provinces" with members owing their allegiances to provincial interests and thus fundamentally impeding the national government's ability to exercise its exclusive jurisdiction under section 91 of the <u>Constitution Act, 1867</u>.

(xiii)   The Government of Canada's right to legislate in areas of its own exclusive jurisdiction will now be contingent upon the consent and goodwill of provincial authorities and a provincially controlled Senate, thus constituting an abdication of its exclusive powers under the Constitution

B] THE SUPREME COURT OF CANADA

(i)   Pursuant to section 101 of the <u>British North America Act</u> (now section 101 of the <u>Constitution Act, 1867</u> which authorizes the federal parliament "to provide for the constitution, maintenance and organization of a general court of appeal for Canada", the Federal Parliament, by statute, established the Supreme Court of Canada in 1875.

(ii)   Historically the judges of the Supreme Court of Canada have been selected and appointed by the Governor in Council, that is, by the federal cabinet.

(iii)   Neither the <u>Supreme and Exchequer Courts Act 1985,</u> S.C. 1875, c.11, nor the <u>Supreme Court Act,</u> R.S.C. 1970, c.S-19, requires appointments to the Supreme Court of Canada to be ratified by the Senate or the House of Commons or a legislative committee.

(iv)   On December 23, 1949, appeals from the Supreme Court of Canada to the Judicial Committee of the Privy Council were abolished by S.C. 1949 (2nd sess.), c.37, s.3.

(v)   Under the Accord the federal government has relinquished its exclusive jurisdiction to select and appoint judges to the Supreme Court of Canada.

(vi)   Under the Accord the governor general in council "shall", except when the Chief Justice is appointed from among members of the Court "appoint" a person whose name may have been submitted by each province.

(vii)   Where the appointment is made from Quebec the governor general in council "shall" appoint a person whose name may have been submitted by the Government of Quebec.

(viii)   Where the appointment is made from any other province the Governor General in Council "shall" appoint a person whose name may have been submitted by the government of a province other than Quebec.   There is no constitutional requirement for the other provinces to submit names for appointments if they so choose.   If a name is submitted which is unacceptable to the Queen's Privy Council for Canada the federal government shall choose from a list from another province.

(ix)   Between 1976 and 1985 the Parti Quebecois was in power in the Province of Quebec. The Parti Quebecois was and is a party committed to the dismemberment of Canada.

(x)   During this time the federal government was able to make two appointments to the Supreme Court of Canada from Quebec. Had the Accord been in force at that time the federal authority would not have had the power to make the aforesaid appointments without leave of the Quebec Government.

(xi)   Under the Accord, each province can choose not to put forward names for appointment to the Supreme Court of Canada or can continually put forward names which will not be acceptable to the Queen's Privy Council for Canada.

(xii)   The Accord does not provide for any constitutional mechanism to resolve any conflict in the circumstances described aforesaid.

(xiii)   Clause 9 of the Accord (section 41(g) of the <u>Constitution Act, 1867</u>) states an amendment to the Constitution of Canada in relation to the Supreme Court of Canada can only be effected through unanimous consent of the Parliament of Canada and the legislative assembly of each province.

(xiv)   In addition to the statement of fact pleaded in the preamble of this paragraph and sub-paragraph A, as well as the statement of fact pleaded in paragraph 10 below, the plaintiff states the Accord undermines section 101 of the <u>Constitution Act, 1867</u>. By requiring unanimity to amend clause 6 of the Accord (section 101A - E of the <u>Constitution Act, 1982</u>), and by providing no constitutional mechanism to resolve any stalemate in the appointment procedure, the Accord inevitably threatens the very constitutional existence of the Supreme Court of Canada itself. The plaintiff states that in the event that the Government of Quebec refuses to submit a candidate for appointment to the Court in accordance with clause 6 of the Accord (Section 101 C (3) of the <u>Constitution Act, 1982</u>) or such candidate is unacceptable to the Queen's Privy Council for Canada, the Supreme Court of

Canada will not be constitutionally constituted. Furthermore the plaintiff states the inevitable crisis will become permanent because the province creating the problem will not resolve it by conforming to the unanimity provisions of the Accord for constitutional amendment.

11.   The plaintiff states the Accord is so imprecise, ambiguous and broad as to destroy the integrity of the division of powers between the federal and provincial levels of government. The plaintiff states the Courts will be unable to delineate and preserve valid power in segregated form. Without limiting the generality of the foregoing the particulars of the aforesaid are as follows:

A]   SPENDING POWER

(i)   The Accord does not specify which level of government sets national objectives under clause 7 of the Accord (Section 106A of the <u>Constitution Act, 1982</u>).

(ii)   The Accord does not specify who determines whether the provincial plan meets national objectives.

(iii)   The Accord does not specify whether national objectives mean standards.

(iv)   The Accord does not define the difference between a "provincial program" and a "provincial initiative", if any.

(v)   The Accord does not provide a definition for the word "compatible".

(vi)   The Accord does not provide criteria to determine the difference between being "compatible with a provincial program" as distinct from a "provincial initiative".

(vii)   The Accord does not provide for a formula to determine whether a province can have an objective compatible with national objectives but have a substantially different view as to the best means of achieving the objective.

B] DISTINCT SOCIETY

The integrity of the division of powers between the federal and provincial levels of government is further threatened by the imprecision and vagueness of the provisions regarding the recognition of Quebec as a distinct society. Representatives of the Government of Canada have stated that the recognition of Quebec as a distinct society is a mere formality which recognizes a social and historical fact and in no way disturbs the balance of power between the Federal Government and the Government of Quebec. In addition the said representatives have stated that the distinct society clause does not dislodge the supremacy of the <u>Canadian Charter of Rights & Freedoms</u> (hereinafter referred to as the "<u>Charter</u>"). Without limiting the generality of the foregoing, the plaintiff states the aforesaid statements have been seriously contradicted by numerous statement and representations of the various political parties in Quebec, the particulars of which are as follows:

(i)   While the French language is a fundamental characteristic of Quebec's uniqueness it is not the sole characteristic relevant to the distinct society clause. There are other aspects such as Quebec's culture and its institutions, whether political, economic or judicial. The distinct society clause will allow Quebec to be confirmed as a French society. [Premier Robert Bourassa]

(ii)   English rights will no longer be a constituent part of Quebec, but purely a limit on the powers to be exercised by the National Assembly. [Premier Robert Bourassa]

(iii)   The reason why Quebec does not want the distinct society clause defined is because definition would confine and hamper the National Assembly in promoting the aforesaid uniqueness. It must be noted that Quebec's distinct identity will be protected and promoted by the National Assembly and government and its duality preserved by the legislators. It cannot be stressed too strongly that the entire Constitution, including the <u>Charter</u>, will be interpreted and applied in the light of the clause proclaiming Quebec's distinctiveness as a society. As a result, in the exercise of Quebec's legislative jurisdiction it will be able to consolidate what has already been achieved and gain new ground. [Premier Robert Bourassa]

(iv)   There will be no more erosion of Quebec's power over language. The Accord provides for an absolute protection. As a result Quebec is entitled and obligated to assert the French fact in Quebec. [Premier Robert Bourassa]

(v)　　We have for the first time in 120 years of federalism managed to provide constitutional underpinnings for the preservation and promotion of the French character of Quebec. [Premier Robert Bourassa]

(vi)　　The only road that Quebec is taking is that of strengthening and consolidating the French language. [Premier Robert Bourassa]

(vii)　　The distinct society clause is fundamentally and essentially founded on the French language and culture. [Quebec Intergovernmental Affairs Minister Gil Remillard]

(viii)　　The distinct society clause has no other origin than that of putting to an end an historical aberration by returning to the very source of the federation, which is the free and voluntary union of two peoples. [Federal Energy Mines & Resources Minister Marcel Masse]

(ix)　　The distinct society clause is a significant clause and should be exploited to the utmost. This would lead to result that the provincial premiers who signed the Accord would not be very happy with. [Former Parti Quebecois Minister Claude Morin]

(x)　　If the recognition of Quebec as a distinct society turns out not to mean anything, Quebecers will realize it and begin fighting again. [Former Parti Quebecois Minister Claude Morin]

(xi)　　If we can get more power, why not? Maybe the distinct society is just a psychological baby's rattle thrown to Quebecers; maybe the courts will decide it is more than that. As a sovereign state Quebec would function in French with one language and one culture fundamentally French. [Parti Quebecois Leader Jacques Parizeau]

12.　　The plaintiff states, as pleaded in the preamble of paragraph 10 and specified in sub-paragraphs A and B therein, that Premier Bourassa has formally acknowledged the ambiguity and threat to the division of powers. The plaintiff states that the following statement by the Premier Bourassa in the Quebec National Assembly was intended to apply to comments by the Premier such as those pleaded aforesaid:

"According to jurisprudence, the statements, the intentions

of the person writing the Constitution can be very useful [in the] interpretation that can be made by the courts."

13.   Section 91(3) of the Constitution Act, 1867 gives the Parliament of Canada exclusive jurisdiction to enact laws for the purpose of "the raising of money by any mode or system of taxation". By operation of clause 7 of the Accord (Section 106A of the Constitution Act, 1982) the Government of Canada shall financially compensate a provincial government that chooses not to participate in a national shared cost program from funds raised pursuant to the Government of Canada's exclusive jurisdiction under section 91(3) of the Constitution Act, 1867. The plaintiff states this severely restricts and threatens the Government of Canada's ability to spend federal funds as it deems appropriate and necessary for the national interests. The plaintiff further states this constitutes an improper delegation and transfer of power of the federal government's exclusive jurisdiction under section 91(3) inasmuch as the federal government cannot do circuitously and indirectly that which it cannot do directly.

14.   The plaintiff states that the cumulative effect of paragraphs 9, 10, 11 and 12 herein constitutes a significant decentralization of Canada which threatens the very existence of Confederation. Representatives of the Government of Canada have stated that the Accord does not have the effect of decentralizing Canada. Other parliamentarians, academics and leading citizens have stated a contrary view. The conflict referred to herein can be demonstrated in the following assertion of former Justice of the Supreme Court of Canada, the Honourable Willard Estey:

> "My instinct is that it is decentralizing and should therefore be viewed by Canadian citizens with some suspicion. You could ruin Confederation - there is no question about it. That is why it is being nibbled at and attacked. I think we would be better off to stay where we are."

15.   The plaintiff states that the rights and freedoms established under the Charter are, at present, guaranteed and are subject only to those limitations set out under section 1 of the Charter.

16.   The plaintiff states that clause 1 of the Accord (section 2 of the Constitution Act, 1867) provides inter alia, that the guaranteed rights and freedoms set out in the Charter are now to be read subject

to the Province of Quebec's legislative and governmental mandate to preserve and promote the distinct identity of Quebec.

17.   Clause 1 of the Accord (section 2 of the Constitution Act, 1867) in addition to being a substantive constitutional provision is a constitutional rule of interpretation designed to fortify Quebec legislation against Charter challenges.

18.   The plaintiff states that clause 16 of the Accord provides that clause 1 of the Accord shall not affect the interpretation of sections 25 or 27 of the Charter. No other section of the Charter is protected from the effects of clause 1 of the Accord.

19.   The provisions of the constitution of Canada are not interpreted so as to create redundancies but rather full and purposive meaning is given to every word of the Constitution. Furthermore, the courts will not read sections of the constitution to provide for protections not expressly guaranteed.

20.   The plaintiff pleads the doctrine of espressio unius est exclusio alterius and states that the requirement that some Charter rights and freedoms be read subject to clause 1 of the Accord while other Charter rights and freedoms are not so affected creates a constitutional hierarchy.

21.   The plaintiff states that clause 16 of the Accord, in expressly recognizing the preeminence of only select sections of the Charter, and in failing to so acknowledge the preeminence of other Charter rights and freedoms, has effectively undermined the guaranteed nature of Charter rights and freedoms. These rights and freedoms would no longer be subject only to limitations under section 1 of the Charter whereas sections 25 and 27 of the Charter would remain subject only to section 1 considerations.

22.   Clause 3 of the Accord (section 95B(3) of Constitution Act, 1867) states that any agreement between the Government of Canada and a Province regarding immigration and aliens is subject to the Charter. The plaintiff states that where the drafters of the Accord intended the protection of the Charter to apply as a whole they so provided and that in the absence of specific protection, Charter rights are vulnerable.

23.   In addition, section 33 of the Charter permits Parliament or the legislature of a province to expressly declare in an Act of Parliament, or of the legislature, as the case may be, that the Act or a provision thereof shall operate notwithstanding a provision included in section 2 or sections 7 to 15 of the Charter. Therefore any actions which would have the effect of overriding Charter rights must, at present, be expressed and carried out through the section 33 mechanism. Under the Accord, Charter rights can be overridden circuitously through the distinct society clause (clause 1 of the Accord). The plaintiff states that such an indirect means of circumvention of Charter rights is contrary to the constitutional standard of express legislative ratification contemplated in section 33 of the Charter.

24.   By the way of an example of the aforesaid, the plaintiff states that the combined effects of clauses 2 and 16 of the Accord undermine the equality rights of women as protected under section 15 and 28 of the Charter.

25.   The plaintiff states that section 15 of the Charter provides, inter alia, for equality of all individuals before and under the law and the right to equal protection and equal benefit of the law without discrimination based on sex. Section 28 of the Charter provides that all rights set out in the Charter are to be guaranteed equally to female and male persons.

26.   The Plaintiff states that section 28 of the Charter is an interpretative clause in that it gives instructions to the court as to how different sections of the Constitution are to be read. Furthermore sections 15 and 28 represent a recognition of collective as well as individual rights within the Charter.

27.   The plaintiff states that the combined effect of clauses 2 and 16 of the Accord would permit legislation to be passed by the province of Quebec that could override women's equality rights as entrenched in sections 15 and 28 of the Charter. Furthermore any minority rights not protected under section 25 and 27 of the Charter are also at risk and are capable of being undermined by Quebec legislation passed to preserve or promote its distinct identity.

28.   The plaintiff states that the proposed constitutional recognition of Quebec's role to preserve and promote its distinct identity represents, as a constitutional amendment, a fundamental part of

the constitutional compromise in the Constitution Act, 1867. Accordingly clauses 2 and 16 of the Accord would not be subject to Charter review.

29.   Notwithstanding the aforesaid, it has been stated by representatives of the Government of Canada that Charter rights are not affected by clauses 2 and 16 of the Accord. Other parliamentarians and academics have stated the contrary. The conflict referred to herein is demonstrated in the following assertions:

(i)   Concerning the equality provisions in the existing Charter of Rights and Freedoms, we are very concerned that an interpretation can be placed on the new Accord that would in fact depreciate from rights currently existing under the Charter of Rights and Freedoms. By specifying what is not affected by clause 2 you imply very strongly that all other matters are. [Premier Frank McKenna]

(ii)   Clause 16 of the Accord could put in jeopardy, in Quebec, the fundamental freedoms (freedom of speech, thought, opinion, the press, peaceful assembly, association), democratic rights, mobility rights, legal rights, equality rights, the right to separate or denominational schools and minority language education rights. [Senator Eugene Forsey]

(iii)   It is not the intention of the First Ministers and drafters of clause 16 of the Accord to in any way derogate from the equality rights of women and minorities as set out in the Charter. [Prime Minister Brian Mulroney]

(iv)   The Charter of Rights and Freedoms has not been amended, nor is there anything in this Accord that overrides it. The sections concerning Quebec's distinct society and Canada's linguistic duality are interpretative. They do not override the Charter. [Senator Lowell Murray]

(v)   Because multiculturalism and native peoples related to groups with a cultural aspect and raised collective as opposed to individual rights it was thought appropriate to put in clause 16 of the Accord. [Senator Lowell Murray]

(vi)   If we accept clause 16 of the Accord for the section 27 and sections 35 and 25, should we add section 28? I may be mistaken, but I think those clauses are there only by prudence; they are not strictly necessary, in my opinion. If it is there for (a) and (b), why not (c)? I agree with you; that is the difficulty. [Professor Gerald Beaudoin]

(vii)   My feeling is that clause 16 was drafted for political purposes. I would say that in law and in logic there is no reason why sections 15 and 28 of the Charter should not be there. In law there is no reason why sections 25 and 27 should be there. [Robert Decary]

(viii)   The adoption of the Accord with its distinct society provisions will make it more politically legitimate for Quebec to invoke the s.33 notwithstanding clause. [Premier Robert Bourassa]

(ix)   The Charter is subservient to the distinct society clause. To state otherwise is to betray Quebec. [Premier Robert Bourassa]

30.   The plaintiff therefore states that, by virtue of the combined effect of clauses 1 and 16 of the Accord, the guaranteed status of all Charter rights and freedoms not expressly protected under clause 16 are in jeopardy.

31.   Accordingly, in the event that this Honourable Court does not grant the declaratory relief set out in paragraphs 32 (a) - (e) below, the plaintiff requests declaratory relief in regards to the effect of the Accord on the Charter.

32.   The plaintiff specifically pleads that there was an entire absence of consensus ad item between the parties to the Accord. The particulars of this lack of consent are set out in paragraphs 9(A)(iv), (vi), (ix) and (x), 9(B)(xiv), 10B(i) - (xi), 13, and 29(i) - (ix) herein.

33.   The plaintiff proposes that this action be tried at Toronto in the Province of Ontario.

WHEREFORE THE PLAINTIFF CLAIMS AGAINST THE DEFENDANTS:

34.

(a)   A declaration that the Government of Canada lacks the authority to transfer its fundamental jurisdiction and power to the provinces as provided in the "1987 Constitutional Accord";

(b)   A declaration that the Government of Canada lacks the jurisdiction to relinquish its exclusive authority to appoint the Senate of Canada by transferring the said power to the provinces so long as the Senate retains an absolute veto over legislation emanating from the House of Commons;

(c)　　A declaration that the Government of Canada lacks the jurisdiction to relinquish its exclusive authority to appoint justices to the Supreme Court of Canada by transferring the said power to the provinces and by creating the constitutional foundation which could bring the very existence of the Supreme Court into question;

(d)　　A declaration that the Government of Canada lacks the jurisdiction to adopt an amending formula that irrevocably entrenches the aforesaid transfer of power.

(e)　　A declaration that the "1987 Constitutional Accord" is null and void because it is so imprecise, ambiguous and broad as to destroy the integrity of the division of powers between the federal and provincial levels of government.

(f)　　A declaration that clause 1 and clause 16 of the "1987 Constitutional Accord" do not affect the guaranteed nature of <u>Charter</u> rights and freedoms or their limitations as established under section 1 of the <u>Charter</u>.

(g)　　Pursuant to section 24(1) of the <u>Charter</u>, such further and other remedies as this Honourable Court deems appropriate and just.

Dated at Toronto, Ontario, this 2nd day of May, 1988.

(Signed) Timothy Danson,
Counsel for the Plaintiff
Timothy Danson, Morris Manning and Edward Greenspan,
Barristers,
c/o 250 Dundas Street West,
Suite 202,
Toronto, Ontario, M5T 2Z5

Timothy Danson
Morris Manning
Edward Greenspan
Counsel for the plaintiff.